Tourism Development:
Environmental and Community Issues

Edited by

Chris Cooper

International Centre for Tourism and Hospitality Research,

Bournemouth University, UK

and

Stephen Wanhill

International Centre for Tourism and Hospitality Research

Bournemouth University, UK and Research Centre of Bornholm, Denmark

JOHN WILEY & SONS

Chichester · New York · Weinheim · Brisbane · Singapore · Toronto

Copyright © 1997 by John Wiley & Sons Ltd,
Baffins Lane, Chichester,
West Sussex PO19 1UD, England

National   01243 779777
International   (+44) 1243 779777
e-mail (for orders and customer service enquiries): cs-books@wiley.co.uk
Visit our Home Page on http://www.wiley.co.uk
or http://www.wiley.com

Other Wiley Editorial Office

John Wiley & Sons, Inc., 65 Third Avenue,
New York, NY 10158-0012, USA

WILEY-VCH Verlag GmbH, Pappelallee 3,
D-69469 Weinheim, Germany

Jacaranda Wiley Ltd, 33 Park Road, Milton,
Queensland 4064, Australia

John Wiley & Sons (Asia) Pte Ltd, 2 Clement Loop #02-01.
Jin Xing Distripak, Singapore 129809

John Wiley & Sons (Canada) Ltd, 22 Worcester Road,
Rexdale, Ontario M9W 1L1, Canada

Library of Congress Cataloging-in-Publication Data

Tourism development : environmental and community issues / edited by
  Chris Cooper and Stephen Wanhill.
        p.   cm.
    Papers from the biennial conference of the International Academy for the Study of Tourism held June 1995, in Cairo, which were also published as a special issue of Progress in tourism and hospitality research in 1996.
  Includes bibliographical references (p. –) and index.
    ISBN 0-471-97116-2 (pbk. : acid-free paper)
    1. Tourist trade—Congresses. I. Cooper, Christopher P. II. Wanhill, Stephen. III. International Academy For the Study of Tourism. IV. Progress in tourism and hospitality research.
  G154.9.T6845 1997
  338.4′791–dc21   97-17409
                                                                                      CIP

British Library Cataloguing in Publication Data

A catalogue record for this book is available from the British Library

ISBN 0-471-97116-2

Typesest by Alden Multimedia Ltd, Northampton
Printed and bound in Great Britain by BPC Wheatons, Exeter
This book is printed on acid-free paper responsibly manufactured from sustainable forestation, for which at least two trees are planted for each one used for paper production

Tourism Development:

Environmental and Community Issues

7 Day Loan

Contents

Preface

The contents of this book comprise the papers which were presented at the biennial conference of the International Academy for the Study of Tourism. The conference was held in Cairo in June, 1995 on the theme of environmental and community issues in tourism development. The conference takes the form of a small gathering of leading tourism scholars in the world and represents state-of-the-art thinking and debate in the field. Each of the papers published in this book addresses an important issue in the area of environmental and community considerations in tourism development. In addition to appearing in this book, the papers were also published as a special issue of *Progress in Tourism and Hospitality Research* in 1996.

List of Contributors

Brian Archer, *Department of Management Studies, University of Surrey, Guildford, Surrey, GU2 5XH*

Richard W. Butler, *Department of Geography, University of Western Ontario, London, Ontario, Canada*

Chris Cooper, *International Centre for Tourism & Hospitality Research, Bournemouth University, Dorset House, Talbot Campus, Fernbarrow, Poole, Dorset BH12 5BB*

Graham M. S. Dann, *Department of Travel, Tourism & Leisure, University of Luton, Park Square, Luton, Bedfordshire LU1 3JU*

Kadir H. Din, *Director, Centre for General Studies, Universiti Kebangsaan Malaysia, 43600 Bangi, Selangor Darul Ehsan, Malaysia*

Donald E. Hawkins, *School for Business & Public Management, The George Washington University, 817 23rd Street NW, Washington DC 20052, USA*

Mitch Leventhal, *The International Institute of Tourism Studies, School of Business and Public Management, The George Washington University, 12704 Bushey Drive, Silver Spring MD 20906 USA*

Wendy L. Oden, *The International Institute of Tourism Studies, School of Business and Public Management, The George Washington University, 7431 Digby Green, Kingstown VA 22315 USA*

Douglas G. Pearce, *Department of Geography, University of Canterbury, Christchurch, New Zealand*

John J. Pigram, *Executive Director, Centre for Water Policy Research, University of New England, Armidale, NSW 2351 Australia*

Krzysztof Przeclawski, *Wilcza 55/63 - 37, 00-679 Warsaw, Poland*

Valene L. Smith, *Department of Anthropology, California State University, Chico, CA 95929-0400, USA*

Turgut Var, *Department of Recreation, Park & Tourism Sciences, Texas A&M University, College Station, TX 77843-2261 USA*

Salah E. A. Wahab, *Mamal Al Sukkar Street No. 16, Garden City, Cairo, Egypt*

Stephen Wanhill, *School of Service Industries, Bournemouth University, Poole BH12 5BB*

Introduction – Tourism Development and Sustainability

Stephen Wanhill

WORLD TOURISM

The undoubted growth in the economic prosperity of Western countries together with the travel revolution brought about through holidays with pay, lower international transport costs in real terms and information technology, has seen world international tourist arrivals grow by an overall rate of 7·3% per annum over the last four decades, from just over 25 million in 1950 to around 456 million in 1990. This growth has not been without fluctuations caused by shocks and cycles in the world economy, but what has been remarkable is the resilience of the industry.

The overall volume did fall back in the mid 1970s in response to the world fuel crisis but then recovered well to achieve in 1980 about what was expected of it from the forecasts made in the early 1970s. The beginning of the 1980s saw a flattening out of growth, but again tourism came back strongly to be well over the target of 410 million set for 1990. By the mid 1990s, world arrivals stood at 567 million, in spite of the various political conflicts in Europe, Africa and the Middle East.

Europe dominates international tourist movements. Seven European countries (France, Spain, Italy, Austria, UK, Germany and Hungary) are amongst the world's top ten tourist destinations, though since the 1960s Europe has been losing market share. Over the past two decades, the growth destinations have been in Asia and Australasia, and we have seen an increasing importance attached to long-haul travel. Nevertheless, it must be remembered that about 80% of all international tourism is short haul to neighbouring countries. For holiday travel this percentage is much higher, at around 90%, but we can expect this share to fall in response to the continual reduction in real and relative terms of long-haul air fares.

Forecasts of international tourist arrivals up to 2000 are currently predicting a world total around 660 million. It is always tempting to revise forecasts quite dramatically as economic circumstances change but, for tourism, this should be resisted on the grounds that the industry has demonstrated its resilience in the past, and that a good part of this resilience is due to the fact that unemployment and recession fall more heavily on the lower socio-economic groups and less heavily on the higher socio-economic groups who tend to dominate international travel. Political events, military encounters and terrorism are more likely to disrupt international travel, but even here the spillover effects are not all negative. Thus Europe gained market share from Africa and the Middle East as a consequence of the Gulf War, and the events in the former Yugoslavia resulted in the elimination of over-capacity in other Mediterranean resorts. The upshot is that continued tourism growth is putting increasing pressure on destinations and raising questions as to whether this growth is sustainable in terms of tourism environments and host communities. To set the scene in this respect and within the context of this book, Przeclawski (Chapter 9) proposes a code of ethics for all those engaged in the activity of tourism.

Market Segmentation

This rising volume of tourism is not a uniform mass; it is made up of a variety of groups. Market segmentation is the process whereby the totality of tourism is divided into a range of sub-markets.

Such grouping must be identifiable and measurable so that trends may be monitored. Groups must also exhibit a degree of stability in the characteristics and behavioural patterns so that they may be targeted collectively by the marketing process.

At a national level, the most common method of segmenting tourism statistics is by purpose of travel. The most basic classification is given as follows:

- holiday
- business
- visiting friends and relations (VFR)
- other, e.g. study, sports events, medical

The reason for this is that these groupings constitute different expressions of demand. Thus holiday tourism is paid for out of discretionary income and is therefore sensitive to aggressive pricing policies. It is commonly resort-based, seasonal and receptive to promotional campaigns. On the other hand, business tourism is much less price-sensitive, city-oriented, short stay and not susceptible to marketing unless for trade fairs, exhibitions and conferences. Visiting friends and relatives (VFR) traffic is relatively price-sensitive, less likely to use serviced accommodation, longer-stay, relatively low spend per day and not susceptible to promotion in terms of destination choice (Cooper *et al*, 1993). In respect of world international arrivals, around 70% of the traffic is for holiday purposes, 14% for business and the remaining 16% for VFR and other purposes.

Over time, the nature of holiday tourism has changed. During the 1950s, the holiday was largely centred around the traditional summer break at a coastal resort, but rising affluence, longer holiday periods and an increasing desire to travel have led to an increase in the amount of market segmentation. Tour operators have responded to changing consumer preferences by diversifying their portfolio of products. This in turn has spread the risk through generating all-year business. Longer holiday periods have not, in the main, lead to longer holidays but rather more frequent holiday taking, particularly short breaks. The latter are more likely to be taken in the home country, whereas the ideal main holiday is often considered to be abroad. However, the European traveller is now sufficiently aware to take pan-Europe short breaks, often to city destinations to enjoy the cultural resources that they offer. Over the past decade or more, there has been considerable growth in cultural tourism and both cities and particular regions have been given considerable revitalisation as local governments and the private sector have recognised their importance as tourist destinations. Accompanying this has been the growth of speciality shopping areas interspersed with places to eat and drink, and street entertainment to improve the leisure experience of visitors as well as that of the local population. In this respect, Smith (Chapter 13) provides a specific case study which analyses the issues surrounding tribal tourism in the USA.

The growth of technology, a matter which is discussed by Hawkins (Chapter 5) in terms of the changing manner in which the product is communicated to the consumer, has made instant reservation and confirmation possible, to the point where the customer expects an immediate response and, if one is not forthcoming, chooses some other product. Technology will lead to increasing integration between the different sectors of the industry to allow the customer to put together 'bespoke' packages all on the same system. This will not be so much aimed at the domestic visitor, who because of familiarity with the product still tends to book direct, but the overseas visitor who will want to be able to book immediately the product seen in the promotional literature. Technology has also brought down the real cost of travel, and in so doing has brought countries closer together. Thus long haul has come nearer to short haul, which in turn has permitted the former to grow faster than the latter.

The World Commission on Environment and Development (1987) defines sustainability as 'development that meets the needs of the present without compromising the ability of future generations to meet their own needs'. This concept is infiltrating the policy framework of many government organisations and agencies, primarily through concern expressed for the natural environment. It is evident that the public is becoming more aware of the perceived adverse effects of tourism on the environment and it has become fashionable to 'go green'. Some operators have consciously taken the decision to reduce their consumption of natural resources to the benefit of the organisation and staff alike. Others have used the concept that *green* tourism is equated with 'soft' tourism, which has low impact and is therefore acceptable, as little more than a marketing tactic. Dann (Chapter 8) uses the term 'greenspeak' to show how the marketing departments of the travel trade easily adapt their promotional literature to match their customers' rising interest in environmental matters. Green tourism, ecotourism or alternative tourism (the words are often used synonymously) are in essence small scale solutions to what is a large scale problem, namely the mass movements of people travelling for leisure purposes. Curtailing this growth on a world scale does not seem to be a series option (Wheeller, 1992), so there is a requirement to continue to create large 'resortscapes' capable of managing high density flows. Here, Wall's concern (Chapter 1) for examining the impact of tourism in a holistic way, as opposed to just the economic effects, is very relevant.

Sustainable Tourism Development

In its most basic form, the concept of sustainability draws in the environment as an issue for the economics of tourism, a matter which is critically discussed by Archer (Chapter 3). The situation is illustrated in Figure 1: suppose that in the initial situation the local economy is at A and the desire is to increase employment and local income. The adverse position is where such a policy can only be accomplished by a move from

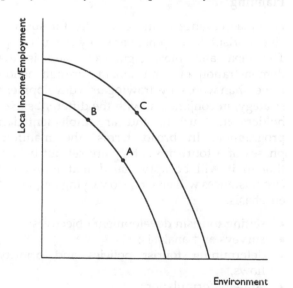

Figure 1. The concept of sustainable development.

A to B which trades off employment against environmental quality. The concept of sustainable tourism development argues that economic growth and environmental quality should not be and are not mutually exclusive events. Cooper (Chapter 12) shows how they go hand in hand by reviewing the environmental consequences of resorts in economic decline. By changes in technology to improve the use of resources in the production process and controlling waste it is possible to reach a position such as C in Figure 1. Going green can build a platform for long-term growth by offering a better product, saving money, and raising the public image of the industry. Sustainable development thus offers a mechanism to escape the 'limits to growth' syndrome illustrated by a move from A to B.

However, of concern to researchers in the field is that, by knowing that some future technology may allow destinations to maintain economic growth and correct for damage to the environment, this may offer policy makers the opportunity to postpone action and continue with private market solutions. Too often there is talk of high quality tourism yet performance is measured in visitor numbers. As several Mediterranean resorts have found to their cost, the unfettered operation of the market may lead to results which are contrary to what are desired. What often happens is that a combination of real estate speculation and the prospect of a rapid pay-back on invested capital causes the accommodation sector to outpace the capacity of the resources required to support a balanced tourism development programme. This is portrayed in Figure 2, where it may be seen that accommodation supply is running ahead of demand and, in so doing, overloads the water supply, creates labour shortages, crowds the beaches and stretches the tolerance of local people as measured by the contact ratio. The latter is the level of the local population divided by the number of tourists present on an average day during the peak month. The outcome is not the integrated tourism development that distils the essence of the country in its design, but a rather crowded, over-built and placeless environment with polluted beaches. Although such a result is somewhat paradoxical in that it is not in the long term interests of the tourist trade, it arises from individual economic agents failing to take account of the external effects of their actions on the tourism resource. Thus a strategy which appears rational from the standpoint of the individual may not be rational from the perspective of the community (Hardin, 1969); the market system, in this respect, is deemed to have failed.

With this in mind, Butler (Chapter 2) reviews the notion of carrying capacity and argues that, despite the many imponderables, researchers should attempt to give clear measurement guidance to practitioners, who are often left with the simple prescription of limiting numbers as they see no alternative.

Partnership

It should now seem self-evident that making tourism work requires a development partnership between the private commercial sector, non-profit organisations, public sector and host community, recognising that tourism and the environment are interdependent and can be mutually reinforcing. This is a significant shift from some of the free-wheeling market oriented supply-side economics that was being expounded in the 1980s. How prophetic the words of Schumacher (1975) now seem:

> What matters is the direction of research, ... towards an harmonious co-operation with nature rather than a warfare against nature; towards the noiseless, low-energy, elegant and economical solutions normally applied in nature rather than the noisy, high-energy,

brutal, wasteful and clumsy solutions of our present-day sciences.

The principles of balanced or sustainable tourism development have been accepted by the British Government and the way forward has been well laid out in the report by the appointed task force on tourism and the environment (English Tourist Board and the Employment Department Group, 1991):

- the environment has an intrinsic value which outweighs its value as a tourism asset. Its enjoyment by future generations and its long term survival must not be prejudiced by short term considerations;
- tourism should be recognised as a positive activity with the potential to benefit the community and the place as well as the visitor;
- the relationship between tourism and the environment must be managed so that it is sustainable in the long term;
- tourism must not be allowed to damage the resource, prejudice its future enjoyment or bring unacceptable impacts;
- tourism activities and developments should respect the scale, nature and character of the place in which they are sited; and
- in any location, harmony must be sought between the needs of the visitor, the place and the host community.

Planning

Policy acceptance of the principles for sustainable tourism development are only the first step. The next and most significant step is the demonstration of commitment through action rather than words, by drawing up a development strategy, in conjunction with the different stakeholders in tourism, and an implementation programme. In broad terms, the manifold phases of a tourism strategy are set out below, though it will be appreciated that individual circumstances will give rise to varying degrees of emphasis:

- setting tourism development objectives;
- surveys and analysis;
- determining tourist policies and priority flows;
- strategy formulation;
- impact assessment;

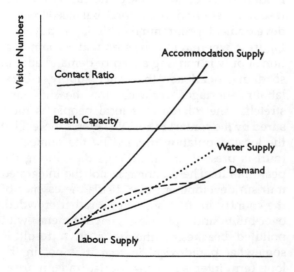

Figure 2. Tourism capacity constraints.

- policy and project implementation;
- monitoring.

A number of case examples are presented in this book. Pigram (Chapter 11) recounts the 'greening' of tourism in Australia and provides a comprehensive review of best practice in relation to environmental management and tourism. The position of the environment in the context of a national tourism plan can be found in Wahab's exposition of tourism in Egypt (Chapter 4) and, at the regional level, Var discusses the development of an ecotourism strategy for Texas. Community development issues are taken up by Smith (as noted earlier) and Din. Using Malaysia as the location, the latter examines the options for the equitable development of tourism through local involvement.

Organisation

In respect of central government, the world-wide significance of tourism as a mechanism for economic development has meant that it is an investment opportunity that few can afford to ignore. But, since the tourist industry does not control all those factors which make up the attractiveness of a destination and the impact on the host population can be considerable, it is necessary that the options concerning the development of tourism should be considered at the highest level of government and the appropriate public administrative framework put in place to ensure sustainable development. Typically, the tourist industry is fragmented into a myriad of agencies and businesses, with manifold objectives and performance criteria, and so there is a need for a centralised body to give direction. In some instances, this may only be a trade association in the form of a Visitor and Convention Bureau but, as a rule, the greater the importance of the industry to a country's economy the greater is the involvement of the public sector, to the point of having a government ministry with sole responsibility for tourism. It is often the case that the planning powers with respect to tourism are devolved to local government, while the executive arm of government is transferred to a non-ministerial public body in the form of the National Tourist Office (NTO). In this respect, Pearce (Chapter 7) presents the findings of innovative research into the regional structure of tourism organisations in

Spain and Wanhill (Chapter 6) offers a case study showing how environmental and community matters are accounted for within the policy formulation of an NTO.

Regulation

The theme of regulation pervades many of the chapters in this book and the balance of the differing views in the tourism literature is in favour of public sector intervention on the premise that the issues surrounding sustainable tourism development are too significant to be left to self-regulation. Amongst practitioners, it is commonly said that there are two things that the tourist industry responds to; one is legislation, the other is money. Thus a combination of monetary rewards or penalties, through, say investment incentives or specific taxes or licenses, and legislative controls in the form of planning restrictions on land use, buildings and access, may be used to drive the industry in the direction dictated by public policy.

Within the developed economies, given their economic framework, there appears to be a growing policy preference for market solutions based on the polluter-pays principle (Pearce *et al*, 1989; Sinclair, 1992). Prices should reflect the marginal economical costs of production plus the marginal environmental costs plus (in the case of an exhaustible resource) the marginal user costs. The sum of these represents the marginal social cost. The difficulty is that many tourism products, especially outdoor recreation areas, have properties akin to 'pure' public goods so that consumption is non-excludable. Thus if the facility is to be provided at all, it must be made available to all, without exception, and free at the point of use. In such situations, there is little choice other than to try to regulate visitor flows in sensitive areas, influence behaviour and/or to follow a programme of continual repair and maintenance.

The different approaches to the impact of visitor pressure on tourism environments are shown in Figure 3. *DD* is the demand schedule and at low rates of consumption the marginal social costs (MSC) consist merely of the marginal economic costs (MEC) of usage. Thus up to V_1 current consumption does not interfere with future consumption or damage the resource. If only current demand is considered then the resource would be used to the level V_2 with visitor expenditure at the destination settling at point B. This results in resource depletion to the extent that the MSC is as high as A. The market solution is to drive consumption back to V_3 by imposing a tourist tax CD on usage to compensate for the renewal costs of the resource. For specific activities this may be achieved by imposing the requirement for participants to hold a licence, over and above the daily user charge. In more general circumstances this is not so straightforward; travel taxes and taxes on bed occupancy are much blunter instruments and their introduction in the past has had more to do with raising government revenue than payment for the costs of visitor crowding.

The problem with the market solutions is that, apart from finding mechanisms for the polluter to pay, estimation of social costs may be extremely speculative and the risk of irreversible damage to the natural resource high. Although sustainability may be defined in terms of a constant capital stock, man-made capital and natural capital cannot be directly substituted and hence the concept has more affinity with the natural environment. In this situation, conservation requires that demand is driven back through planning controls to V_1. The argument runs along the lines that market instruments do not correct the damage inflicted on tourism environments through over-use, but simply licence individuals and organisations to do it. However, society cannot afford to be over-zealous in limiting visitor numbers. CAC represents the

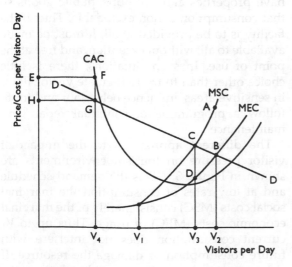

Figure 3. Control versus market solutions.

combined average cost curve of the tourism plant in the community. If demand is forced back to V_4 this plant is no longer viable and, in order to survive in the longer term, it has to be subsidised by an amount $EFGH$. The practical realities of this aspect can be found in situations where local planning has limited revenue earning activities on tourist sites to the detriment of the whole project. It is often not appreciated that tourism enterprises typically have high capital costs in relation to operating expenses and so the ability to service debt out of earnings is critical to long term growth.

The experience in Britain has been that rarely have visitors or tourist businesses been charged directly for the social and environmental costs generated by their actions. The money is paid indirectly through general taxation and most of the burden of coping with congestion, litter and visitor management falls on the public sector, particularly local authorities. To this extent, the British Department of the Environment tries to take account of the influx of visitors in its support grant for local authorities. The government task force (English Tourist Board and the Employment Department Group, 1991) looked at a tourist or bed tax but did not see this as a realistic option to pursue, although the Government did introduce an air travel tax in 1994, but the rates were higher for outbound than inbound tourism, which indicates that this was primarily a revenue-generating instrument. Nevertheless, the task force concluded that:

> 'The tourism industry should seek to ensure, so far as is practicable and compatible with the principles of sustainable tourism, that visitors contribute directly towards the costs which their activities cause'.

A compromise solution is to set up 'honesty' boxes and encourage donations, a common method adopted by cathedrals and churches. However, in sensitive areas where visitor management techniques either fail to regulate demand or become too expensive, it may be necessary in the future to assign quotas, say, V_1 in Figure 3 to tourist enterprises, yet at the same time allowing market forces to work by levying a graduated tourist charge on those businesses exceeding their quotas. The object here is to position the community as near as possible to point C on the diagram. To ensure that allocations are adjusted in an optimal manner, businesses will be allowed to buy and sell quotas. Lindberg and Huber (1993) see the possibility of auctioning off licences to tour operators in those areas, particularly national parks, where there is a high degree of admission control.

Clearly, the model depicted in Figure 3 is not static. In times of growth this is of benefit, for it is politically less painful to refuse planning consent for new projects than it is to regulate existing operators. Over time it is expected that new technologies and visitor management techniques will enable a shift in the MSC curve to the right. This should allow a greater number of visitors to be handled at a lower cost to the environment (see Butler, Chapter 2 for a more expansive discussion), which is, after all, what sustainable tourism development is about.

REFERENCES

Cooper, C., Fletcher, J., Gilbert, D. and Wanhill, S. (1993), *Tourism: Principles and Practice*, London: Pitman.

English Tourist Board and the Employment Department Group (1991), *Tourism and the Environment: Maintaining the Balance*, London: Glasgow and Associates.

Hardin, G. (1969), The tragedy of the commons, *Science*, **162**, 1243–1248.

Lindberg, K. and Huber, R. (1993), Economic issues in ecotourism management, in Lindberg, K. and Hawkins, D. (Editors), *Ecotourism: a Guide for Planners and Managers*, North Bennington, Vermont: The Ecotourism Society.

Pearce, D., Markandya, A. and Barbier, E. (1989), *Blueprint for a Green Economy*, London: Earthscan.

Schumacher, E. F. (1975), *Small is Beautiful: Economics as if People Mattered*, New York: Harper and Row.

Sinclair, M. T. (1992), Tourism, economic development and the environment: problems and policies, in Cooper, C. and Lockwood, A. (Editors) *Progress in Tourism, Recreation and Hospitality Management*, Chichester: Wiley, Vol 4, 75–81.

Wheeller, B. (1992), Is progressive tourism appropriate?, *Tourism Management* **13**, 1, 104–105.

World Commission on Environment and Development (1987), *Our Common Future*, Oxford: Oxford University Press.

Rethinking Impacts of Tourism

1

Geoffrey Wall

ABSTRACT

Current work on impacts of tourism has deficiencies which hamper the development of cumulative knowledge and the practical application of that knowledge. While much is known about the consequences of tourism for destination areas in a general sense, much less is known about the types of tourism which stimulate these changes and the contexts in which these changes occur. As a minimum, more comprehensive typologies of tourism are required, incorporating types of tourists, community characteristics, the nature of visitor–resident interactions and the role of culture brokers. More radically, it may be advisable to develop a research paradigm which acknowledges explicitly that tourism is usually only one among a number of agents of change impacting upon communities and that it is artificial to abstract tourism from this broader context.

THE NATURE OF TOURISM IMPACTS

It is contended that much work on the impacts of tourism is simplistic and that a more sophisticated perspective is required if understanding is to be advanced. While much is known about the consequences of tourism for destination areas in a general sense (Mathieson and Wall, 1982), much less is known about the types of tourism which stimulate these changes and the contexts in which these changes occur. Thus, much more needs to be done in describing aspects of tourism and associated impacts in a more rigorous manner.

The Desirability of Impacts

Impact is often used as a perjurative term and it is often assumed that impacts are likely to be negative. However, residents of destination areas often want tourists to come and want them very much: destination areas seek tourism development and advertise to attract tourists. They do this because they want their lifestyles to change. They want jobs, higher incomes, increased tax revenues and better opportunities for their children. Of course, the benefits may be largely economic and may sometimes be illusory, and there may be adverse consequences, often of an environmental or socio-cultural nature, associated with acquiring the benefits. Thus, trade-offs are likely to be involved. Are the benefits worth the costs? As an aside, it is worth pointing out that it is not possible to maximise the benefits and, at the same time, to minimise the costs, as many writers continue to suggest (Van Lier and Taylor, 1993). It is not possible to maximise and minimise at the same time.

Prospects of change are often viewed with dismay by outside observers who bemoan the modifications in the traditional lifestyles of indigenous peoples. However, it should not be assumed that such peoples do not want change, especially when exposed to alternative lifestyles. Furthermore, it should also not be assumed that indigenous communities that have existed largely unchanged for centuries are in harmony with their environment. Many such peoples have short life-spans, high death rates, inadequate food supplies and suffer from ill-health. They may be quaint and appear to be happy to the outsider who may be reluctant to see them change and would be happy if they retained their marginalised positions (Oakes, 1992). However, should legitimate aspirations for change be denied? Paradoxically, in a tourism context, residents of destination areas may be encouraged to retain their traditions in order that they can develop! The situation is extremely complex, but the main points I wish to make are that impacts are often desired, are extremely difficult to assess, may require the acceptance of trade-offs and, in a policy context, may involve the development of strategies to mitigate undesirable impacts.

The Context of Impacts

The impacts of tourism can be viewed as arising from the type or types of tourism involved, the characteristics of the communities in which tourism is taking place and the nature of resident–visitor encounters. Furthermore, investigations of tourism cycles suggest that impacts in a destination area are likely to change with time as the nature of tourists, the community and resident–visitor interactions also change (Butler, 1980). Furthermore, much change associated with tourism may be cumulative as a number of small enterprises is developed in sequence in close proximity, each having a minor impact when viewed alone, but together having far-reaching consequences. Cumulative impact assessment is a challenging topic which is beginning to attract the attention of those charged with conducting and evaluating impact assessments, although it has yet to receive much recognition in the tourism literature (Shoemaker, 1994). While environmental impact assessments for specific tourism developments such as resorts and marinas have an important place, it should be recognized that tourists are mobile and their impacts are not confined to the bounds of such establishments, for example having implications

for transportation termini through which access is provided and attractions which are visited (Butler, 1993). Thus in addition to impact assessment, monitoring of change may be required and mitigation strategies may be required to reduce the magnitude of environmental consequences (Nelson *et al.* 1993).

While much work has documented the impacts of tourism, often under economic, environmental and socio-cultural headings, few authors have taken the trouble to document adequately the types of tourism, the community characteristics or the nature of host–guest encounters which give rise to these impacts. In fact it would be worthwhile to review the tourism impacts literature in an attempt to establish more precisely the contexts in which authors have documented specific impacts. Failure to provide such information or to take note of it adequately has resulted in:

(1) Communication failures. If one person is thinking of impacts of downhill skiing, while a second is concerned about sunbathing on a beach, and a third is contemplating visiting an historic site, is it any wonder that they come up with differing evaluations of impacts and talk past each other?

(2) Contradictory findings. The findings in the literature are not consistent. Thus, for example, some authors lament the destruction of culture as a result of tourism and others point to the role of tourism in stimulating cultural revival (McKean, 1973, 1989; Noronha, 1976; Picard 1983; Udayana University and Francillon, 1975). Who is correct? Of course, both perspectives may be correct, but in different circumstances and to varying degrees. However, as suggested above, little attempt appears to have been made to ascertain what types of tourism in what type of community and in what type of host–guest interaction give rise to specific impacts.

(3) Limited policy relevance. The general failure to specify adequately the contexts in which impacts occur means that the impacts literature provides limited guidance to decision-makers. In general, it fails to indicate how many people, of what type, doing which activities, in communities with specified characteristics, in specific forms of

host–guest interaction result in particular consequences. This is not the same as calculating carrying capacities which has its own problems (Wall, 1982), but an understanding of use–impact relationships is essential for establishing carrying capacities (if you believe they exist!) and limits of acceptable change (Stankey and McCool, 1984), or for implementing concepts such as the tourism or recreation opportunity spectrum (Driver *et al.*, 1987).

While this is not the place to review the carrying capacity literature, it is worth pointing out that the determination of appropriate levels of use is as much a value judgment related to the goals set for the site as a technical problem. While many researchers have eschewed the search for a magic number, which can be approached with impunity and exceeded at peril, recognising that management is required from the time that the first tourists arrive, if not before, and that trade-offs will be required, many managers still seek a simple solution to a complex problem through belief that a single inherent capacity exists and that this number can be determined by technical means. Such a perspective puts power in the hands of consultants who are hired as experts to determine the non-existent number. On the other hand, perspectives such as limits of acceptable change have the potential to empower local people if they are permitted to provide input on the acceptability of possible trade-offs.

(4) Culture brokers. Resident–visitor interaction may be mediated by culture brokers with implications for social, environmental and economic impacts. While a literature on cultural brokers is emerging slowly (Lew, 1992) and an extensive literature on interpretation exists (Machlis and Field, 1984), very little of this deals explicitly with the role of culture brokers in influencing impacts of tourism in destination areas.

(5) Saliency. The saliency of impacts refers to the importance of impacts, usually according to the views of residents of destination areas and usually ascertained through public opinion surveys. The interpretation of survey results is often facile. For example, because most people acknowledge that increased tourism is likely to be associated with increased litter and fewer spontaneously identify changing land values, it does not follow that litter is a more important problem than land values. Furthermore, the litter problem is not difficult to resolve (for people can be paid to pick it up) when compared with land values which may be expected to increase or decline depending upon one's perspective and are very difficult to manage.

(6) Aggregated and disaggregated measures. Different types of impacts are measured in different ways. Thus for example, economic impacts may be recorded in currency units or units of employment, environmental impacts may be assessed through concepts such as species diversity or coliform counts, and social impacts may be assessed through surveys whose results may be presented according to the proportions of respondents agreeing or disagreeing with particular propositions. In such situations it is virtually impossible to come up with a single summary measure and to determine whether the benefits exceed the costs.

This is an intractable problem for benefit–cost analyses. However, it may be less critical for managers who require disaggregated data rather than a single combined index to inform their decisions. It is a paradox that, as described in the discussion of carrying capacity above, many continue to seek a single number when disaggregated information is much more useful for decision-making and the evaluation of the inevitable trade-offs.

Thus, it is suggested that the existing impacts literature has a number of deficiencies and, as a minimum, there is a need to:

- verify the tourist typologies which exist, most of which have not been based upon detailed empirical investigations (Murphy, 1985, p. 5–8);
- develop classifications of destination area communities;
- examine the nature of resident–visitor interactions including the extent to which they are mediated by culture brokers;
- place the recording and monitoring of impacts in the context of all of the above.

- assess the utility of the widely discussed related planning and management concepts.

If such steps were taken, the quality of impact analyses and their comparability would be greatly improved and the body of knowledge might be cumulative rather than a series of case studies as is presently largely the case. The resulting investigations might also be more useful to planners and managers. However, by themselves they are insufficient to bring about more fundamental modifications in perspective which are required.

A FADING PARADIGM OR WHO IS DOING WHAT TO WHOM?

Either explicitly or, more often, implicitly, tourism is viewed as an external force imposed upon a static community, causing change in that community and leading ultimately to the establishment of a new equilibrium. This is what Wood (1980) has termed the billiard ball assumption.

In fact, none of the components of the billiard ball assumption is usually tenable. As has already been suggested, tourism is not simply an external force and tourism may be sought and welcomed by members of destination areas. In practice it is extremely difficult to distinguish between internal and external forces of change. Furthermore, few communities are static and vibrant cultures are likely to be in a continual state of flux for a diversity of reasons and not simply because of the onset of tourism. In addition, it is virtually impossible, and perhaps unrealistic, to separate the consequences of tourism from other causes of change which may be occurring in the same place at the same time. However, since it is usually impracticable to study everything at the same time, it is often pragmatic to abstract tourism from the broader context of change to make investigation more manageable. However, the milieu in which those changes occur should not be forgotten and, ideally as has been argued above, should be incorporated into the analyses. As will be illustrated below, residents of destination areas are not simply acted upon: some respond to opportunities and thus play an active role in contributing to and directing change. Thus, in

this post-modern world, destination areas are exposed to global and local forces of change as well as factors operating at intermediate scales making the attribution of cause and effect a particularly difficult challenge.

The above perspectives will be illustrated with examples from Bali, Indonesia. In particular, the latter point of indigenous response to tourism opportunities will be illustrated through reference to the creation of 'homestays' (bed and breakfast establishments) by residents of Bali and through discussion of the involvement of the informal sector in Balinese tourism.

TOURISM IN BALI

Space does not permit a detailed explication of the history or current status of tourism in Bali (Picard, 1992, Wall and Dibnah, 1992). Suffice to say that tourism has become an extremely important sector of the Balinese economy and it also intersects with and has implications for most other economic sectors. Tourism has grown so rapidly in the last 25 years since the construction of an international airport that, if the craft industries associated with tourism are included, it now contributes in excess of 30% of the gross provincial product and one estimate in the early 1990s suggested that the figure may now be as high as 40% (Bali Tourism Development Corporation, n. d.).

While tourism has been a major agent of change in Bali, it has not been the only one. For example, Bali has experienced the green revolution, the introduction of family planning, rural electrification and increased exposure to electronic media. Balinese culture has not been static, but has been modified by many outside forces, such as the influences of European artists who chose to settle and work in Bali, the impositions of colonial powers and the employment opportunities associated with tourism (Vickers, 1989). Expressions of Balinese culture have been adopted as symbols of national identity by government spokespersons in Jakarta (Picard, 1990) and the culture of Bali has become one of the island's most important resources for tourism.

Cultural tourism (pariwisata budaya) is the official tourism product and policy. However, tourism is outside the complete control of the

Balinese and even Indonesian authorities and the development of tourism in Bali have been strongly influenced by the advice received from international agencies. Off-island investors, western anthropologists and the movie industry have created the image of an island paradise.

Outsiders, particularly western visitors, have long viewed Balinese culture as being unique and special (Vickers, 1989). By definition, international tourists come from elsewhere and their decisions to visit are influenced by local and international events and situations. For example, a slow world economy and the Gulf War dampened the demand for international travel in 1991, leading to low occupancy rates and an over-supply of tourist accommodation in Bali. Tourism plans have concentrated upon large investments in an international airport and five-star hotels and much of the investment in tourism infrastructure in Bali is not Balinese.

In spite of the strength of outside influences, the Balinese have found ways to participate in tourism. Residents of Bali have sought to benefit from the economic opportunities which tourism has brought. These opportunities have occurred in both the formal and informal sectors, in part and full-time positions, including the establishment of hotels, restaurants and guide services and employment in such businesses, as well as the manufacture and sale of craft products, the undertaking of cultural performances and the production of fruit and vegetables to feed the visitors (Cukier-Snow and Wall 1993, Cukier and Wall, 1994b). One among many such responses has been the development of 'homestays' in which Balinese families take visitors into their homes in much the same way as bed and breakfast accommodation has proliferated in parts of the western world. A second response is the increase in the number of vendors who sell products and services to tourists in an informal manner. These two examples are described briefly below.

'Homestays' as an Indigenous Response to Tourism

'Homestays' are usually family-owned and operated, and accommodation usually consists of a room with two single beds with a bathroom, and breakfast. They are generally cheap (averaging approximately Rp. 10,000 per night single,

Rp. 12,000 double, or US $ 5 and $6, respectively) and supply inexpensive accommodation for a low-budget clientele. However, they also afford views of traditional housing compounds and family life and cater to the demand from some tourists for interaction with the Balinese. As Stringer (1981) has pointed out in a western context, bed and breakfast establishments are seen not only as a form of commercial accommodation, but are also viewed by both operators and patrons as a means of establishing interpersonal relationships.

Hassall and Associates (1992) suggest that there were, as of 1992, 1663 rooms for rent in homestays in Bali, but this is likely an underestimate. Hussey (1986, 1989), drawing primarily upon a sample of 50 accommodation establishments in Kuta in 1984, demonstrated that even in situations in which resources may appear to be limited, existing resources will be used effectively by local people if they see an opportunity to engage in entrepreneurial activities which will improve their economic situation. Aided by the availability of a white sand beach, proximity to the airport, government promotion of Bali and, at least initially, absence of competition from professional developers, local entrepreneurs were able to meet the relatively low standards sought by 'budget' tourists. Successful involvement resulted from a willingness to take risks and liquidate resources, the ability to recognise changes in tourists' demands, and the manipulation of 'traditional' resources such as the residence, land, gold, agrarian products and family social networks, singularly or in combination, in order to establish business to meet a growing demand from foreign visitors.

A recent study of 'homestays' in Peliatan, a village near Ubud in south-central Bali, confirms and updates Hussey's findings (Long and Wall, 1995; Wall and Long, 1996). All but one of 24 'homestays' investigated were owned and operated by resident families. They had been in operation for between 1 month and 18 years, although 11 had been in operation for 1 year or less, and two were under construction. They had between one and nine rooms for rent, although most were quite small, 17 having four or less rooms for rent. Prices per room ranged between Rp. 5000–20,000 per night single with cold water, and Rp.10,000–30,000 with hot and cold water (although only four establishments had rooms with hot water), and were only slightly more expensive for double occupancy. In half of the establishments all work was done by family members, seven relied primarily on hired help, and the remainder used a mixture of family and hired workers. Twelve respondents claimed to have had previous experience in some sort of tourist business or in a tourist area, but two admitted that they were currently uncertain of what they were doing and were learning on the job. No formal job training was reported. With respect to plans for the future, 16 wanted to build additional rooms and two wanted to add hot water.

It should be evident from the above that the accommodation establishments in the Peliatan study area constitute examples of indigenous responses to tourism. Most were small, locally owned and operated, and most had a short history. Whether the latter reflects rapid growth or the instability of small establishments is not known.

The research, like that of Hussey (1986) mentioned above, clearly demonstrates the desire and ability of at least some Balinese to cater to tourists. 'Homestays' require a relatively low initial capital outlay and, in the study area, this type of business was potentially accessible to any family with a spare room or the space to build one, for small rooms and a lack of hot water were generally acceptable to the existing clientele. However, it is unfortunate that returns to investors in the study area are unclear: operators generally lacked formal management and pricing skills, and actual prices paid varied since bargaining is a part of most transactions. Most likely, 'homestay' operation was a supplementary income for many operators.

Informal Sector Employment

Employment in the informal sector has not received the attention which it deserves from tourism researchers and planners (Cukier-Snow and Wall, 1993). Tourism plans in developing countries often ignore the informal sector entirely or try to eliminate the participation of the informal sector in satisfying the needs of tourists. It is true that some forms of informal activity, such as prostitution, may be deemed undesirable, but there are many others which provide legitimate economic opportunities for individuals who might otherwise have difficulty in participating in the tourism economy.

In a study of vendors in Bali, Cukier and Wall (1994a) found that most such workers were male. The majority were unmarried teenagers or young adults with limited formal education but substantial language skills, which they had picked up on the job. While many hawkers felt that they had few alternative employment opportunities, most enjoyed their work and, although hours were long, they were generally well remunerated, at least by Indonesian standards. In fact, this was the main attraction of the position. Many vendors viewed their current employment as a means of acquiring the skills necessary to gain access to employment in the formal sector. However, it is unclear how many are successful in this objective. Nevertheless, in countries of the South, where there may be great challenges in making a living, vending can provide above-average incomes and hawking products to tourists may be an acceptable and remunerative activity. It is one way in which some local people create opportunities to become involved in the tourism economy.

IMPLICATIONS OF THE BALINESE SITUATION

Vibrant cultures are not static and there are divergent opinions concerning changes in the outward manifestations of Balinese lifestyles resulting from tourism (see above). Differences of opinion are difficult to resolve because of the problems involved in measuring and evaluating the significance of changes. For example, Balinese ceremonies are now often more ornate than in the past. Does this mean that Balinese people are now more religious or is this merely a reflection of rising living standards? Somewhat similarly, a growing number of Balinese, particularly in urban areas, purchase rather than make their daily offerings. What is the cultural significance of this? It has been suggested that modifications in clothing styles and diet (replacement of rice by bread) are occurring in resort areas (Manuabe *et al.* 1990). Are these problems and which of them is most important? Could such behaviours be measured and used as indices of cultural change?

CHANGE, IMPACTS AND OPPORTUNITIES

Changes, whether economic, environmental or socio-cultural, are inevitable and it is likely that rapid rates of growth in tourism will accelerate change. Which changes are acceptable? Which are unacceptable? Who will or should decide these questions? What strategies can be put in place to manage change? From the perspective of culture, clear answers to these questions can only be derived if there is a strong sense of identity and self-worth. If people do not know or are not comfortable with whom they are and where they have come from, it is difficult for them to arrive at decisions on what is sacred and to be protected at all costs, and what is profane and can be shared with visitors. Fortunately, the Balinese have a well-developed sense of identity. It remains to be seen if it is sufficiently strong, and if decision-making processes will permit them, to incorporate the inevitable changes associated with burgeoning tourism on their own terms.

TOWARDS A NEW RESEARCH DIRECTION

It has been argued that the words 'impacts' and 'change' have extremely similar meanings. However, the former tends to be more emotive than the latter and usually conjures up images of negative change, ignoring the fact that tourism is often wanted by some members of destination areas because of certain positive changes which may be anticipated.

Furthermore, tourism is unlikely to be the only agent of change in operation in a particular place or at any point in time. At the same time, some residents of destination areas are not simply impacted upon, but create and respond to opportunities associated with tourism. Thus a broader conceptualization of change than the narrower perspective of impacts is required if the consequences and opportunities associated with tourism are to be more fully appreciated.

Some brief thoughts on fruitful research directions and procedures which respond to these concerns will now be provided.

It is suggested that much may be gained by considering tourism as one among many agents of change. Thus, as a starting point, one might attempt to document all major changes that have occurred in study communities over a period of time. The findings could then be shared with members of the community for validation. In this way one could ascertain which changes are regarded by them as being of greater or lesser importance, whether tourism is considered to be a major or minor agent of change, and which changes are ascribed to tourism and which to other forces. At the same time one would acquire both an etic and an emic, or external and internal, views of change. Such investigations would benefit greatly from careful documentation of the types of tourists under consideration, destination community characteristics, the nature of host–guest interactions and the roles of culture brokers or, in other words, the development of a more sophisticated tourism (as opposed to tourist) typology. Also, the incorporation of the results of impact studies in decision-making for planning and management will be furthered by relinquishing the thoughtless application of simplistic concepts such as carrying capacity.

SUMMARY AND CONCLUSIONS

The current work on impacts of tourism has deficiencies which hamper the development of cumulative knowledge. It has been argued that it is simplistic to view tourism as an exogenous force impacting upon a static destination area. A description of some aspects of tourism in Bali, Indonesia, demonstrates that as tourism has expanded with considerable input from 'outsiders', residents of Bali have found opportunities to participate in tourism development. Tourism is often sought and invited, and residents respond to take advantage of the opportunities which it affords. Such complex situations are not handled well by the existing impacts paradigm. As a minimum, enhanced understanding of the consequences of tourism will require the development of more comprehensive typologies of tourism, incorporating types of tourists, community characteristics, the nature of visitor–resident interactions and the role of culture brokers. More radically, it may be advisable to develop a research paradigm which acknowledges explicitly that tourism is usually only one among a number of agents of change impacting upon communities and that, while necessary for pragmatic reasons, ultimately it is artificial to abstract tourism from this broader context.

ACKNOWLEDGMENTS

The materials on Bali were collected with the support of the Bali Sustainable Development Project, which has been funded by the Canadian International Development Agency.

REFERENCES

Bali Tourism Development Corporation (n.d.), *Tourist Resorts in Indonesia: The Nusa Dua Concept*, Bali: BTDC.

Butler, R. (1980), The concept of a tourist area cycle of evolution: implications for management of resources, *Canadian Geographer*, **24** (1), 5–12.

Butler, R. (1993), Pre- and post-impact assessment of tourism development, in Pearce, D. G., and Butler, R. W., (Editors), *Tourism Research: Critiques and Challenges*, London: Routledge, 135–155.

Cukier, J. and Wall, G., (1994a) Informal tourism employment in Bali, Indonesia, *Tourism Management*, **15** (6), 464–467.

Cukier, J. and Wall, G., (1994b), Tourism employment in Bali, Indonesia, *Tourism Recreation Research*, **19** (1), 32–40.

Cukier-Snow, J. and Wall, G. (1993), Tourism and employment: perspectives from Bali, *Tourism Management*, **14** (3), 195–201.

Driver, B. L., Brown, P. J., Stankey, G. H. and Gregoire, T. G. (1987), The ROS planning system: evolution, basic concepts and research needs, *Leisure Sciences*, **9** (3), 201–212.

Hassall and Associates (1992), The Tourism Sector. Comprehensive Tourism Development Plan for Bali, Denpasar, Bali, Annex 3.

Hussey, A. (1986), Resources for development, tourism and small-scale indigenous enterprises in Bali, Honolulu: University of Hawaii PhD Thesis, Department of Geography.

Hussey, A. (1989), Tourism in a Balinese village, *Geographical Review*, **79** (3), 311–325.

Lew, A. (1992), Perceptions of tourists and tour guides in Singapore, *Journal of Cultural Geography*, **12** (2), 45–52.

Long, V. and Wall, G. (1995), Small-scale tourism development in Bali, Indonesia, in Conlin, M., and Baum, T., (Editors), *Island Tourism: Management Principles and Practice*, New York: John Wiley and Sons, Inc., 237–257.

Machlis, G. E. and Field, D. R. (1984), *On Interpretation: Sociology for Interpreters of Natural and Cultural History*, Corvallis: Oregon State University Press.

Manuabe, A., Sunarta, N. and Prata, P. (1990), Tourism development in Bali and its impacts, *Proceedings of the International Seminar on Human Ecology, Tourism, and Sustainable Development*, Bali: Bali-HESG, 145–151.

Mathieson, A. and Wall, G. (1982), *Tourism: Economic, Physical and Social Impacts*, London: Longman.

McKean, P. (1973), Cultural involution: tourists, Balinese, and the process of modernization in an anthropological perspective, Providence: Brown University, Phd Thesis, Department of Anthropology.

McKean, P. (1989), Towards a theoretical analysis of tourism: economic dualism and cultural involution in Bali, in Smith, V., (Editor), Hosts and Guests: The Anthropology of Tourism, Philadelphia: University of Pennsylvania Press (2nd ed), 119–138.

Murphy, P. (1985), *Tourism: A Community Approach*, New York: Methuen,

Nelson, J. G., Butler, R. and Wall, G., (1993), *Tourism and Sustainable Development; Monitoring, Planning, Managing*, Department of Geography Publication Series no. 37, Waterloo: University of Waterloo.

Noronha, R. (1976), Paradise reviewed: tourism in Bali, in De Kadt, E., (Editor), *Tourism: Passport to Development?* Oxford: Oxford University Press, 177–204.

Oakes, T. (1992), Cultural geography and Chinese ethnic tourism, *Journal of Cultural Geography*, **12** (2), 4–17.

Picard, M. (1983), Community participation in tourist activity on the island of Bali: environment, ideologies and practices, Paris: UNESCO–CNRS.

Picard, M. (1990), Kebalian Orang Bali: tourism and the uses of 'Balinese culture' in new order Indonesia, *Review of Indonesian and Malaysian Affairs*, **24**, 1–38.

Picard, M. (1992), *Bali: Tourisme culturel et culture touristique*, Paris: L'Harmattan.

Shoemaker, D. J. (1994), *Cumulative Environmental Assessment*, Department of Geography Publication series no 42, Waterloo: University of Waterloo.

Stankey, G. H. and McCool, S. F. (1984), Carrying capacity in recreational settings: evolution, appraisal and application, *Leisure Sciences*, **6**, 453–474.

Stringer, P. (1981), Hosts and guests: the bed and breakfast phenomenon, *Annals of Tourism Research*, **8** (3), 357–376.

Udayana University and Francillon, G. (1975) Tourism in Bali – its economic and socio-cultural impact: three points of view, *International Social Science Journal*, **27** (4), 721–725.

Van Lier, H. N. and Taylor, P. D. (1993), *New Challenges in Recreation and Tourism Planning*, Amsterdam: Elsevier.

Vickers, A. (1989), *Bali: A Paradise Created*, Berkeley and Singapore: Periplus.

Wall, G. (1982), Cycles and capacity: incipient theory or conceptual contradiction? *Tourism Management*, **3** (3), 188–192.

Wall, G. and Dibnah, S. (1992), The changing status of tourism in Bali, Indonesia, *Progress in Tourism, Recreation and Hospitality Management*, **4**, 120–130.

Wall, G. and Long, V. (1996), Balinese 'homestays', an indigenous response to tourism opportunities, in Butler, R., and Hinch, T. (Editors), *Tourism and Native Peoples*, London: Thomson Business Press, pp. 27–48.

Wood, R. E. (1980), International tourism and cultural change in Southeast Asia, *Economic Development and Cultural Change*, **28** (3), 561–581.

The Concept of Carrying Capacity for Tourism Destinations: Dead or Merely Buried?

R. W. Butler

2

ABSTRACT

Tourism inevitably impacts upon destinations. One of the central concepts in the management of such impacts is that of carrying capacity. However, this chapter argues that destinations have been poorly served by the development of the concept of carrying capacity into growth management techniques such as limits of acceptable change and opportunity spectrums. This is particularly the case for destinations dependent upon natural characteristics for their appeal. The chapter argues that adoption of such techniques leads to creeping incremental development and changes the profile of the visitor towards those more tolerant of higher use. The chapter argues for a return to the idea of identifying maximum appropriate numbers of users.

INTRODUCTION

All forecasts of tourism predict continued growth at the global scale (WTO, 1995), and, by implication, increased levels of use at destination areas. At the same time there are increasing reports of crowding, of decline in quality of landscapes, physical plant and satisfaction of visitors in many established destinations. It is hard to escape the conclusion that at least a part of this problem lies in the fact that many destinations are now operating beyond their carrying capacity, however that term may be defined. In the recreation literature there has been extensive work on the carrying capacity of destination areas, and this research has changed considerably in its approach over the last three decades. The focus has moved from the idea of determining a specific maximum number of users (Wagar, 1964) towards concepts such as the 'limits of acceptable change' and 'opportunity spectrums' (Clark and Stankey, 1979; Stankey et al., 1985; Butler and Waldbrook, 1991) which place an emphasis on management policies meeting visitor expectations and preferences rather than determining limits to use.

Although these approaches have received widespread support in the literature and by management agencies since their introduction in the late 1970s (Williams and Gill, 1991), it is argued in this chapter that such approaches, in fact, serve destination areas poorly in the long run, especially those areas which are most dependent upon natural characteristics for their attractiveness and appeal. Discussion in the chapter focuses on the proposition that the adoption of such practices results in a form of creeping incrementalism of development, and with it cumulative change, shifts in tastes and types of tourists, and essentially a shifting of capacity limits in favour of ever higher levels of use. This process has left destination areas potentially exposed to overuse and, unless corrective actions can be taken, inevitable radical change and possibly ultimate despoliation. It is argued that there should be a return to the concept of identifying maximum appropriate numbers of users, and if necessary the limitation of the numbers of visitors and the amount and type of development permitted. If such steps are not taken, then it is concluded that there is little chance of controlling or mitigating the impacts caused by excessive levels of visitation, with no hope of retaining those elements which were once the major attractions of these destinations.

RESEARCH ON CARRYING CAPACITY

Growing Awareness of Capacity Issues

The application of the concept of carrying capacity in recreation and leisure studies has evolved in stages, first from what might be categorised as irrelevancy to a topic of considerable attention, and then to one of potential, if indirect, concern. In the decade following the First World War, when mass tourism can be said to have really begun, many destinations were busy, often operating at capacity or overcapacity at peak periods, but few people were worried by this. The phenomenon of mass tourism was new, few tourists knew what to expect, crowds at the then relatively few established holiday resorts were expected and even required for a satisfactory mass-tourism experience (Ogilvie, 1933). At the more elite destinations, crowding or business was also seen as a feature of success and even exclusivity, and given what was then the recent development of many facilities, overuse had had little time to take effect.

The years of economic depression in the early 1930s saw periods of underuse, and the idea of concern about crowding and capacity problems disappeared until the economic recovery in the second half of the decade. At this time, however, most operators and tourists were so glad that

economic troubles were over that they were prepared to put up with some crowding after years of little business or no holidays. The end of the decade saw other things on people's minds than problems of capacity tourist destinations.

The 1940s were not a time for contemplating the evils of overcapacity of tourist destinations, and after World War Two few people had time, money or opportunity to crowd holiday destinations, certainly not in most of Europe. The ravages of the war and its effect on transportation and other elements of infrastructure in Europe at least, meant that even if the levels of affluence, amount of free time and inclination of people to take holidays had been high, facilities were not in place to allow them to travel widely. Much of the leisure travel that took place in the immediate post-war years was confined to established holiday resorts, especially those mass resorts which had escaped the effects of war, and new facilities such as holiday camps, designed to cater for low- to middle-income domestic mass tourism. Absence of private vehicles in much of Europe and rationing of goods still further curtailed the ability to travel, particularly for leisure purposes. Thus overuse of destinations was not an issue, and those destinations with heavy visitation both expected and desired such levels of use.

It was the 1950s which first saw the real explosion of tourism in its modern form, especially in North America, but overuse was still not an issue in most locations. Crowds were still viewed as a sign of success and any environmental impacts were either not noticeable because of their recency, or, in tune with 1950's philosophy, not viewed as significant. Only a very few authors such as Clawson (1959) noted the explosive growth of recreational and leisure travel in the 1950s and mused on the possible implications of such levels, primarily in North America, which had recovered from the war much more rapidly than had Europe or Asia.

The 1960s saw a marked change in attitudes and awareness with respect to the potential effects of rapid growth in tourism and recreation. These attitudes can be related to a general growing concern with the effects of development on the environment, dramatised in such works as *Silent Spring* by Carson (1962) and *Limits to Growth* by Meadows *et al*. (1972). They were mirrored by the development of concerns over increasing leisure use and resulting impacts in many natural areas, particularly in North America.

The Emergence of Research on Carrying Capacity

It was the decade of the 1960s which witnessed the beginning of extensive research activity on the subject of carrying capacity, especially by geographers working with the US Forest Service such as Lucas (1964a, b) and Wagar (1964), with a particular focus on wilderness and remote locations. In such areas, of course, environmental and social impacts were easily and quickly visible, and thus of considerable concern to both resource managers who were expected to offer wilderness and high-quality experiences to visitors, and to the visitors who had expectations of high-quality environments and solitude when visiting such areas. There is little evidence in the tourism literature of the 1960s of concerns over capacity limitations, with one or two exceptions. One is in the writings of Wolfe (1964, 1966) who drew attention to the rapid growth rate of tourism and its potential effects on destination areas, including the ability to transform the appeal of an area from inherent to man-made attractions (Wolfe, 1952). Another is the continued commentary of Clawson (1963) on the problems of providing sufficient opportunity for a rapidly increasing number of visitors to many recreation and tourism areas. His concerns were echoed by Darling and Eichorn (1966) in the context of national parks. One noticeable and rather unique work of this period was a study conducted for the Irish Tourist Board (An Foras Forbatha, 1966) by the United Nations. This was one of the very first studies which attempted to define limits to tourism use on the basis of the physical characteristics of the destination area. In this pioneering study various features and characteristics of destination areas in County Donegal were allocated numbers of visitors they were thought to be capable of absorbing or accommodating. It is interesting to note that this study focused almost entirely on the environmental aspects of capacity and did not deal with the social characteristics of the visitors or the host populations, nor with the economic capacity of the destination communities to absorb the effects of tourism.

The 1970s continued to see very little attention paid to the topic of capacity in the context of tourism, which is perhaps surprising in view of the fact that this decade saw the beginning of a critical examination of the effects of tourism on destination areas, and the development of a now considerable body of literature on the impacts of tourism on host communities and environments (Bryden, 1973; De Kadt, 1973; Young, 1973; Smith, 1977). However, this focus did not extend to the direct consideration of the relationship between levels of use and level and nature of impacts. It did see major and highly significant developments in the context of capacity studies in the recreation field. What is of particular relevance was the beginning of a shift from the search for precise limits and numbers of users which could be sustained by an area, to an approach which recognised a number of alternative capacity levels, some of which were based on human preferences (Lime and Stankey, 1971). This line of research represented a fundamental shift in thinking and established a new focus for theory and research which has remained predominant for the two decades following. This shift has seen resource managers pay increasing attention to allowing levels of use which were viewed as acceptable by most managers and users, at some potential cost to many environments and which certainly has seen the quality of some recreational experiences decline or be re-established at levels lower than those at which they had previously existed.

In the 1980s the rejection of the search for specific numbers was reflected in much of the research, epitomised best in Washbourne's (1982) appropriately titled paper, 'Wilderness recreational carrying capacity: are numbers necessary?', and the idea of managing destination areas on the principle of norms and expectations of visitors continued (Graefe *et al.*, 1984). Probably the most significant piece of research in this context is the Limits of Acceptable Change report of the US Forest Service (Stankey *et al.*, 1985), which introduced the argument that it was more appropriate and feasible to concentrate on identifying levels and rates of acceptable and unacceptable change in destination areas rather than trying to identify specific numbers of users who could be accommodated in these areas. This approach has remained one of the mainstays of capacity research in recreation over the last decade and has been incorporated in a variety of forms into many management plans. The recreation literature in the 1980s reflects almost entirely this changed attitude to capacity research, and is admirably summarised by Stankey and Manning (1986), and placed in a conceptual context by Shelby and Heberlein (1986). In the current decade there has been relatively little change in the thinking on carrying capacity in the recreation field. Where the concept is utilised at all, it has normally been through the application of management concepts reflecting social and perceptual norms of managers and users, as for example in National Parks and wilderness areas in North America (Hendee *et al.*, 1990; Kuss *et al.*, 1990).

It is unfortunate, although as will be noted, understandable, that little of the extensive research in the recreation literature (Vaske listed over 3000 articles and papers on this topic in 1992) has been incorporated into tourism research. In the tourism literature there has appeared a large amount of writing on the impacts and effects of tourism, much of which was lucidly brought together in what has become the standard text on the subject by Mathieson and Wall (1982), which still provides the most comprehensive and conceptually satisfying discussion of the topic. Implicit in that volume is the unwritten philosophy that all tourism results in some form of impacts, and that effects will vary depending on the nature of the host region and population, as well as the nature and dimensions of tourism. There was also continued brief discussions of capacity in most of the standard books on tourism such as Pearce (1987, 1989) and Murphy (1985) which appeared in this decade, and certainly acknowledgment that too many tourists caused problems, but little detailed investigation of the topic. O'Reilly (1986) discussed some of the concepts and issues involved, Walter (1982) raised the issue of social limits to tourism, and Hovinen (1982) related the links between capacity and Butler's (1980) resort cycle, a topic also discussed by Wall (1983). Getz' articles (1982, 1983), however, are the only ones which paid specific attention in trying to identify variables and indicators relating to this topic in the context of tourism in the 1980s.

The 1990s, however, have seen something of a revival or, more accurately, the development of interest in the problem of capacity of tourism destination areas. Whether this is related to the recent interests in sustainable development or not is hard to state categorically. However, a number of pieces on this subject have appeared in the literature, for example, Saleem (1994), Hawkins and Roberts (1994), Johnson and Thomas (1994) and Martin and Usyal (1990), which use the term capacity and appear to accept the necessity of limiting numbers. Saleem (1994) produces a statistical model of the carrying capacity for a tourism destination, incorporating a number of primarily social and economic variables. Martin and Usyal (1990, p. 329) explore the relationship between carrying capacity and the tourism life-cycle, arguing that 'it is impossible to determine tourism carrying capacity outside of the context of the position of the destination area in the lifecycle'. Johnson and Thomas (1994) take a more limited economic viewpoint in raising relevant and generally ignored issues about the ability of local economies to absorb tourism development and expenditures. Hawkins and Roberts (1994) are almost alone in examining the environmental issues involved with tourism development, incorporating these with the quality of the tourist experience in the context of marine tourism. Long *et al.* (1990), in their survey of rural resident attitudes towards tourism, echo the findings of others (Brougham and Butler, 1981; Liu *et al.*, 1987, for example) in reporting that attitudes of residents were not consistent with respect to numbers of visitors or level of development, but that at a point which they were able to identify, resident attitudes became more negative and remained so with respect to tourism. One of the implications of Long *et al.*'s research (1990) is to suggest that there is a perceptible limit to the numbers of visitors who were acceptable to, and desired by, the local population, a view expounded by Doxey (1975) almost two decades earlier. Similar issues are raised by Craik (1995), who argues strongly for the adoption of conditions or indicators to identify the matrix of impacts of tourism to determine limits in the context of culture.

In summary, therefore, approaches to research on carrying capacity over the past four decades have moved from ignoring the topic, to a search for specific numbers, to management approaches based on social and experimental expectations.

Only in the last half decade or so have researchers in tourism, as distinct from colleagues in recreation and leisure, paid specific attention to the issue, but in general most tourism researchers appear not to be familiar with the extensive literature already existing in recreation publications.

DISCUSSION

Capacity and Sustainability

It may be that the slight but perhaps significant increase in interest by tourism researchers in carrying capacity in this last decade is related to other developments, including the way the public, decision-makers and academics are looking at the environment and the use made of it. The enthusiasm with which the idea of sustainable development (World Commission on Environment and Development, 1987) has been adopted suggests that many observers recognise that there are limits to consumption and environmentally unfriendly actions. One may argue that the popularity, if not the true application of the concept of sustainable development, is really a call for the recognition and acceptance of capacity limits in a different guise. The well-being of future generations can only be ensured if this generation leaves the environment in a fit state to sustain itself; in other words, if it is not taxed to over capacity. The definitions of the two concepts have much in common. Sustainable development involves meeting the needs of the present without negatively affecting the needs of future generations (WCED, 1987), while the varying definitions of carrying capacity in recreation and tourism generally contain the concept of limits of use to which an area can be put before there is significant and appreciable decline in both the quality of the resource and the quality of the experience for the user. Hovinen (1982) defined it as the maximum number of visitors an area could accommodate without there being excessive deterioration of the environment or declining visitor satisfaction, a definition supported closely by Mathieson and Wall (1982). O'Reilly (1986) argued justifiably for the inclusion of the social, cultural and economic capabilities of the destination in such definitions.

The broad nature of sustainable development may explain in part why the tourism industry and associated public sector agencies have embraced the concept with such enthusiasm. (Another reason may relate to Wheeller's (1992, 1993) excellent and valid comments on the marketability of the concept of sustainable tourism and its prostitution.) Other writers (Sadler, 1988) have commented on the strong links between this concept and tourism, and the need to develop guidelines and limits to development; however, they have generally fallen short of recommending the identification of limits or a specific carrying capacity, possibly because of recollections of the previous abandonment of the term, and possibly because it implies real ceilings and limits to development. These are things a growth-oriented private sector industry and most governments still find generally unacceptable, a point emphasised by Craik (1995) in the context of the cultural effects of tourism.

Yet one can argue strongly that the idea of limits in the form of ceilings or of maximum permissible numbers are not at all alien to many forms of leisure. It is accepted, even if with annoyance, that most leisure facilities have fixed capacities, as anyone trying to get a ticket for a major sporting event, such as the Olympic Games opening and closing ceremonies, or to watch the Rugby or Soccer World Cup finals, would testify. It is acknowledged that infrastructure will sometimes be beyond capacity limits, as traffic jams on highways or congestion at airports illustrate. (The 1996 Olympic Games in Atlanta have demonstrated this problem all too clearly.) It is even accepted that natural areas and heritage features can receive too much use and that closed periods or restrictions on numbers of visitors to them may be necessary, as seen in the closing of Stonehenge and the Lascaux caves, the limits placed on the number of rafts allowed on the Grand Canyon at any one time, and the necessity to book in advance to secure a campsite at many popular parks in North America.

Lack of Acceptance of Capacity Principles

It is appropriate to ask why there is apparent unwillingness to accept that the same principles apply to tourist destinations as they do to other leisure destinations and facilities. There are a number of reasons for the abandonment of the idea of a specific capacity of a tourism or recreation area. First and foremost is the realisation that there rarely, if ever, can be a single definitive figure which realistically represents the maximum number of visitors who should visit a site over a particular period of time, since different types of users cause different types of impacts and have different preferences and expectations. The appreciation of this fact came about in the 1960s, and subsequently led to the conclusion that capacity was best regarded as a management concept, dealt with in terms of policies, objectives and acceptable levels of change, rather than through the imposition of limits on numbers.

Second, certainly in the context of tourism, if less so in the case of recreation, is the fact that tourism normally represents a form of free enterprise, of capitalism and competition, and in the minds of many involved in the industry, the less external control on the private sector the better. In the case of tourism, where the resources and infrastructure are often in private hands, then the rationale for government intervention and regulation is weaker than in the case of, for example, wilderness recreation areas on public land.

Third, and related to the above, is the absence of clear responsibility for the quality of the resources of many destination areas being assigned to any one agency or individual, a good example of the privatisation of a common, as noted by this author in an earlier paper (Butler, 1991), and by Healy at more length in 1994. In the absence of such responsibility it is almost inevitable that a *laissez faire* approach operates, often with virtually no regulation beyond normal planning controls. As Healy (1994) notes, in the case of tourism landscapes in particular, there is often susceptibility to overuse and resource damage. Both Butler and Healy draw comparisons with Hardin's now classic analogy of the 'tragedy of the commons' (1969), where the absence of responsibility and control resulted in the inevitability of resource decline through overuse.

Again, related to this, not only is there often absence of control and responsibility, but there is rarely a clear and effective method of enforcement of limits, even if they could be identified and accepted. There is not much point in producing capacity figures if no agency or group is interested in introducing them and no-one capable of enforcing them.

Part of the problem of accepting the implications of carrying capacity is undoubtedly the appreciation that the concept of capacity implies limits, and limits tend to mean no growth beyond a certain level. To the private sector this means a potential loss of profits and/or a decline in current levels of income. It means in most cases more competition for a declining or smaller number of visitors and their expenditure, if the result of the acceptance of the capacity concept is a ceiling on the number of visitors. As noted earlier (Butler, 1991), the argument that smaller numbers of tourists to a destination can maintain overall expenditure at the same level as that obtained from larger numbers of lower spending visitors only works if there are enough high-spending tourists to make up the loss of expenditure caused by a decline in total numbers, and at the global scale this is clearly impossible.

This is often a concern shared by the political sector. A decline in visitation to a destination, whether possibly related to overvisitation or some other reason, is normally responded to by efforts to increase marketing, to diversify the market, to advertise more extensively, to offer inducements and to add attractions to the destination in an effort to make it more 'competitive', and thus restore numbers to their original levels or, even better, to exceed them. The thought never seems to occur to decision-makers that a decline in visitor numbers may be due to the fact that to some visitors at least, the destination has become less attractive and is drawing fewer visitors because it has suffered or is suffering from overvisitation. Increased marketing, in whatever form, even if successful in the short term in stemming a decline in numbers of visitors, will not solve the basic problem, and in a short time it is likely that the destination will again experience a decline in visitation. (This is certainly not to claim that every decline or even many declines in visitor numbers may be caused by visitor perceptions of crowding and the effects of overcapacity, but it is likely that some are due to this.)

CONCLUSIONS

The previous discussion on the development of research on capacity in the context of tourism has revealed that there has been relatively little insensitive study on this topic that has appeared in the academic literature. This absence cannot be blamed on a lack of knowledge about increasing pressure on resources, as an anonymous author noted in the 16th Century,

> But now the sport is marred,
> And Wot ye why?
> Fishes decrease,
> For fishers multiply. (Anon., 1598)

Despite this, and in contrast to the mindset of most academics that their research should lead decision-makers rather than follow their actions, a number of agencies and governments have taken action on limiting numbers of visitors to destinations. Advance booking requirements to mount expeditions to climb Mount Everest and other peaks in Nepal and Bhutan (Shackley, 1993), limits on the numbers of rafts allowed on some major rivers in the United States (Stankey, 1977), limits on the number of cruise boats allowed to be in the harbour in Bermuda and on the number of hotel rooms in that country (Conlin, 1995), restrictions on access to several small towns in mountain areas (Williams and Gill, 1991), and the closure of access to other attractions as noted earlier all bear witness to the fact that decision-makers and those with responsibility for management of facilities recognise that there can be too many visitors to a location.

It is surprising and disconcerting therefore to conclude that researchers appear to be unable or unwilling to do what those operating tourist facilities and destination areas are already doing, namely, to produce maximum numbers which should be allowed to visit specific destinations. At specific sites these limits have been imposed for a variety of reasons, some relating to real or perceived impacts of tourism on destination environments, some because of local population feelings over the level of tourism to which they are being exposed, some on the basis of real or imagined changes brought about in the local communities, and some in order to prevent anticipated changes coming about as a result of tourism. Whether the limits chosen are realistic or not, and whether they are effective or not in reducing or eliminating undesired impacts and change is of less importance than the fact that individuals and agencies in charge of tourism

development in some locations are prepared to place limits on tourist numbers because they see few other choices if they are to avoid or reduce impacts and correct problems ascribed to tourism. In almost all cases, while there may also be a desire to attract or reduce numbers of *specific* types of tourists, the limits which have been imposed have been on *overall* numbers of tourists, despite the belief expressed in the academic literature that absolute numbers are often of less importance than the type of tourist and the activities they engage in.

One may argue that those involved in hands-on management are being more realistic than those undertaking research, and that limiting total numbers, even if total numbers may only be a part of the problem of capacity, will at least reduce the numbers of inappropriate or undesirable tourists, even if it also reduces the numbers of other types of tourists. A recent case in point is the action of English Heritage, which has responsibility for the Roman structure, Hadrian's Wall, in northern England. A new version of the official visitor's map has a popular feature, Steel Rigg, deleted from the previous version of the map in the hope of reducing annual visitor numbers from the current 500,000, in order to prevent irreparable damage. The head of the tourism project is quoted as stating 'Steel Rigg was left off the map on purpose – in fact it's the first leaflet without a picture of the site. It's part of our policy of spreading the number of tourists across different sites to make sure the parts which have been most popular in the past are protected' (quoted in *The Scotsman*, 10 July 1996, p. 7). While this particular action could be regarded as short-sighted and simply moving pressure to other areas, which ultimately will probably suffer the same fate as the non-depicted site, it illustrates the desperation many managers are feeling about extremely high levels of use and subsequent overuse and damage to the sites which they are managing and protecting.

Another method of limiting numbers which appears to work, reflecting the private sector dominance of tourism, is that of price selectivity. Scarce commodities fetch a higher price, at least on the open market, reflecting their rarity and a greater demand than supply. High-quality tourism opportunities, including assured privacy and avoidance of crowding and loss of environmental quality, have always been able to command high prices and thus apply selective entrance on the basis of cost (Butler, 1991; Wheeller, 1992). To the public sector this is generally regarded as anathema and contradictory to the normal rationale for public involvement in the provision of leisure facilities and access to areas, which is to ensure all members of the public can be involved, partake and share the opportunity to participate in activities or visit areas, rather than limiting numbers, and least of all limiting them on the basis of ability or willingness to pay.

In this respect these agencies are addressing one of the major problems which have persuaded many researchers to cease trying to find specific numbers for the capacity of a destination, namely that there are many such numbers, reflecting the characteristics and behaviours of the many types of users. Most researchers have argued that as there exists no single number which can be identified for a destination, except perhaps where there is only one homogeneous type of visitor with similar expectations, experiences and preferences, the search for specific numbers should be abandoned. In reality, however, it may be argued that this assumption, while conceptually correct, may be viewed as irrelevant. A good analogy with capacity is that of a chain, with the limit being the weakest link. Research over the past decades has identified three major elements of capacity, similar to those in the impact literature, environmental, social and physical (infrastructure), to which have been added the economic capacity of a community to absorb expenditure and investment of tourism, and institutional capacity, relating to regulations imposed by public sector agencies, for example with respect to safety (Williams and Gill, 1991; Butler *et al.*, 1992). For problems to emerge in destination areas, these capacity limits do not *all* have to be reached or exceeded. It may well be that exceeding only one of them will be sufficient to trigger a range of problems in the other elements, or be sufficient on its own to cause major problems which may result in a decline in visitation or irreparable environmental or social change. For example, too many tourists in five-star hotels, who are traditionally heavy water users, could result in the overtaxation of water resources, with attendant problems with sewage facilities, which may in turn cause pollution of beaches, pollution of water supplies and a shortage of potable water, which in turn could result in changes in social and economic activities, loss of attractivity of the destination, illness of visitors and hosts; problems which require significant economic investment to correct or overcome, often beyond the ability of the local community.

It can be argued, therefore, that what is necessary is not the identification of critical numbers of each type of user, but rather the establishment of a reasonable estimate of the most sensitive element of capacity for a specific destination, and that such a figure is the level beyond which numbers should not be allowed to rise unless change is acceptable within the destination, and the destination is willing to accept a change in the nature of its visitors and its image. If instead, destinations settle for no response, or for a policy of accepting models such as the limits of acceptable change (Stankey *et al.*, 1985), then they have to accept also that change will only occur in one direction, that of reflecting increased use, and that they are tacitly accepting at least some of the principles of Plog's (1974) and Butler's (1980) models dealing with the evolution of tourism destinations. Adopting an approach which relies on identifying what users regard as acceptable change, and basing usage levels on user norms and expectations can only result in increasing levels of use and development, as those users concerned by development and increasing numbers will go elsewhere and will be replaced by those with higher use threshold levels. Ultimately of course, that argument would result in all areas experiencing major or mass development and visitation, and while this clearly will not happen, many areas *will* experience visitation levels and development beyond what is an appropriate level for many of their elements of capacity. One result will be environments which will not be sustainable, if by sustainable is meant the ability of the environment to maintain itself at existing levels of quality, however those may be defined.

In conclusion, tourism means impacts. Impacts may be desirable or undesirable, or of little concern when they are at a low level. Once undesirable impacts reach a certain level, however, they are likely to become unacceptable and to provoke reaction, either by local residents or by visitors, or both. It is at this point that it can be regarded that one or more elements of capacity has been reached or exceeded. In essence, therefore, to avoid at least some of the negative impacts associated with visitation, it must be ensured that capacity limits are identified and not exceeded. Without such a guarantee, there can be no sustainable tourism, and likely no really long-term tourism in a destination. Williams and Gill (1991, p. 16) note that difficulties with 'numerical carrying capacity indicators arise when efforts are made to link them directly to the management of specific tourism impacts'. They go on to point out that 'There appear to be no comprehensive applications of carrying capacity approaches' (op. cit., p. 28). They suggest that the most common way of incorporating some elements of capacity into development is through growth management strategies, arguing, appropriately in this writer's view, that there has to be 'some prior designation of conditions upon which unacceptable levels of tourism impact can be judged' (op. cit., p. 16).

Semantics apart, whether 'growth management strategies' are a form of sustainable development or acceptance of carrying capacity principles does not really matter. There is still a very real need, one that is becoming more urgent each year as tourism numbers increase, to devise ways of handling tourism pressure. The evidence suggests that a few tourism agencies have appreciated this fact and are endeavouring to solve this problem as best they can, often by limiting total numbers as they see no other alternative. It is unfortunate that they are not being significantly aided by most of the research community, which has tended to either ignore the problem, while expounding extensively on the problem of impacts, or to wash its hands of the problem of capacity by arguing that it does not really exist, and even if it did it would be too difficult to determine. Declaring carrying capacity dead because the problems it raises cannot be solved is, to this writer, a case of premature burial. It appears to be a case of at least some public sector agencies knowing that too many tourists are not good for them, even if the experts cannot agree and prefer to avoid the issue.

REFERENCES

An Foras Forbatha, (1966), *Planning for Amenity and Tourism*, Dublin: Bord Failte.

Anonymous, (1598), quoted in Brougham, J. E., (1969), University of Western Ontario, London, Canada, Unpublished Masters thesis.

Brougham, J. E. and Butler, R. W. (1981), A segmentation analysis of resident attitudes to the social impact of tourism, *Annals of Tourism Research*, **8**, 4, 569–590.

Bryden, J. M. (1973), *Tourism and Development: A Case Study of the Caribbean*, Cambridge, MA: Cambridge University Press.

Butler, R. W. (1980), The concept of a tourist area cycle of evolution: implications for management of resources, *The Canadian Geographer*, **24**, 1, 5–12.

Butler, R. W. (1991), Tourism, environment and sustainable development, *Environmental Conservation*, **18**, 3, 201–209.

Butler, R. W. and Waldbrook, L. A. (1991), A new planning tool: the tourism opportunity spectrum, *Journal of Tourism Studies*, **2**, 1, 2–14.

Butler, R. W., Fennell, D. A. and Boyd, S. W. (1992), *Canadian Heritage Rivers System Recreational Carrying Capacity Study*, Ottawa: Environment Canada, Heritage Rivers Board.

Carson, R. (1962), *Silent Spring*, Boston, MA: Houghton Mifflin.

Clark, R. and Stankey, G. (1979), The recreation opportunity spectrum: a framework for planning, management and research, US Department of Agriculture Forest Service, General Technical Report PNW-98, Pacific North West Forest and Range Experiment Station, Seattle, DC.

Clawson, M. (1959), *The Crisis in Outdoor Recreation*, Washington, DC: Resources for the Future.

Clawson, M. (1963), *Land and Water for Recreation – Opportunities, Problems and Policies*, Chicago: Rand McNally, Resources for the Future.

Conlin, M. V. (1995), Rejuvenation planning for island tourism: the Bermuda example, in Conlin, M. V. and Baum, T. (Editors), *Island Tourism: Management Principles and Practices*, London: Wiley, 181–208.

Craik, J. (1995), Are there cultural limits to tourism? *Journal of Sustainable Tourism*, **3**, 2, 87–98.

Darling, F. F. and Eichorn, N. (1966), *Man and Nature in the National Parks*, Washington, DC: Conservation Foundation.

de Kadt, E. (1973), *Tourism – Passport to Development?* New York: Oxford University Press.

Doxey, G. V. (1975), A causation theory of visitor—resident irritants, methodology, and research inferences, in *The Impact of Tourism*, Proceedings Travel Research Association, 6th Conference, San Diego, CA, 195–198.

Getz, D. (1982), A rationale and methodology for assessing capacity to absorb tourism, *Ontario Geography*, **19**, 92–101.

Getz, D. (1983), Capacity to absorb tourism: concepts and implications for strategic planning, *Annals of Tourism Research*, **10**, 2, 239–263.

Graefe, A. R., Vaske, J. J. and Kuss, F. R. (1984), Social carrying capacity, *Leisure Sciences*, **6**, 4, 395–431.

Hardin, G. (1969), The tragedy of the commons, *Science*, **162**, 1243–1248.

Hawkins, J. P. and Roberts, C. M. (1994), The growth of coastal tourism in the Red Sea: present and future effects on coral reefs, *Ambio*, **23**, 8, 503–508.

Healy, R. G. (1994), The "Common Pool" problem in tourism landscapes, *Annals of Tourism Research*, **21**, 3, 596–611.

Hendee, J. C., Stankey, G. H. and Lucas, R. C. (1990), *Wilderness Management*, Golden, Colorado: North American Press.

Hovinen, G. R. (1982), Visitor cycles – outlook for tourism in Lancaster County, *Annals of Tourism Research*, **9**, 4, 565–583.

Johnson, P. and Thomas, B. (1994), The notion of capacity in tourism: a review of the issues, in Cooper, C. P., and A. Lockwood (Editors), *Progress in Tourism, Recreation and Hospitality Management*, Chichester: Wiley, Vol. 5.

Kuss, F. R., Graefe, A. R. and Vaske, J. J. (1990), *Visitor Impact Management: The Planning Framework*, Washington, DC: US National Parks Service.

Lime, D. and Stankey, G. (1971), Carrying capacity: maintaining outdoor recreation quality, in *Proceedings Forest Recreation Symposium*, New York College of Forestry, Syracuse, 171–184.

Liu, J. C., Sheldon, P. J. and Var, T. (1987), Residents' perception of the environmental impacts of tourism, *Annals of Tourism Research*, **14**, 1, 17–37.

Long, P. T., Perdue, R. R. and Allen, L. (1990), Rural resident tourism perceptions and attitudes by community level of tourism, *Journal of Travel Research*, **28**, 3, 3–9.

Lucas, R. C. (1964a), The recreational carrying capacity of the Quetico-superior area, St. Paul: USDA Forest Service Research Paper LS-15.

Lucas, R. C. (1964b), Wilderness perception and use: the example of the Boundary Waters Canoe Area, *Natural Resources Journal*, **3**, 3, 394–411.

Martin, B. S. and Uysal, M. (1990), An examination of the relationship between carrying capacity and the tourism lifecycle: management and policy implications, *Journal of Environmental Management*, **31**, 327–333.

Mathieson, A. and Wall, G. (1982), *Tourism: Economic, Physical and Social Impacts*, New York: Longman.

Meadows, D. H., Meadows, D. L., Randers, J. and Behrens, W. W. (1972), *Limits to Growth*, New York: Universal Books.

Murphy, P. E. (1985), *Tourism – A Community Approach*, London: Methuen.

Ogilvie, F. W. (1933), *The Tourist Movement*, London: Staple's Press.

O'Reilly, A. M. (1986), Tourism carrying capacity, *Tourism Management*, **7**, 4, 254–258.

Pearce, D. G. (1987), *Tourism Today: A Geographic Analysis*, Harlow: Longman.

Pearce, D. G. (1989), *Tourist Development*, Harlow: Longman.

Plog, S. C. (1974), Why destination areas rise and fall in popularity, *Cornell Hotel and Restaurant Administration Quarterly*, **14**, 55–58.

Sadler, B. (1988), Sustaining tomorrow and endless summer: on linking tourism environments in the Carribean, in Edwards, F. (Editor), *Environmentally Sound Tourism in the Caribbean*, Calgary: University of Calgary Press, ix–xxiii.

Saleem, N. (1994), The destination capacity index: a measure to determine the tourist carrying capacity, in Seaton, A. V. (Editor), *Tourism – State of the Art* Chichester: Wiley, 144–151.

The Scotsman (1996), Plans for Hadrian's Wall win support, 10 July, 7.

Shackley, M. (1993), No room at the top, *Tourism Management*, **14**, 6, 483–485.

Shelby, B. and Heberlein, T. A. (1986), A conceptual framework for carrying capacity determination, *Leisure Sciences*, **6**, 4, 433–451.

Smith, V. (Editor), (1977), *Hosts and Guests: The Anthropology of Tourism*, Philadelphia, PA: University of Pennsylvania Press.

Stankey, G. (1977), Rationing River Recreation Use, in *Proceedings: River Recreation Management and Research Symposium*, USDA Forest Service General Technical Report NC 28, Upper Darby, PA, 397–401.

Stankey, G. and Manning, R. E. (1986), Carrying capacity of recreational settings, in *Literature Review, President's Commission on American Outdoors*, Washington, DC: US Government Printing Office, 47–57.

Stankey, G., Cole, D. N., Lucas, R. C., Peterson, M. E. and Frissell, S. S. (1985), The limits of acceptable change (LAC) systems for wilderness planning, USDA Forest Service General Technical Report INT-176, Intermountain Forest and Range Experiment Station, Ogden, UT.

Vaske, J. J. (1992), VIMDEX, computerized bibliography, University of New Hampshire.

Wagar, J. A. (1964), The carrying capacity of wild lands for recreation, Forest Science Monograph no. 7, Washington, DC: Society of American Foresters.

Wall, G. (1983), Cycles and capacity: a contradiction in terms. *Annals of Tourism Research*, **10**, 1, 268–270.

Walter, J. A. (1982), Social limits to tourism, *Leisure Studies*, **1**, 2, 295–304.

Washbourne, R. F. (1982), Wilderness recreational carrying capacity: are numbers necessary? *Journal of Forestry*, **80**, 726–728.

Wheeller, B. (1992), Alternative tourism – a deceptive ploy, in Cooper, C., and Lockwood, A. (Editors), *Progress in Tourism, Recreation and Hospitality Management*, London: Belhaven, 140–145.

Wheeller, B. (1993), Sustaining the ego, *Journal of Sustainable Tourism*, **1**, 2, 121–129.

Williams, P. W. and Gill, A. (1991), Carrying capacity management in tourism settings: a tourism growth management process, Burnaby, British Columbia: Simon Fraser University, Centre for Tourism Policy and Research.

Wolfe, R. I. (1952), Wasaga Beach: the divorce from the geographic environment, *The Canadian Geographer*, **2**, 57–66.

Wolfe, R. I. (1964), Perspective on outdoor recreation: a bibliographic summary, *Geographical Review*, **54**, 203–238.

Wolfe, R. I. (1966), Recreational travel: the new migration, *The Canadian Geographer*, **10**, 1, 1–14.

World Commission on Environment and Development (1987), *Our Common Future*, Oxford: Oxford University Press.

World Tourism Organization (1995), *International Tourism Overview*, Madrid: WTO.

Young, G. (1973), *Tourism – Blessing or Blight?* Harmondsworth: Penguin.

Sustainable Tourism – Do Economists Really Care?

3

Brian Archer

ABSTRACT

The rapid expansion of tourism from the mid-1960s onwards led in some cases to developments which had deleterious consequences for the long-term welfare of the populations of the affected areas. The climate of thought changed in the 1980s following the publication of many reports, accords and statements. Economists have become increasingly concerned with evaluating the environmental consequences of tourism and have developed new techniques for this purpose. One of these, described in the chapter, is an extension of input–output analysis to incorporate environmental aspects. A second is cost–benefit analysis.

The introduction of commercial jet aircraft in the mid-1960s coincided with first, the growing affluence of North America and the residents of several European countries and secondly, the increasing desire of many people to travel abroad. Together these forces generated a boom in world tourism which continued throughout the 1970s through to the mid-1990s, despite fuel price hikes, world recessions and various wars.

Over these years the prospects of increased foreign revenue, higher levels of income and employment and increased public sector revenues were attractive factors in influencing many governments to permit and encourage the development of new destination regions.

In many cases, growth and development was considered to be a self-justifying end without due regard to any environmental or socio-cultural consequences. Developers and speculators proved more than willing to ignore such side effects in the search for quick profits. As a result, many early developments have had deleterious consequences for the long-term welfare of the resident populations. The literature abounds with examples, some of which are included in a volume edited by de Kadt (1979). Yet over the last two decades, policy-makers, planners, industrialists and economists have become increasingly aware of the imperative need to consider, in addition to economic factors, the environmental consequences of proposed new developments and also the needs, aspirations and rights of present and future generations in the affected areas to be in a position to make their own choices about the use of scarce resources.

What changed the climate of thought? First, since the beginning of the 1980s there has been an increasing output of international reports, accords and statements concerning the present and future well-being of Planet Earth. Some of these documents have been specifically concerned with the role of tourism as an agent of change.

The most influential reports were: the 1980 World Conservation Strategy, which stressed the need for sustainability in the use of natural resources; the Brandt Commission of the same year, which emphasised the need for development to include 'care for the environment'; the WTO Manila Declaration, also in 1980, which *inter alia* pointed out that natural resources are of common heritage; the UNEP–WTO Accord (1982), which stressed the need for tourism development to be environmentally sound; and the Brundtland Report (1987), which indicated a path towards sustainable development with economic growth.

Secondly, partly in consequence of the publication of these reports, the growing international concern for the environmental and socio-cultural consequences of all forms of development stimulated an outpouring of papers by academics and practitioners. In many cases, these papers have helped to arouse public awareness and concern.

The concept of sustainability appeared in many papers and its general acceptance is probably the most beneficial outcome of this outburst of literature. The term itself gained more common usage and acceptance with the publication of the Brundtland Report *Our Common Future* (1987) where it was defined as 'a process of change in which the exploitation of resources, the direction of investments, the orientation of technological development, and institutional changes are made consistent with future as well as present needs', and as 'meeting the needs of the present without compromising the ability of future generations to meet their own needs'.

Canada was one of the countries which responded most quickly to the Brundtland Report. At the Globe '90 Conference held in April 1990 in Vancouver, Canada, the Tourism Stream Action Strategy Commission produced an interesting 'Action strategy for sustainable development'. For those unable to acquire a copy of the Report, a reproduction of the draft is provided in a recent book by Inskeep (1991). Also in Canada, D'Amore (1993) has provided an

interesting account of the progress made in that country towards achieving guidelines, codes of ethics and practical methods of responding to the Brundtland Report.

An authoritative paper by de Kadt (1992) recognises that whereas there is a need for future growth in some countries and regions in order to improve the material well-being of the resident population, 'policy-makers can ... promote sustainability by constantly striving to make the conventional more sustainable' and that many 'alternative forms of tourism' will continue to evolve but, for economic reasons, will 'almost inevitably ... [ride] ... piggy-back on the more cost-effective forms of the conventional, integrated international tourism industry'. His final sentence – 'how to coax that behemoth into less destructive behaviour is surely the main task ahead' – could well itself form the theme of a major conference.

Since the Brundtland Report, in addition to the wealth of written papers, a very interesting but spasmodic correspondence on sustainability in tourism has been conducted by TRINETTERS on e-mail. Indeed some participants in this meeting have contributed substantially to their correspondence. I hope that someone will take the initiative to use this correspondence to form the basis of a publication – it would form a valuable addition to the literature.

However, the purpose of this paper is not to attempt a general synthesis of the state-of-the-art in sustainability, but to consider the role of the economist in this context. Indeed, does the economist have a role? Does the economist even care?

Well this one does. During the 1960s and 1970s economists gained an unenviable reputation because of their support of schemes which subsequently were shown to have deleterious long-term effects in environmental and socio-cultural terms. To what extent were these early economists to blame? Probably not a lot, or at least not as much as may sometimes be assumed.

First, economists are concerned with the allocation of resources which have alternative uses, but it should be remembered that economists *per se* do not lay down *the policy prescriptions* for the use of these resources. Policy is the province of politicians, and politicians prescribe the aims and objectives and the constraints which govern the work given to economists and within which they formulate their recommendations. Secondly, until relatively recently, environmental and socio-cultural factors were rarely included among the aims, objectives or constraints presented to economists. Thirdly, economists *per se* are not equipped either to identify or to measure environmental or socio-cultural factors.

In short, during the 1960s and 1970s economists carried out the tasks they were assigned and which they were equipped as economists to undertake. In fairness to this earlier generation of economists (among whom this speaker qualifies by age) many did point out some of the environmental or socio-cultural factors revealed by their work, but for the most part such factors were rarely evaluated in money terms and many may have been omitted entirely.

What has changed since then? Do economists care about sustainability? I think that much has changed and that economists do care and have endeavoured to expand their range of expertise to encompass the identification and evaluation of many environmental and socio-cultural factors insofar as such factors can be quantified.

This poses one of the major difficulties faced by economists. Economic models exist to evaluate most impact situations, but economists working in isolation are not able to make quantitative assessments of environmental and other factors. An example of the difficulties which can be encountered is some work currently being undertaken at the University of Surrey. One of our projects involves assessing the economic and environmental consequences of tourism development in Mauritius (Fletcher *et al.*, 1996). Constructing an appropriate model was the easiest part of the task. Obtaining good quality environmental data is a different matter.

The Government of Mauritius has a wealth of good data about pollution in the bays and beaches by various sectors of the economy, including two of the major export industries – sugar production and tourism. These data, however, cover a wide spectrum of readings – pH values, particle suspension, etc. How is an economist to choose between 20 or more separate environmental indices and which should be included in the model, and in what form?

This raises the wider issue of modelling. Essentially there are two principal economic techniques which can be adapted to incorporate environmental and socio-cultural factors. The one which is being used in Mauritius is input–output analysis. This involves constructing a matrix of the purchases and sales made by all economic sectors over a given time period and then, by the use of matrix algebra, analysing the effects of injections of export earnings (including tourism receipts), on incomes, government revenue, imports and employment in each sector of the economy. The technique measures *secondary* effects in addition to the primary direct effects.

What is being done in addition is the attachment of an additional matrix of environment factors which can be pre-multiplied by the inverted Leontief matrix to yield the secondary environmental consequences of export changes. The principal problem, already mentioned, is to identify and measure the environmental factors in a form suitable for inclusion in the model. It is not intended that any monetary evaluations will be assigned to these factors, but that they will be expressed in units which are meaningful to environmental researchers.

A second major technique available to economists is social cost–benefit analysis. This should not be confused with financial appraisal. Whereas financial appraisal places the emphasis on the financial revenue and costs which accrue to the developers and operators of a project, cost–benefit analysis considers the benefits and costs received by the community or country as a whole. To a developer or operator such benefits and costs are external to the financial analysis, whereas in cost–benefit analysis such effects are intrinsic to the study. In essence, cost–benefit analysis takes a longer and deeper view than financial analysis; it is concerned with the community as a whole, including future generations.

The literature on cost–benefit is quite extensive and a general flavour of the concepts and their application can be gleaned from authors such as Prest and Turvey (1965), Layard (1972) and Little and Mirrlees (1969). The technique has been used widely and can be employed to simultaneously investigate a large number of alternative uses of the same resources, including a continuance of the *status quo*. Indeed the greater the number of alternative uses that are investigated, the more meaningful and helpful are the results. The principal weakness of the approach, as previously mentioned, is the inability of economists *per se* to recognize, assess and measure factors such as ecological implications which do not have readily apparent monetary values.

In essence, social cost–benefit analysis involves assessing and measuring (in a common monetary unit) the consequences of proposed forms of development. All of the identified and measured benefits and costs are discounted back to their present value to provide a common yardstick of measurement. One of the measures recommended is the foreign exchange equivalent value of the money in the hands of the government (Little and Mirrlees, 1969). The discount rate used in social cost–benefit analysis is quite different from that used by private sector developers. Whereas the latter use a discount rate which reflects both the rate of borrowing money and the risk factors involved, social cost–benefit analysts use a rate which is intended to reflect *society's* valuation of net benefits in the present time rather than in the future, i.e. a discount rate can be chosen which takes into account future requirements and the needs of future generations.

Thus, for example, in the case of a proposed airport development in Cyprus (Wanhill and Archer, 1976), the principal monetary benefits were identified as the net foreign currency likely to be obtained from the expenditure of additional tourists, the foreign currency likely to be obtained by exporting additional fruit as a consequence of siting the new airport close to the major fruit producing regions, and the other net benefits accruing to some of the domestic population from the development. The principal cost factors were the opportunity costs of using the necessary factors of production (land, labour and capital) and other resources to construct and then to operate an airport rather than in their best possible alternative uses. Among the alternative uses explored in the study was retaining these factors in their existing uses – the land was under occasional pastoral usage, the majority of the labour force concerned was either unemployed or only seasonally employed, and the available capital was a mixture of overseas investment funds (which might not have been available for alternative uses within Cyprus) and domestic savings. The most productive alternative use was identified as irrigated agriculture. The discount rate was selected after consultation with the Cyprus Government and lay within the guidelines recommended by UNDP. In this particular study no major externalities or spill-over effects were identified.

Indeed the identification and measurement of externalities are for economists the most difficult aspect of social cost–benefit analysis. Pollution of beaches is a common occurrence in tourism development and economists can assign a monetary value to such occurrences and to the costs of taking preventative or remedial actions. Indeed it is possible to 'internalise' this type of cost to the developers themselves by legally enforcing them to take measures to prevent the occurrence of such situations. Nevertheless, many externalities, notably ecological effects, are much harder for economists and indeed others to identify or evaluate. Unless such effects can be anticipated and the costs of preventative action be evaluated, it is impossible to include them within the numerical analysis.

It may be, for example, that a proposed development involves the destruction of a specific habitat and in consequence the possible eradication of a particular species of fauna or flora. If, in such cases, some ecologists place an infinite monetary value on the preservation *in situ* of this threatened species, then it could be argued that the environmental costs of the proposed development would be greater than the net economic benefits, however great these may be. On the basis of this premise, the development should not be allowed to proceed.

In such a situation, however, an economist would not accept the premise that preserving the habitat had an infinite value. Instead he would wish to calculate and include in the analysis the total costs of re-creating the threatened habitat in another suitable location and of preserving the threatened species. Similarly, an investigation of proposed mining developments in a national park in the United Kingdom (Zuckerman Commission, 1972) considered the net benefits accruing to the region over a long time span. During the period of active mining considerable environmental and other costs would be incurred, especially the impact on the aesthetic appearance of the area. If, however, at the end of the active mining period, the area were to be completely restored at the expense of the developer, then after a few years there would be few if any traces of the development. In this case the magnitude of the net present value of the benefits depended partly upon the value attached by the affected population to the environmental damage incurred over the period of mining operations rather than over an indefinitely prolonged period of time.

Long-lasting environmental damage is a different consideration. Advances in technology have made it possible for most forms of pollution and many other violations of the environment to be avoided, ameliorated or rectified at a subsequent date. As previously mentioned, such damage can be minimised by imposing legal restrictions and/or financial penalties to 'internalise' the cost to the developer. Admittedly, in some cases, long-term damage may occur and it is essential that a monetary valuation of such damage should be included as a cost in the cost–benefit analysis. The onus is on environmentalists to give a valuation to such occurrences. Merely bemoaning the events or placing an infinite valuation on the affected resources is unacceptable, either politically or scientifically. Nor is it acceptable to place the onus solely on economists to estimate a value in the absence of any hard environmental data.

Similarly, social scientists must be prepared to identify and to place a valuation on any expected changes in socio-cultural patterns which might result from a proposed development. As a minimum social scientists should endeavour to produce a ranking order of such changes – there appears to be little scientific merit in ex-post studies which describe outcomes as being 'good' or 'bad'. What is needed is the degree of acceptability of any anticipated changes in order to assist economists in assessing the social benefits and costs involved. Again, the most adverse aspects of some expected changes can be offset by forethought and planning, and the costs involved can be 'internalised' within the costs of development. In Mauritius, for example, in order to prevent the disruption by tourists of sega dances organized by local communities, tourist satisfaction is achieved by organising visits by sega dance troupes to the major hotels. Examples of such ersatz provisions for visitors exist in many tourist destinations.

A second difficulty to be resolved in undertaking a social cost–benefit analysis is to define the beneficiaries, i.e. is the study concerned with the benefits and costs to the whole resident population of the country or to some sub-set of this population, e.g. a defined local area or region? It may well be the case that the balance of benefits and costs of a proposed development will be quite different for people living in the area most affected compared with the population of the country as a whole. Thus, for example, a major tourist development in a given region of a country may generate considerable net economic advantages to the country as a whole, but may have several deleterious environmental and socio-cultural effects in the region most affected. Quite different results can be obtained if the social cost–benefit study is carried out from a national rather than regional or local perspective. In cases where local communities are worse off whilst the country as a whole gains net benefits, the costs of compensating the local community should be included in the social cost–benefit calculations.

The successful application of techniques such as cost–benefit analysis and input–output analysis to the study of sustainable tourism is possible only within a favourable climate of thought. The early economists in general accepted the prevailing political attitude that growth itself was a sufficient motivation to justify development; yet the changing climate of thought in the 1980s and 1990s has focused attention on limitations to growth and on the need to constrain growth where the deleterious effects of further growth on the environment and the socio-cultural life of the population are thought to outweigh the purely economic benefits. Even so, the less developed economies of the world require some growth to meet the legitimate aspirations of their citizens and the relief of poverty in some areas.

Finally, this writer would like to draw attention to a point which he raised at a conference in Malta (Archer, 1993) and which is still pertinent today.

> . . . there is a strong onus on academics in all disciplines to make a determined effort to devise methods of identifying, assessing and quantifying the direct and secondary effects of tourism developments. This is an extremely difficult task and one to which economists can contribute. It is not, however, a task which economists can undertake in isolation. Economic techniques exist and can be adapted for this purpose, but economists are

not equipped to produce the necessary input data.

Economists do care and are willing to join with others to resolve the definitions, to perform the requisite modelling and to assist others in the identification and measurement of data.

REFERENCES

Archer, B. H. (1993), Sustainable tourism – an economist's viewpoint, *1993 Conference of Sustainable Tourism in Islands and Small States, Foundation for International Studies*, Valetta, Malta, 18–20 November.

Brundtland Report (1987), *Our Common Future*, WCED (World Commission on Environment and Development), Tokyo Declaration, 27 February, Oxford: Oxford University Press.

D'Amore, L. J. (1993), A code of ethics and guidelines for socially and environmentally responsible tourism, *Journal of Travel Research*, **31**(3), 64–66.

de Kadt, E. (Editor) (1979), Tourism: Passport to Development?, Oxford: Oxford University Press.

de Kadt, E. (1992), Making the alternative sustainable: lessons from development for tourism, in Smith, V. L. and W. R. Eadington (Editors), *Tourism Alternatives*, Philadelphia, PA: University of Pennsylvania Press.

Fletcher, J. E., Cooper, C. P., and Archer, B. H. (1996), *The Economic and Environmental Impact of Tourism in Mauritius*, Port Louis: Government of Mauritius.

Inskeep, E. (1991), *Tourism Planning*, New York: Van Nostrand Reinhold.

International Union for the Conservation of Nature and Nature Resources (IUCN) (1980), *World Conservation Strategy*.

Layard, R. (Editor) (1972), *Cost Benefit Analysis*, Harmondsworth: Penguin.

Little, I. M. D., and Mirrlees, J. (1969), *Manual of Industrial Project Analysis in Developing Countries*, Vol. 2: *Social Cost–Benefit Analysis*, Paris: OECD.

Prest, A. R., and Turvey, R. (1965), Cost–benefit analysis: a survey, *Economic Journal*, **75** (300), 683–735.

UNEP/WTO (1982), *Joint Declaration between the UNEP and the WTO*, Madrid: WTO.

Wanhill, S. R. C., and Archer, B. H., (1976), Financial and cost–benefit analysis, in Sir Frederick Snow International Limited et al., *Larnaca International airport and an airport in the Paphos district*. Technical report 2, financial investment and cost–benefit analysis Chapter 3.

WCED (World Commission on Environment and Development) (1987), Tokyo Declaration, 27 February. *Our Common Future* (the Brundtland Report), Oxford: Oxford University Press.

World Tourism Organization (WTO) (1980), *Manila Declaration on World Tourism*, Manila.

Zuckerman Commission (1972), Report of the commission on mining and the environment, London: HMSO.

Tourism Development in Egypt: Competitive Strategies and Implications

Salah E. A. Wahab

ABSTRACT

Tourism is witnessing a profound change in the next decade due to new megatrends characterizing typologies, demand, product development, environmental safeguards, community participation and sustainability requirements. Moreover quality services, more than pricing policy, are becoming decisive in the choice of destinations. This chapter, stressing tourism development in Egypt, the leader of Middle East tourism, illustrates the diversity and quality of the tourist product of Egypt, the prevailing tourist trends, the various constraints and tourism development strategies. The future of tourism in Egypt looks brighter in the light of regional cooperation.

OVERVIEW

International tourism traffic is unevenly distributed among the major tourist regions of the world among which Europe leads (337·2 million tourist arrivals, accounting for 59·5% of the world inbound tourism in 1995), with the Middle East trailing last but one (11·0 million tourist arrivals, accounting for 1·94% of the world inbound tourism). Egypt inbound tourist traffic accounts for 28% of the total tourist traffic to the Middle East, reaching in 1995 around 3·13 million tourist arrivals which registered a 21% increase over the number of tourist arrivals in 1994. Egypt's share of the tourist market is still smaller than might be expected considering its natural endowments and historical attractions.

Egypt is the storehouse of history as it possesses unique cultural and archaeological patrimony and remnants of the oldest civilization known in history, dating back more than 6000 years.

Since antiquity, it was a destination for travellers and emigrants. It is one of the traditional tourist destinations that knew tourism in its modern sense in the mid-nineteenth century, when Thomas Cook organized its third group tour outside Great Britain to Egypt after Europe and the United States. The British aristocracy used to spend the whole or a major part of the winter season in Egypt until World War II.

When the revolution broke out in July 1952, Egypt's holiday traffic totalled 75,000 tourists spending over 2·2 million tourist nights with an average length of stay of 30 nights. In the sixties, Egypt started to embark on an ambitious tourist development and marketing program under the leadership of the state Tourist Administration and the Egyptian general organization for

Tourism and Hotels. In 1965 Egypt's tourist traffic totalled 600,000 tourists with 10·4 million tourist nights at an average length of stay of 17·3 nights.

Due to the wars in 1967 and 1973, the Egyptian tourist traffic declined while world-wide tourist competition became more acute. The open-door policy of the government under the late president Sadat resulted in a slow revival of tourism, starting in 1975.

Only since 1986, when the economic liberalisation policy of the Egyptian Government manifested itself in private enterprise encouragement, has tourism started to achieve steady progress ratios with tourist development projects becoming highly valued by various segments of the population. The government's recognition of the role of tourism in the national economy became a vital force in the enhancement of tourism. A thorough review of investment incentives led to the replacement of law no. 34 of 1974 with law no. 230 of 1989 on investments, which included more encouraging measures represented by a longer tax holiday for projects in remote areas (10 years) as well as allowing full foreign investments in some productive sectors instead of restricting such foreign investment to 49% of invested capital. Tourism is one of these sectors.

The targets of the second 5-year plan (1987–1992) were exceeded in mid-term. The 1992 target of 2·5 million tourists was overtaken in 1989 and the accommodation target of 50,000 rooms was passed in 1990. Although tourism is the fastest growing sector in the economy since 1987, its contribution to GDP is still less than 3%.

Egypt's tourism potential suffers numerous constraints, among which is the high cost of air travel from the main tourist-generating countries of USA, Japan and Northern Europe, the relative high cost of travel package, the shortage of competitive marketing efforts coupled with a long-standing case of weak budget allocations for tourist promotion in targeted overseas markets, and the poor image of the Middle East as an unsafe and insecure region. All these factors are current obstacles to tourism expansion.

The setbacks in Egyptian tourism because of the Gulf War (1990) as well as the inopportune terrorist attacks supported by some groups settling in neighboring countries that started in 1992 affected to a certain extent the Egyptian national economy.

Data on foreign tourism traffic to Egypt are collected on a regular basis by the Central Agency for Mobilisation and Statistics and released to the Ministry of Tourism. The data are based on the international definition of tourist, and are categorised by nationality, month of arrival, modes of transport, type of accommodation used and bank transfers. The Ministry of Tourism publishes a yearly statistical report encompassing all relevant data on inbound tourism traffic to Egypt. Some statistics on domestic tourism movement are also included, but are yet far from complete.

The Egyptian Hotel Association maintains and publishes an annual report grouping all types of tourist accommodation establishments, whether they be regular hotels of various levels and locations, tourist villages or floating hotels. The EHA data show that the number of hotels of various types and levels in Egypt reached 732 hotels containing around 63,000 hotel rooms and 121,350 beds up to September 1995. Additionally, there are about 22,180 hotel rooms under construction in various Egyptian tourist areas, pertaining to 176 accommodation establishments (Egyptian Hotel Association, 1994).

Inbound tourist traffic to Egypt in 1995 registered a growth ratio of 21·38% over 1994, while the number of tourist nights increased in the same period of 1995 by 32·5%. American tourists number grew by 23·35%, the number of European tourists increased by 45·6% and the number of Arab tourists fell by 9·47%. Statistics of certain other nationalities recorded a rising trend, namely the Swiss (59·6%), the Italians (78·6%), the Japanese (17%), the Brasilians (104%), the Hungarians (79%) and the Russians (66·2%).

THE TOURISM PRODUCT OF EGYPT

Since the dawn of Egyptian tourism, history and archeology were the main attraction for overseas visitors. The beaten track of tourism in Egypt included four focal points, namely greater Cairo, Menia, Luxor and Aswan including Abou Simbel. It was inevitable in the sixties to start developments on the Red Sea and the Mediterranean coasts where three pilot projects were constructed and marketed, namely the Sidi Abdel Rahman Hotel on the Mediterranean, and the Ein Sokhna Hotel and the Hurghada Hotel, both on the Red Sea.

Cairo is the tourist base of Egypt. Its old Islamic quarter, containing the large mosques of Al-Azhar, Al-Hussein and others, the bazaar (the Khan el Khalili) and the Citadel, form a major tourist attraction. Regardless of its appeal to the large segments of tourists, overcrowding has caused some degradation of this quarter that was regarded as a rival to the great remnants of the Phaeronic civilization. Nevertheless, this quarter is still very much liked by tourists in general and scholars in particular. Similarly, the old Cairo Coptic quarter to the south of the city center is rich in evidence of the Christian era. In Giza (south of Cairo) there lies the three great pyramids and the sphinx which are among the main features of Egyptian tourism and a landmark in its archaeological attractions. The Pyramids area was cleaned and smartened up in the last 5 years. All unsightly buildings in the precincts have been removed and entrance to the area is now fully controlled by ticket.

An essential feature of Cairo is its prime location on the Nile which is considered a striking attraction and a scene of ever-changing interest. The riverside as well as various types of floating restaurants became a feature of the Nile that attracts both tourists and residents. The government is exerting a serious effort to improve the Cairo waterfront.

Cairo is a metropolis of 12 million resident inhabitants, with more than three million cars. It has four universities, namely Al-Azhar University (1100 years old), Cairo, Ein-Shams and Helwan Universities. It is known as the historic city of a thousand minarets as it contains more than 800 mosques and 100 churches.

Cairo has about 12,000 hotel rooms of various levels divided into five-star (49·4%), four-star (18·4%), three-star (24·2%), two-star (20·6%) and one-star (19·1%).

Luxor is considered the major archaeological center in Egypt as it embodies the great temples of Karnak and Luxor on the East bank, the Kings and Queens tombs, the Colossi and the Hatchipsout temple (where the opera Aida was performed in November 1994) on the West bank. Luxor's dramatic setting on the River Nile and the mountains of the Western desert in the background gives the city a special flavor. The main problem with Luxor is that thousands of its visitors want to visit the tombs. As only 11 tombs are open for visitation, government authorities have now created a visitors' center on the west bank of the Nile where tourists are given the opportunity to see in motion pictures the history of the whole area, then visit some replicas of the most famous tombs. Only a few hundred of all visitors can visit the original tombs after paying the necessary visit fees, which tend to be expensive. The reason for such rearrangement is the fear of tomb degradation and in particular the danger that tomb paintings may fade as a result of the humidity of visitors' breathing. The future of the Luxor visitor center, however, shall be finally decided in the next few months as there is a strong opposition to the proposed system.

Luxor has 3900 hotel rooms of which 1351 rooms of the five-star category represent 10·5%, 892 rooms are of the four-star level, 585 rooms are of three-star level, 510 rooms are of the two star category and 244 rooms are of one-star quality.

Aswan also has many important archaeological sites, including the recently restored Philae Temple, the Kalabsha temple, several temples lying on the road to Abu Simbel, the Abu Simbel temples, the Kom Ombo temple, the Edfu Temple, etc. Lake Nubia, the largest fresh water lake in the world, extends for 280 k and has an average width of 40 k. The Nile cataracts and islands form an unforgettable natural scenery that is partially used for tourism development projects.

The main problem with Aswan is its hot climate in summer, which is often preceded by sand storms in the spring (khamaseen). Consequently the tourist season is rather short and therefore an average year-round hotel rate of occupancy is relatively low. An original solution to such a problem are the Nile cruises which operate mainly between Aswan and Luxor. These cruises could serve as a supplementary means of accommodation in the winter season in both Luxor and Aswan. Tour operators use these cruises to extend the stay of tourist groups by an extra two or three nights.

Sinai became a much preferred tourist destination for overseas and domestic tourists. Both the south and north of Sinai now accommodate over 4000 operational rooms in hotels and tourist villages, in addition to 2000 under construction or in the pipeline. In the south of Sinai the main attraction, beside seaside recreational activities and desert safari, is scuba diving where more than 10 foreign-operated diving clubs are active. The newly established extensive road network in Sinai facilitates ground transportation and movement between the southern coast of Sinai and the mid-Sinai attractions encompassing Mount Moses, St Catherine's monastery, the cave valley as well as the various other religious and archaeological sites. Access to north Sinai (the Mediterranean coast) is also easy by land transportation and by plane.

There are other numerous tourist regions in Egypt, including diverse natural, cultural, archaeological and recreational attractions. Examples of these are the Red Sea coast encompassing Ein Sokhna, Hurghada, Safaga, Quseir, Mersa Alam, etc, Lake Nubia in the south of the Nile Valley, the New Valley, Ryan Valley and Fayoum, Beni Suef, Menia, Sohag, the North-West Coast, Port Said and the Suez Canal Zone, Mersa Matrouh and others.

It may be safely said that the tourist product of Egypt is multi-faceted and affords multiple tourist typologies appealing to a wide range of overseas visitors. These include archaeological, recreational, beach, religious, conventions, adventure and eco-tourism, sporting, hunting, business, etc.

The diversification of tourist attractions and facilities in Egypt was the outcome of its geographical location in the heartland of the world, its natural endowments, its rich historic background and lastly a policy of tourist development that extended from the sixties up to the present time with some interruptions because of the various impeding wars and negative events. It is noteworthy that beach tourism development started as early as 1920 in Alexandria and extended to the North-West coast and to the Red Sea in 1965. At present, there are about 38 hotels and tourist villages on the North-West coast from Alexandria to Mersa Matrouh as well as nearly 40 hotels and tourist villages on the Red Sea coast, in addition to 20 hotels and tourism villages in the south of Sinai.

TRENDS OF THE TOURIST TRAFFIC TO EGYPT

Tourism to Egypt has been dominated for a long

time by two distinct trends: Arab and foreign. The Arab market consists of visitors mainly from Saudi Arabia, Kuwait, Libya, Syria, Jordan and Sudan, accounting for 37·6% of the overseas tourist traffic to Egypt in 1993. The foreign market consists of visitors from Western and Eastern European countries, the USA, Canada, Latin America, East Asia and the Pacific, South Asia and Africa. All these accounted for 62·4% of the overseas tourist traffic to Egypt in 1993. The European tourist movement alone formed 47·5% of the total tourist traffic to Egypt, while tourist traffic from North and Latin America constituted only 7·4% and tourists from Asia and the Pacific formed 6% in 1993. Growth in tourist arrivals and in tourist nights in the past few years is summarised in Table 4·1. However, the overall average increase in arrivals of 39·7% between 1987 and 1993 masks fluctuations and regional variations. The annual average increase of 10·55% in the same period is well above the average increase in international tourist traffic (6·4%), irrespective of supervening events that affected tourism in Egypt and the Middle East.

THE INSTITUTIONAL SETTING

Since 1967, the Ministry of Tourism (MOT) has been the main authority dealing with tourism in Egypt, which succeeded the state Tourism Administration. The Ministry of Tourism is presently overstaffed with a purely mechanistic organisation. It is therefore in need of a thorough reshuffle in order to introduce a semi-systems approach to its organisation so that it can become more efficient in responding to the newly emerging changes in tourism. In cognizance to the existing deficiencies, the MOT is being streamlined to improve efficiency and strengthen its technical expertise to be able to cope with the structural changes and technical developments that are imposed by increased fiercer competition in planning, marketing and support from an increasingly stronger private sector. One of the major steps in streamlining the MOT was the creation of the Tourist Development Authority (TDA) in 1991. The TDA is becoming an active instrument in tourism development, drawing on private expertise more than depending on full-time appointed personnel.

The MOT oversees four semi-autonomous

Table 4·1. Trends in Egyptian tourism by origin: 1987–1995.

Tourist arrivals (thousands)									
	1987	1988	1989	1990	1991	1992	1993	1994	1995
Middle East	477·6	469·0	731·4	829·4	931·2	924·8	767·3	819·1	741·5
Africa	192·3	204·8	238·5	326·6	172·5	204·1	187·1	152·8	130·4
Americas	149·0	164·1	200·5	179·1	119·8	224·4	187·4	182·3	228·8
Europe	863·0	1011·7	1188·8	1123·2	889·9	1664·9	1205·7	1252·5	1811·0
Asia–Pacific	112·1	119·2	143·4	141·0	99·7	187·3	157·8	160·9	219·4
Other	0·3	0·7	0·8	0·8	0·8		0·2	0·3	0·21
Total	1794·9	1969·5	2503·4	2600·1	2214·2	3206·9	2507·7	2581·9	3131·3
Tourist nights (millions)									
Middle East	5·4	5·58	7·72	7·25	7·81	6·99	4·98	5·71	5·789
Africa	2·40	2·19	2·05	2·51	1·46	1·47	1·07	1·07	1·05
Americas	0·95	1·05	1·27	1·81	0·70	1·31	1·00	1·00	1·46
Europe	6·23	8·04	8·52	7·90	5·47	10·97	7·20	6·65	10·74
Asia–Pacific	0·86	1·00	1·01	1·10	0·75	1·07	0·80	0·96	1·98
Other	0·01	0·01	0·01	0·01	0·01	0·09	0·12	0·23	0·38
Total	15·86	17·86	20·58	19·94	16·23	21·83	15·08	15·43	20·45

governmental organizations: (a) the Egyptian General Authority for the Promotion of Tourism, responsible for promoting tourism in both international and domestic markets; (b) the Public Authority for Conference Centers which manages the Cairo Conference Center; (c) the Tourism Academy which monitors all training institutions in the tourism sector; and (d) the Tourism Development Authority. According to law no. 203 of 1991, the Public Sector Authority, which was under MOT supervision, became a holding company reporting to the Minister of Public Business Sector. This holding supervises five affiliated companies that are expected to be gradually restructured and privatised under the on-going government privatisation policy. These changes are expected to help strengthen and consolidate the tourism sector if the private sector is to become more efficient and entrepreneurial.

The tourism private sector is represented by the Egyptian Federation of Tourist Chambers and its four chambers, namely the Chamber of Hotel Establishments, the Chamber of Travel Agencies, the Chamber of Tourist Establishments and the Chamber of Handicraft Industries. This structure has been created by law no. 85 of 1968 as amended by law no. 124 of 1981.

In the various tourist governorates, regional organisations for tourism promotion have been created since 1957 (Presidential decree no. 691) and have been operational ever since. Their impacts upon the tourism sector have been practically negligible, although a few are relatively more active than others.

This tourism institutional setting in Egypt should be reviewed in depth in order to provide for the necessary changes in organisation, staffing, motivation, operational rules, and in monitoring its impact upon tourism.

Employment in the Egyptian tourism industry totals 150,000 direct jobs in addition to almost an equal number of indirect jobs. Thus the tourism work force in Egypt, estimated at 300,000, represents 2·4% of the total Egyptian work force.

CONSTRAINTS IN THE TOURISM SECTOR

Long-term Planning

Presently, tourism's contribution to the Egyptian national economy has made it the second foreign exchange earner after remittances of Egyptians residing abroad. However, a written document on National Tourism Policy has not been issued yet and therefore development strategies are mainly the work of the MOT and TDA which may change according to the Minister's wish. The National Tourism Policy should be the expression of the State's will and has to be embodied in a legislative document approved by Parliament. Therefore it can be safely said that the planning capabilities of MOT are inadequate in terms of providing the integrated plans needed for the stable development of the sector. The tourism sector still lacks the reliable and comprehensive database needed for indicative planning and investment by public and private sectors. Statistical tables of tourist arrivals by nationality, month, means of transportation, length of stay, tourist nights, etc, are insufficient and comparatively inaccurate as the international definition of a tourist is not correctly followed. Expenditures by tourist levels and activities, regional tourist flows, employment statistics and investment expenditure by project are virtually lacking. Planning for the sector is based on global figures and the interface at the planning stage between the physical and financial aspects is notably weak. Moreover, criteria for project evaluation and rating are not always consistent with the international classification system, especially in certain remote areas in Egypt. Tourism development projects are approved for investments without careful attention to the impact of the planned outlays on the national budget. Inflation rates are sometimes underestimated in feasibility studies which results in large gaps between planned and actual investments. It is hoped that the TDA can shortly provide streamlining to these deficiencies in order to promote accuracy. This would mean: (a) providing reliable information on the sector particularly in terms of investment planning; (b) strengthen land use and environmental planning functions; and (c) ensure the complementarity of public and private sector investments.

Institutional and Jurisdictional Complexity and Overlapping

One of the major impediments to private investments in tourism development in Egypt is the overlap between several jurisdictions. The MOT and TDA, the Ministry of Development, the General Investment Authority, and the various governorates are the main jurisdictions which have a right of intervention in tourism development. The task of coordination and drawing lines of demarcation between these government agencies is complex and therefore difficult to achieve. The reason for this is that each of these jurisdictions has its own law that allows it competence in one or more aspects in tourism

development. The Presidential decree (no. 712 of 1981) which gave the MOT an extended mandate in tourism facilitation, research, development, industry control, tourism marketing, coordination and policy did not prevent such overlapping developing. In 1988, a Prime Ministerial Decree (no. 933) gave MOT the right to plan the development and coordinate the provision of infrastructure and facilities for all areas designated as tourism zones. These zones are mostly desert areas predominantly situated outside the boundaries of populated cities in the Nile Valley, Red Sea and the South Sinai Governorates. As this decree cannot bring an amendment to the problem of existing institutional and jurisdictional ambiguity, law no. 7 of 1991 was enacted to grant jurisdictional authority over the designated tourism zones to a national tourism authority. This authority became the TDA. However, real coordination between the various ministries and agencies on the needs of the tourism sector is still a difficult problem. Hopefully, this is soon going to change after the government has recognised the importance of tourism as a productive sector in the Egyptian economy after terrorist attacks caused a slow down in tourism in 1993.

The Interdepartmental Supreme Council for Tourism is another case that deserves attention. Reorganised by the Presidential decree no. 216 of 1985, the Supreme Council for Tourism headed by the Prime Minister was convened only four times in 8 years while it should have met four times a year. Its decisions were not implemented, regardless of their approval by the Council of Ministers. One of its most important decisions was to declare tourism a special-status sector that would bypass the jurisdiction of Governorates and leave it to Central Government. This decision has not yet been enforced.

DEVELOPMENT STRATEGIES AND PRIORITY ACTION PLAN

A national strategy for tourism supply development was adopted by the TDA and identified as a development goal:

> The institution of an environment is where the tourism sector can accomplish its optimal sustainable development potential on a sound regulatory, technical, social, economic financial and environmental basis.

The strategy debated the fact that tourism in Egypt to date has focused on traditional visits to the antiquity sites. It therefore stressed the need for diversifying the product and offer the visitors the opportunity to combine culture and leisure activities, by encouraging the development of a wide variety of visitor attractions and facilities. To do so, the strategy included carrying out a survey of the tourism sector, and the preparation of a priority action plan.

The main objectives of the priority action plan were to:

- offer a vision for future tourism development based on an analysis of international tourism markets and demand in relation to national assets and resources;
- identify priority development areas based on an examination of potentially developable sites;
- define development requirements, including infrastructure and environmental and investment needs; and
- define implementation priorities and plans.

Environmental Management

As stated by the World Bank in its world development report (1992): 'without adequate environmental protection, development will be undermined, and without development, environmental protection will fail'. The tourism development strategy adopted by the Ministry of Tourism places a primary concern on environmental aspects. Environmental management is an integral component of the development process. Particular consideration is also given to the protection of the unique heritage of Egypt, and the role both the past and the present must play in setting tourism development goals.

Planning Approach

In the preparation of the priority action plan a hierarchical planning approach has been used (Fig. 4·1). The approach involved an examination of the development potential from the largest spatial planning unit to the smallest. Five hierarchical levels were examined. The top, or *national*, level is Egypt itself. All decisions at

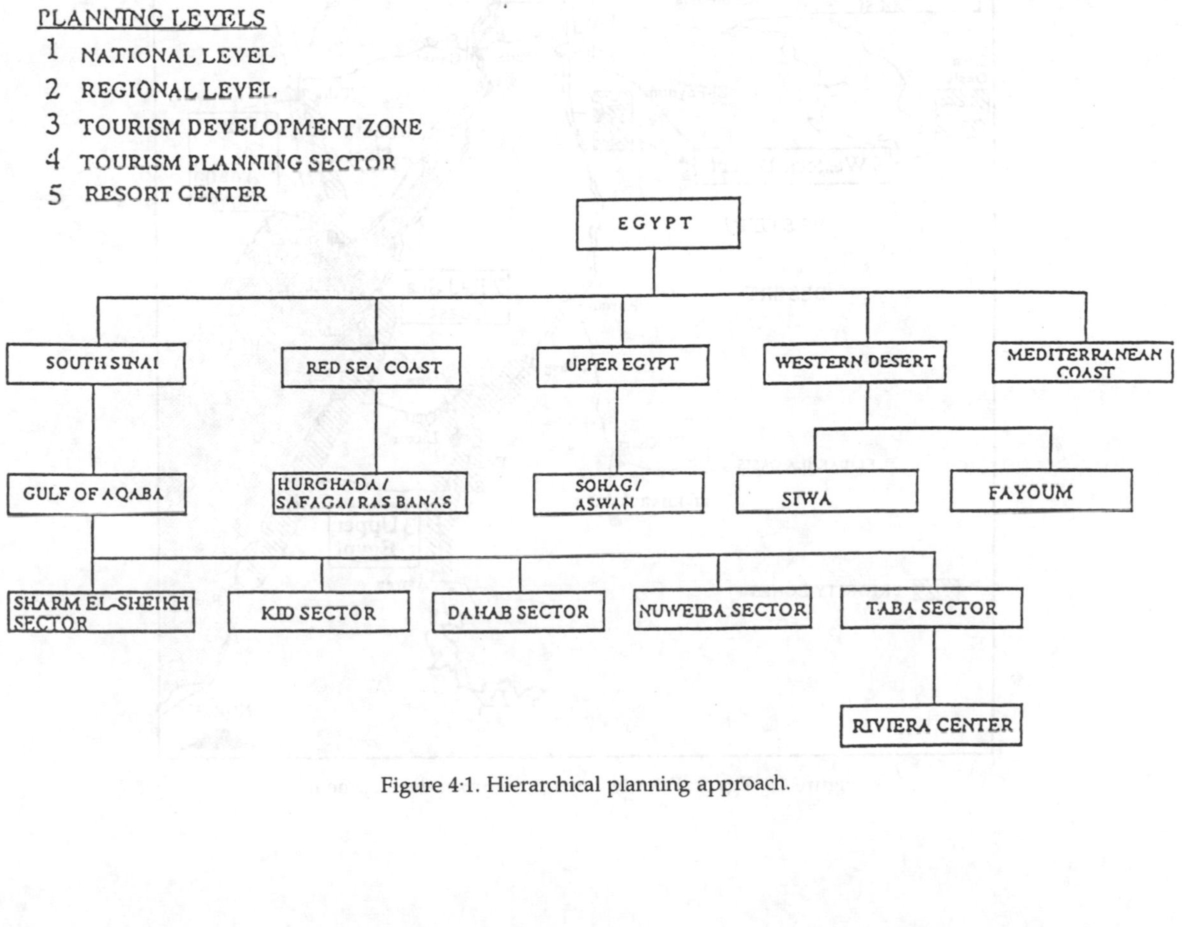

PLANNING LEVELS
1 NATIONAL LEVEL
2 REGIONAL LEVEL
3 TOURISM DEVELOPMENT ZONE
4 TOURISM PLANNING SECTOR
5 RESORT CENTER

Figure 4·1. Hierarchical planning approach.

lower levels have to take into account national objectives and policies that affect tourism development as well as prevailing national conditions.

Next is the *regional* level, which provides an overall framework for consideration of the priority areas and involves basic strategy decisions as to where to apply national resources for development.

Zones, the next level, are similar in scope to regions except that their boundaries are defined to reflect more specific development objectives.

Zones are divided into sectors. A *sector* is an area with homogenous characteristics about 30–70 k in length, usually encompassing an established community and more than one smaller area suitable for development as a resort center. The needs of infrastructure at the sector level can be defined relatively precisely.

Finally, the smallest planning unit is the *center*. A resort center is defined as a specific tract of land encompassing several sites for hotels, recreational facilities and commercial activities forming an integrated development.

The importance of this planning approach is that it allows projects be prepared and evaluated within their proper context. An investor, for example, will be able to identify a project based on a full understanding of its priority at the national level, of how it relates to other projects at the regional level, and of how future plans at the local level will affect the investment decision. The ministry used this approach to formulate the development programme and define the priority zones to be provided with infrastructure within the next 3 years.

Development Priorities

Priorities established by the Ministry for tourism development include the Egyptian Coast of the Gulf of Aqaba, the zone from Hurghada to

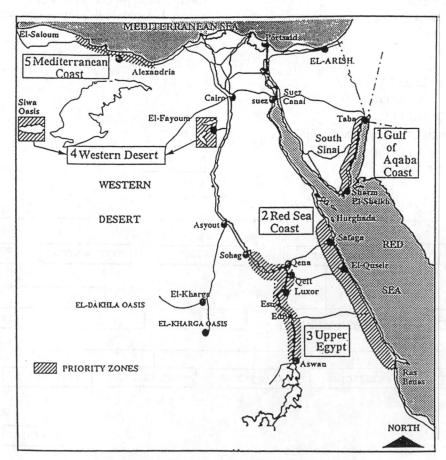

Figure 4·2. Egypt: Priority zones for tourism development.

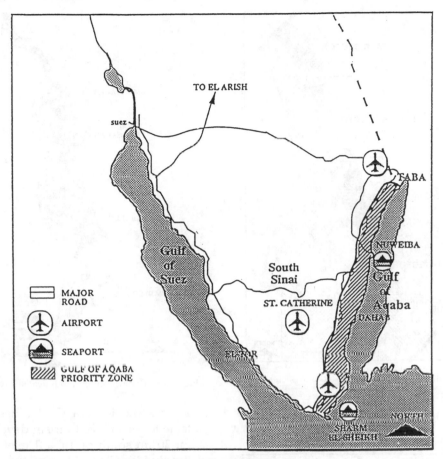

Figure 4·3. Egypt: South Sinai governorate.

Safaga on the Red Sea, Nile cruises from Sohag to Aswan and yachting tourism (see Fig. 4·2).

Gulf of Aqaba

The Gulf of Aqaba as a zone stretches from Ras Mohammed at the southern extreme of the Sinai Peninsula to Taba in the north (Figs 4·3 and 4·4). Its major settlements are Sharm El Sheikh, Dahab and Nuweiba. The zone is served by two airports, two sea ports and a scenic regional road. The zone possesses internationally renowned diving sites and a number of exceptionally beautiful sandy beaches. The national park at Ras Mohammed is recognised as one of the two greatest coral barrier-reef formations in the world. The Gulf is also known for its highly colorful and diverse marine life which includes more than 150 species of corals and 1000 species of fish. In addition, at Nabaq a large mangrove covers 5 km of the coastline serving as a habitat for a wide variety of birds and aquatic life. A

great spectacular sight in Sinai is the huge migration that occurs every spring and autumn as thousands of eagles, buzzards and vultures together with flocks of storks, cranes and pelicans fly past to or from their African winter habitats.

The Gulf of Aqaba coastal region has been divided into five tourist development sectors. The identified sectors are Sharm El-Sheikh, Wadi Kid, Dahab, Nuweiba and Taba. The sectors have been further examined and developable areas within each sector have been identified.

Taba Sector. As an example, five centers have been identified within the Taba sector as priority centers for development. For each center, an indicative master plan has been prepared to identify suitable land use and provide development guidelines (Fig. 4·5).

Riviera Center. One of the priority areas along the Gulf of Aqaba is known as the Riviera Center

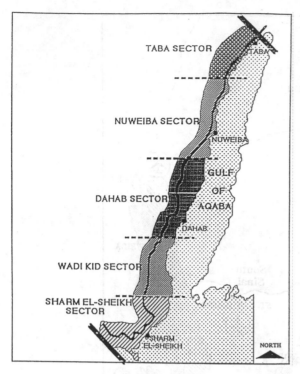

Figure 4·4. Gulf of Aqaba zone divided into sectors.

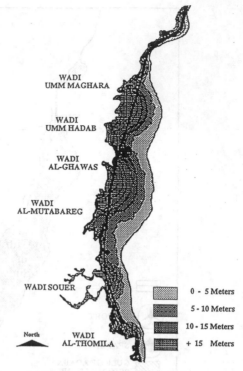

Figure 4·6. Riviera center: analytical study (topography).

(Fig. 4·6). The Riviera Center has been found suitable for extensive tourism development. It is about 30 km south of Taba. Development plans of the Riviera Center east of the regional road encompasses about 1600 acres of land. Averaging 2 km in width, the Riviera contains 9 km of gently sloping, virgin coastal beach, with offshore coral reef formations and inland mountains which range up to 2000 m in height. The beach front varies from water level to 10 m above the sea. Natural slopes of 2–4° allow maximum views of the gulf.

Two hills on the beach front provide landmarks and serve as natural divisions creating three distinct development areas. This natural subdivision is also suitable for the phasing of construction. Thus three main entrances from the existing regional road to the site have been proposed, with the major hotels located at these entrances to minimise traffic flow through the area and complement the natural features provided by the hills.

For planning and construction purposes, the center is thus viewed as three development areas separated by the two hills. A town center containing a hotel, restaurants, shops and other facilities is proposed in the middle to provide the

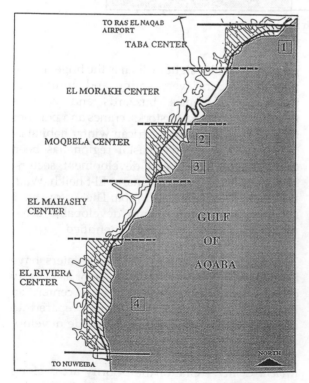

Figure 4·5. Taba sector divided into centers.

main focus for village life and commercial activities. Smaller sub-centers are designed to serve the north and south villages. The northern-most point of the Riviera provides an excellent location for a marina and a hotel complex.

Moqbela and Homayra Center. The next priority center is just north of the Riviera. It consists of two adjacent sites: Moqbela and Homayra. Moqbela and Homarya are two distinct geographic areas separated by an attractive hill. Moqbela, which comprises the southern sector, is a vast fan-shaped area of gently sloping land and sandy beaches. It is about 3·5 km in length. 2·0 km in depth and has an area of 800 acres (over three million square meters). In the Homarya section to the north, a narrow valley zigzags across from west to east, opening onto a flat coastal plain at the water's edge. The surrounding hills form an unusually protected secluded area of about 40 acres (170,000 m^2).

Homarya has been identified as an excellent site for a major tourist marina, to be developed in phases. The first phase will contain a five-star hotel and accommodate about 200 boats of various types and sizes. It will also provide the required maintenance and repair facilities and infrastructure services.

Homayra is planned to be developed in conjunction with a major tourist resort at Moqbela. The Moqbela development is planned to include five hotels, tourist villages, a main town center containing a full range of shops and services in addition to smaller sub-centers, a major diving center and a championship golf course and tourist housing.

Taba Center. Next is the Taba Center which is approximately 1·5 km long and 0·5 km in average depth. It is situated along the northern tip of the Gulf of Aqaba at the Egyptian–Israeli border.

The area abounds in natural assets: white sandy beaches; crystal clear water; dramatic cliffs; historic sites (Salaheddin Fortress on Pharoas island); a wealth of coral reefs and marine life; as well as a favorable year-round climate.

The site is adjacent to the coastal highway that runs along the entire edge of the Gulf of Aqaba from the Egyptian–Israeli border in the north to Sharm El-Sheikh in the south. The international airport is about 25 km from the site.

For planning purposes, the Taba Center has been divided into three sections. Upon completion, it will contain about 1500 rooms for tourists, a world-class gambling casino and tennis complex, a major regional commercial center, a diving center and tourist housing. The entire resort will be served by an open beach 100 m wide running the length of the development.

Red Sea – Hurghada–Safaga Sector

The coastal area of the Red Sea zone, from Hurghada to Safaga, ranks as a top priority sector for tourist development. This sector enjoys the additional advantage of being near the famous antiquity sites at Luxor, only 240 km away. This includes the temples of Karnak, Luxor, Hatshepsut and the tombs of Tut Ank Amun and Ramses the second.

Within the Hurghada–Safaga sector, two centers have been identified for immediate development. These are Sahl Hasheesh and Ras Abu Soma.

Sahl Hasheesh Center. Sahl Hasheesh is a spectacular natural bay of sandy beaches. It is about 7 km long and 2 km wide. It contains about 32 million square meters of developable gently sloping site, offering panoramic views of the Red Sea from every corner. It is about 20 km south of the international airport of Hurghada and is served by the regional scenic coastal road. The area is also known for its world famous diving sites, coral reefs and marine life.

Planning concept: the proposed master plan is based on three nodal points (two hotels and a town center) connected by a ribbon-type beach development along the length of the site. In conjunction with this beach development, two secondary, self-sufficient residential golf developments and apartments in park-like settings, starting approximately 1 km from the beach, represent a multi-directional development. The town center will provide all the services needed for year-round living as well as the recreational amenities one would expect at an international resort community. The town center would include multi-storey residential blocks, water front shops and restaurants, traditional shopping bazaars and a large resort hotel and casino.

All key infrastructure facilities, namely potable water, electric power, roads, sewage treatment and communication systems will be designed and furnished in an integrated manner.

A flexible phasing plan has been formulated to maintain a sensitivity towards the tourist market and competitiveness with other tourist centers. The phasing is organised in such a way that each phase will separately constitute an attractive tourist image which fits into the general development framework of the completed community.

Abu Soma Center. The peninsula of Ras Abu Soma is located about 40 km south of Hurghada international airport. It contains about 30 million square meters of developable land, of which 10 million square meters have been designated for immediate development.

Soma Bays consists of a series of fine sandy beaches, which benefit from the added protection of an outlying coral island and coral reefs. It is renowned in the region for its diving sites and deep-sea fishing.

Planning concept: a master plan has been prepared for the phased development of the Soma Bay site. The master plan calls for the development of the site in phases starting with a 1·5 million square meter development comprising four resort hotels, 50 resort villas, a marina with accompanying restaurants, and commercial activity will support this first-phase development with all necessary infrastructure.

The peninsula's development is expected to expand in subsequent phases to cover the entire 10 million square meter site with:

- 15 resort villages and hotels to be built on individual beachfront lots ranging on surface area from 90,000 to 120,000 square meters;
- three marinas with adjoining restaurants and commercial/retail outlets;
- clusters of resort housing developments;
- a central sporting facility, including an 18 hole golf course;
- utility centers servicing the overall development with all necessary infrastructure.

Nile Cruise Tourism
Development in this area aims to improve services to the current 183 floating hotels, and provide infrastructure and other services for up to 300 by the year 2000. The Nile cruises are a significant feature of traditional tourism, and great attention is given to the environmental impact of greater numbers of tourists and increased use of the Nile.

The priority components of the project include:
(1) development and improvement of the existing docks and berthing facilities by supplying the necessary services and infrastructure, and building new berthing facilities to avoid overcrowding;
(2) construction of facilities for repair, servicing and building floating hotels;
(3) establishing a center for navigation control, and for the provision of health, safety, fire and other emergency services;
(4) development of some islands for recreational purposes;
(5) development of tourist sites and attractions, and renovation and beautification of surrounding areas.

Yachting Tourism
Yachting tourism is an area of great potential which has not yet been developed, particularly in view of Egypt's unique geographical position, and historical and natural riches.

Two sites have been identified as suitable to become the first in a chain of marinas which will eventually extend from Port Said on the Mediterranean to the Red Sea and the Gulf of Aqaba. The first marina site is in Port Said, which has all the special characteristics of a coastal city and could become a stopping point for yachts cruising in the Mediterranean. The second marina site is in the Gulf of Aqaba, south of Taba at Homayra, and will serve as an eastern outlet for a chain of yachting facilities.

Investment Climate and Privileges

The Government of Egypt is committed to an economy based on market forces, and in order to enhance the investment climate, Law no. 230 of 1989 adds further privileges and guarantees for investors. These include the right of repatriation of profits, and tax exemptions ranging up to 10 years.

Several investment opportunities for the private sector have been identified and includes the development of new tourist centers and marinas and also the right to acquire shares in current projects.

While investment requests were approved in an *ad hoc* manner without due regard to the adequacy of infrastructure support and environmental protection, the previous shortage of a proper regulatory framework has resulted in uncontrolled development on the Red Sea Coast, land speculation, some spoilage of the coast line in Hurghada and crowded cruise operations on the Nile that caused a cut-throat price competition in slack seasons. The TDA, however, in cooperation with the Agency of Environmental Protection, is presently exerting serious efforts to overcome these problems and provide for a future enforceable development standards to ensure sustainability.

The enforceability of development standards should not counteract the privatisation trend that provides for gradually deregulating the tourism industry to allow the private sector to operate freely in a competitive environment. The private enterprises should play a larger role in the design, finance, ownership, implementation and operation of tourism facilities.

Limited Access to Long-Term Financing

One of the noticeable obstacles to tourism development is the fact that the business community in Egypt still has limited access to long-term financing, particularly from the international capital and credit markets. Egypt is undergoing debt rescheduling, and lending with guarantees by export credit agencies is scarce. Moreover, direct foreign investments in tourism projects and resource financing are still inadequate in spite of the guarantees provided by the Government under Investment Law no. 230 (1989) against expropriation and nationalisation as well as the guarantees to repatriate annual profits. The most recent economic reforms suggested by the IMF are expected to restore the confidence of international commercial lenders in Egypt and thus improve access to long-term loans. Quite astonishingly, although the availability of financing in the domestic market was limited by the credit ceilings imposed by the Central Bank since February 1991 and high interest rates (22–25%), tourist development projects are still comparatively on the increase.

THE FUTURE OF EGYPTIAN TOURISM

The MOT has succeeded in allocating a large budget for overseas tourism marketing totalling US$42 million in 1994–1995. A reasonably conceived promotional plan was designed, concentrating on six priority tourist-generating markets, namely the USA, the UK, Germany, France, Italy and Japan. This is believed to bring about a boosting of the tourist image of Egypt and thus an upsurge in its inbound tourist traffic.

With the necessary restructuring of tourism institutions to become more effective along with the creation of a reliable system of tourism management information, the full implementation of the manpower development strategy led by the Tourism Academy, the policy reforms to surmount aforementioned constraints, and with sound environmental management to safeguard tourist resources and thus promote sustainability, Egypt should become one of the major tourist destinations in the world.

Terrorism, which is on the verge of being eradicated, is no longer an impediment to the growth of tourism in Egypt. The success of the newly emerging regional cooperation talks between the Middle Eastern countries, namely Egypt, Israel, Jordan and Palestine, would lead to a rational and large-scale tourism development in the region. Moreover, the potential Middle Eastern market and the large-scale tourist projects, such as the Red Sea riviera, would be to the benefit of all countries concerned.

Given the competitive tourist advantage Egypt enjoys and the promising future of peace in the region, the future of tourism in Egypt looks brighter. The Middle East is bound to have a better image internationally and tourism will not be as vulnerable as it has been.

SELECT BIBLIOGRAPHY

Bryden, J. (1973), *Tourism and Development, a Case Study of the Commonwealth Caribbean*, Cambridge, MA: Cambridge University Press.

Defert, P. (1972), Les Resources et les activities touristiques, essai d'integration, *Les Cahiers du Tourism*, C-19.

de Kadt, E. (1979), *Tourism Passport to Development*, Oxford: Oxford University Press.

Economist (1991), Report on Egypt, International Tourism Reports no. 1, 53–71.

Edgell, D. L. (1987), International Prospects (1987–2000), Washington, DC: US Department of Commerce.

Edgell, Q. L. (1990), *International Tourism Policy*, New York: Van Nostrand Reinhold.

Egyptian Hotel Association (1994), *Hotel Guide, 1994/ 1995*, Cairo.

Hudman, L., and Hawkins, D. (1989), *Tourism in Contemporary Society*, Englewood Cliffs, NJ: Prentice Hall.

Mathieson, A., and Wall, G. (1989), *Tourism: Economic, Physical and Social Impacts*, Harlow: Longman.

Ministry of Tourism (MOT) (1993), *Tourism in Figures*, Cairo. Ministry of Tourism (MOT) (1994), *Promotion Plan*, Cairo.

Pearce, D. (1989), *Tourism Development*, Harlow: Longman.

Wahab, S. (1987), National Report no. 127, Economist International, Tourism Reports no. 1, 19–31.

Wahab, S. (1975), *Managerial Aspects of Tourism*, Turin: ILO Turin Center.

Wahab, S. (1975), *Tourism Management*, London: Tourism International Press.

Wahab, S., Crampon, L., and Rothfield, L. (1976), *Tourism Marketing*, London: Tourism International Press.

Wahab, S. (1979), *Studies in Tourism Planning*, Cairo.

Waters (somerest) (1994), *The Travel Industry Yearbook*, New York: Child and Waters.

WTO (1994), *Integrated Planning*, Madrid, Spain.

The Virtual Tourism Environment. Utilisation of Information Technology to Enhance Strategic Travel Marketing

Donald E. Hawkins, Mitch Leventhal and Wendy L. Oden

5

ABSTRACT

This chapter provides a descriptive overview of the use of the Internet and applications of World Wide Web technology in the travel and tourism industry at a moment in time[†]. Emphasis is placed on informing tourism practitioners and academics about present developments in Web technologies and current applications within the travel and tourism strategic planning and marketing process. Several examples of travel-related Web sites are provided that illustrate applications within the industry. Additionally, the authors explore future opportunities and industry trends relating to the adoption of electronic information technologies into the next decade.

[†] All website addresses cited in this article were current as it went to press. Unfortunately, due to the dynamic nature of the Internet Web, some sites may have moved or vanished subsequent to publication. Should the reader encounter addresses which appear to be nonfunctional, we suggest that they search by company name or title using a major Internet search engine.

INTRODUCTION

A technological tsunami is sweeping across the tourism industry, and it will have profound implications on the travel experience. Tourism enterprises, distribution channels, governments, researchers and consumers are struggling to keep up with the ripple effects of an unprecedented wave of electronic communication, multimedia developments and information technology advances. Indeed, technology in tourism is evolving so rapidly that this paper, which was initially presented in Cairo in June 1995, had to be completely updated prior to its publication here.

Interactive electronic technology can potentially unify the tourism industry, which historically has been characterised by many fragmented small- and medium-size enterprises. New information technologies hold the power to foster global collaboration, cooperation and strategic alliances within the industry, along with new marketing opportunities.

Due to advances in information technology, a new approach is emerging in which strategic travel marketing focuses on the *individual* rather than on the *mass market*, tailoring messages and products to specific consumer needs, and resulting in more cost-effective, efficient and productive marketing outcomes.

THE GROWTH OF THE INTERNET

This new wave of change has been pushed by the explosive growth of the Internet. The Internet is an international network of networks, all running TCP/IP (transmission control protocol/Internet protocol), connected through gateways and routers, and sharing common name and address spaces. It is predicated on open architecture, and exists to facilitate sharing of resources and collaboration among anyone, anywhere, anytime, who has connectivity.

Although originally designed for use by the military, government agencies and universities, the advent of the World Wide Web (Web), hypertext transfer protocol (HTTP) and graphical browsers (i.e. Netscape and Microsoft Internet Explorer) have changed the complexion of the Internet entirely. The Internet is now an explosively growing narrowcast medium for education, entertainment and commerce.

Lottor's comprehensive longitudinal study of the growth of Internet servers indicates an overall increase from 376,000 in 1991 to almost 9·5 million in January 1996. During the 6 months prior to that month, US servers grew by 34% while growth worldwide stood at about 42%. Although almost 64% of Internet servers remain in the US, the rate of growth is considerably greater outside of North America. The number of computers set up specifically as Web servers has grown astronomically, from 17,500 in July 1995 to 75,743 in January 1996 – representing a 432% increase over 6 months. More recently, the April estimate of total Web servers has skyrocketed to 114,572 (Lottor, 1996).

Network Solutions, a private firm contracted by the National Science Foundation to oversee US Internet domain name registration (popularly known as the 'InterNIC'), reports a phenomenal increase in the number of unique domains. In 1993, only 8700 names were registered worldwide, compared to 37,565 in December 1994, and over 340,000 in April 1996 (Mills, 1996). Domain names increased 66% in the first 4 months of 1996 (Metzger, 1996).

Today, millions are tapping into the Internet, and thousands of new users are being initiated every day. Estimates of use vary widely, although all sources agree that growth is steep. By the year 2000, some experts predict that 52 million people will be accessing the Internet worldwide (Swisher, 1996a). No matter what the estimate of current use, all agree that it is only a matter of a few years before the magic 100 million users is reached.

People in more than 140 countries are using computer bulletin-board systems, Usenet and other interactive systems to form alliances with others who share a common interest. This online community is giving rise to electronic commerce. Businesses are adopting Internet technology in increasing numbers. In 1993, over half of the Fortune 1000 companies had an e-mail address (Klinghagen, 1995). In 1996, over 87% of domain names registered belong to commercial organisations (Mills, 1996).

PARADIGM SHIFTS

The Web represents a technological advance on a par with Gutenburg's printing press. It is profoundly changing the way in which humans organise, use and retrieve information, how they think about information, and even how they interact with one another. The following transformations are currently underway and will have momentous impact in the coming years.

Document Centric vs Application Centric

The significance of Internet technology on business development worldwide has to be viewed in the context of the earlier PC revolution and the subsequent widespread adoption of local area networks (LAN). Both share the same paradigm – empowerment through group- and enterprise-wide collaboration, and worldwide access to resources.

Computing is witnessing a fundamental shift toward a document-centric desktop computing paradigm; this is in contrast to today's application-centric paradigm. Just as many people were getting comfortable with LANs and database servers, this document-centric world arrived that is based on HTTP (hypertext transfer protocol), and which supports a new client-server model. HTTP, the language of the Web, runs on top of TCP/IP – the Internet's basic transport mechanism – and permits discrete documents to have unique addresses accessible by anyone, anywhere, anytime.

The Emergence of 'Intranets'

In addition to providing an easy interface for communicating with the world over the Internet, HTTP is ideal for 'intranets' – closed or 'fire-walled' networks which serve individual companies or organisations. Because of its simplicity, this document-centric technology offers significant savings over last generation application-centric distributed databases. Because HTTP is the same for both Internet- and intranet-based websites, organisations can easily make selected documents available to the world without any arcane software conversions or manipulations. An added attraction is full platform-independence – documents appear identical under Windows, Mac, OS/2 and UNIX.

All types of organisations are beginning to discover that with TCP/IP technology, they can accomplish even more information sharing at lower cost than with more traditional groupware solutions. As esoteric as it may seem, the most efficient way of storing, distributing and providing remote access to information within any organisation and throughout the world is via a Web server. Thanks to uniform resource locators (URLs) – simply put, Web addresses – users can specify any publicly accessible object on the Internet and retrieve it. These documents contain hyperlinks which facilitate rapid access to other locations in the same document, other documents on the same website, and to documents on other sites anywhere in the world.

The Boeing Company has created a nationwide intranet for its 96,000 U.S. employees (Tittle and Stewart, 1996). The World Travel and Tourism Council is working with IBM-Europe to develop a Web site powered by Lotus Notes. The WTTC has established 'EcoNet', a site for information on environmentally sustainable tourism and human resource best practices. The USAir–Quantas–British Airways alliance is also in the process of implementing Lotus Notes as a cooperative tool for joint planning across the alliance (Dingley, 1996). In Canada, the four provinces of the Atlantic (New Brunswick, Newfoundland–Labrador, Nova Scotia and Prince Edward Island) have joined forces to build a Notes-based intranet with Internet links called ACTN (Atlantic Canada Tourism Network) (Jean-Joyce, 1996).

Analysts estimate that 20% of Fortune 1000 companies have launched intranets. Similarly, 16% of all US businesses have installed intranets and another 50% report that they are presently evaluating their options (Tittle and Stewart, 1996). Businesses are discovering that they can now establish a global presence at a fraction of traditional marketing costs; realise a cost-savings in mail, distribution and telephone expenses through online, real-time distribution of detailed product and service information; and improve communication efficiency, document management, training on demand, and business-to-business links through the use of TCP/IP without the associated costs of traditional voice mail, fax and express mail services (Ellis, 1995).

The Potential for Electronic Commerce

Much of the excitement surrounding the Internet can be attributed to predictions of an unlimited, universal electronic marketplace. Such a marketplace would 'level the playing field', allowing small and large companies to compete equally, since in cyberspace it is difficult to determine organisational size. Entrepreneurs are racing to set up shop on the Web, eager to cash in on the 'pot of gold' at the off-ramps leading directly into consumers' homes.

Dramatic sales growth is predicted. In the first quarter of 1995, $47 million in venture capital was invested in Internet-related businesses, compared to $40 million for all of 1994 (Cash, 1995). According to Input, Inc., the overall worldwide Internet market, including intranets, will grow from $12 billion annually in 1995 to $210 billion by the year 2000. Furthermore, by 2000 intranet Web servers will outnumber Internet servers by six to one (Bauer, 1996).

Jupiter Communications' 1996 'Home Shopping Report' estimates that a $7·2 billion online marketplace will exist by 2000 of which $4·5 billion will be Web-based. The remaining $2·7 billion market will be transacted on commercial online services, such as America Online and CompuServe (Heyman, 1996a). According to

InterAdMonthly, fourth-quarter Web advertising for 1995 totaled $12·5 million. Top spenders included American Airlines, AT&T, Microsoft, Honda, Sprint and other blue chip companies. According to ActiveMedia, this year more than $83 million will be spent for website development worldwide. (Resnick, 1996).

While analysts predict that retail sales on the Web will more than triple this year and top $4 billion by 2000, actual online consumer purchases have proceeded at a slower rate of growth than some initially predicted. According to Jupiter Communications, more than 8 million Web shoppers spent $132 million in actual online purchases in 1995 (Martin, 1996). However, a 1996 *Internet World* article estimated all 1995 Web commerce combined totaled $436 million (Resnick, 1996). These disparate estimates are hardly a drop in the $57 billion home-shopping bucket (Martin, 1996). However, sales growth continues at a steady rate. Forrester Research predicts that online shopping revenues will reach $518 million by the end of 1996, and soar up to $6·6 billion by the year 2000. They further estimate that travel will make up fully 24% of all online revenues (Schwartz, 1996).

Preliminary studies of purchasing habits bode well for the travel and tourism industry. Jupiter Communications estimates that nearly one-half (47%) of online buyers spent $1000 or more in the past six months, with 6% reporting expenditures in excess of $1000. Interestingly, the average expenditure came to $235 per online buyer, indicating a willingness to make large online purchases, such as those required by the travel industry (Resnick, 1996).

The Power to Link

While online sales *potential* is very real, its *reality* has often been exaggerated. At the same time, the Internet's inherent 'power to link' global entities in a forum of information exchange across platforms has often been undervalued. As we look ahead to 2000, Internet tools and technologies offer the potential to change the way we do business, and will result in more efficient work processes, new approaches to strategic planning, customised products and support, and more strategic alliances. This 'linkage' power is actually causing commercial activities on the Internet to occur in three big waves: enterprise

(intra-company) communications; business-to-business commerce; and direct, point-of-sale marketing to consumers (Cash, 1995).

The adoption of 'intranet' technologies among organisations within the travel and tourism industry will have major implications for tourism planning, destination management and marketing, through extraordinarily enhanced opportunities for collaboration and coordination.

Consumer Changes

Finally, changing consumer buying behaviors are occurring coterminous with technological advances in the virtual environment. According to confidence measures in the 1993 Yankelovich Monitor, 72% of people surveyed reported that they had great confidence in themselves while 45% had confidence in travel recommendations made by friends. Unfortunately, only 12% had confidence in travel agent recommendations (Yastrow, 1995). This loss of confidence in traditional market intermediaries coincides with the newly arrived ability for travel marketers to go directly to the point-of-sale. In an atmosphere of skepticism, the new consumer will inevitably 'go to the source' – all indications point to the Internet as the preferred shopping environment for the next age. Successful use of Internet technologies will leave the new, self-reliant consumer in control, while at the same time simplifying his decision-making process which will result in more brand loyalty and trust (Yastrow, 1995).

NEW TOOLS DRIVING THE WEB

Internet technology continues to be developed at breakneck speed. Consensus has now been reached that a seamless interface between desktop computers and the Internet is in the offing (Heyman, 1996b). Microsoft intends to fully integrate Web functionality into its next operating system, Windows 97.

Technology-based products will be designed to meet the needs of specific individuals. Personal computers will be replaced by 'Internet appliances'. Already, intelligent agents perform tasks customized for each individual user and advanced security features prevent anyone but the authorised user from signing on and carrying out electronic transactions (Millet, 1996). The following are just a few of today's new technologies that will lead the Web into tomorrow:

- *Distributed object technology* – with its Java programming language (www.javaworld.com), Sun Microsystems is racing to establish itself as the leader for Web-based interactivity. Based on C++, Java allows developers to create miniature applications, known as 'applets', that are transmitted over the Web and which are temporarily used on the client end for carrying out specific tasks. Java offers full 'platform-independence', introducing 'inter-activity' to multimedia Web information regardless of individual computer operating systems (Williams, 1996). Microsoft's ActiveX technology seeks to compete head on with Java. These technologies are fueling an industry dedicated to the creation of 'objects' written in these languages and which can be used as interactive building blocks. Leaders in this area include Next's WebObjects (www.next.com) and its competitor NetObjects (www.netobjects.com).
- *Database integration* – Numerous database solutions now exist for creating robust databases of information that run behind Web pages and that can be user-specified via access through different interfaces. Running common gateway interface (CGI) and application programming interface (API) scripts, these applications allow high level interactivity with databases. One company, The ObjectLinks Corporation (www.objectlinks.com) has developed complete libraries of proprietary objects which permit the construction of powerful, inter-active, database applications which compile Web pages 'on the fly', and which permit high-level database administration to occur through simple forms interfaces.
- *Activity tracking* – Other software programs offer Web usage tracking and sales lead generation through various methods. Market Focus2, software by Intersé (www.interse.com), offers powerful usage analyses of behavior on intranets and websites. It reports on usage, document requests, location of users, number of visits, and more (Patel, 1996). Other leading tracking companies include I/PRO (www.ipro.com) and Web Track (www.webtrack.com).

Marketers are turning to an array of software tools that can use the Internet to find new sales leads and distribute them automatically within a company to maximize their bottom line payoff from venturing into cyberspace. Top products in this category include: WebTrack Internet Marketing Module (Aurum Software, www.aurum.com); ACT! (Symantec Corp., www/symantec.com); MultiActive Maximizer 3.0 (Maximizer Technologies, www.maximizer.com); and ECCO Pro (NetManage, www.netmanage.com).

- *Search engines* – various kinds of automated search systems have emerged on the Web to help users more effectively and efficiently retrieve customized information. Many offer the ability to customize the use of available data bases. Strategic indexing in search engines is a critical marketing step. Leading search engines include AltaVista (www.altavista.digital.com), Lycos (www.lycos.com), Excite (www.excite.com), Infoseek (www.infoseek.com/), WebCrawler (webcrawler.com), and Open Text (www.opentext.com:8080/), among others.
- *Multimedia* – many new tools which expand multimedia capabilities are now emerging. Virtual reality markup language (VRML) is an ASCII-based language that describes three-dimensional worlds (Gross, 1996). Motion Pictures Experts Group (MPEG) video compression technology helps networked systems move large video images easily, reducing the jerky and unpolished look of video transmitted over slow telephone lines (Hayes, 1996). Audio and video 'streaming' technologies from firms such as RealAudio (www.realaudio.com) and Xing (www.xingtech.com) permit real-time transmission of programming. These technologies will become increasingly important as more and more companies adopt interactive multimedia and video teleconferencing in their marketing mix.
- *Intelligent agents* – the idea of Internet-based 'intelligent agents' which act as personal assistants, performing tasks on the user's behalf and tailored to individual needs is becoming increasingly popular. The most common applications of intelligent agents are software programs that deliver Web pages

'off-line'. These programs search for and retrieve information specified by the user in advance and can even perform other specific tasks or make suggestions tailored to the individual's needs. Competitors in this fast-growing niche include Freeloader, Inc. (www.freeloader.com), PointCast, Inc. (www.pointcast.com) and First Floor Software (www.firstfloor.com) (Swisher, 1996b).

- *Groupware* – software architecture that allows users to access networked resources through an easy-to-use interface as well as engage in 'collaborative' computing. This new technology allows groups to interact across space and time. An excellent example of a groupware application has been developed by the US National Center for Supercomputing Applications for the National Performance Review. The net-WorkPlace (calliope.ncsa.uiuc.edu:8080/) is an integrated set of productivity tools which support a virtual office setting, enabling collaboration among members of an on-line team regardless of location, time or computing platform.

  The netWorkPlace interface, through the use of an office builder metaphor, combines common terminology and spatial structure in a telecommuting environment which integrates familiar, pre-existing collaborative tools with newly created tools. Workers can continue to use the software applications with which they are already familiar, on whatever computer platform they already own. This environment is designed to *supplement and enhance* team communication, *not to replace* face-to-face or phone contact.

- *Security software* – a number of firewall vendors are creating security products for the Internet. Border Network Technologies (www.digital.de/ibg/resources/providers/248.html), CheckPoint Software Technologies (www.checkpoint.com/), Raptor Systems (www.raptor.com) and Trusted Information Systems (www.interop.com) offer products to help companies build secure, private networks by providing three key security features: privacy, authentication of data, and integrity of data transmission. Firewall software acts like a lock on the front door to keep intruders from accessing private company data or files of confidential information about clients and suppliers (Haber, 1996).

- *Internet appliances* – many computer giants are betting that there is a market for a low-cost, desk-top computer appliance that will provide easy access to the Internet, as well as a company's internal 'intranet'. This appliance would have the ability to access network-based applications and provide companies with a way to simplify employee computing needs while saving millions in software and support (Bambon, 1995). Companies paving the way include IBM, Oracle and Sun Micro-systems who are all developing appliances that will sell for $500–$1000 each.

INTERNET-BASED STRATEGIC TRAVEL MARKETING APPLICATIONS

Travel marketing can be improved substantially through the use of information systems and decision making tools, particularly if they involve interactivity with key stakeholders involved in the tourism process – businesses, governments, educational institutions, travelers, suppliers, host destination communities and related sectors. Marketing using Internet technologies provides new opportunities to sell travel products and services on a worldwide basis for practically any size business or service provider at a relatively low cost.

Additionally, intranets provide an environment for enhancing collaboration and for sharing knowledge in a private password accessible environment. Use of intranets among tourism enterprises can have major implications for the planning process by creating a coherent environment where the best global expertise available can be assembled in a collaborative planning process.

Internet technology is ideally suited for Delphi panels, through which highly reliable expert consensus can be achieved, and commitment to group decisions attained. Groups can be assembled that previously could not exist due to cost factors of traditional communication channels. Similarly, expertise from other industries can be included that traditionally might have been excluded (Linstone and Turoff, 1975; Kerr and Hiltz, 1982).

Intranets can play a significant role in fostering the growth of sustainable tourism. Automatic feed-back loops can be built-in, enabling tourism planners to be more cognisant of external community factors. Decision making can therefore be more responsive and sensitive to stakeholder needs. Additionally, information shared in the intranet environment can be made available to the general public at any time across the Internet.

Several Websites exist that are making use of the all-inclusive nature of the Internet and in presenting various stakeholder viewpoints relating to local ecotourism, cultural tourism and nature-based tourism planning issues. One of the best examples of a community-based ecotourism Website has been set up by the Jemtland Province in Northern Sweden (www.sbbs.se/hp/hkab). The site is the cooperative project of the City of Stockholm, the Jemtland Provincial government and 40 local ecotourism suppliers. It provides the local villagers' view of ecotourism, as well as guidelines and related links for travelers, lots of information about the local culture and an educational message for travel agents (Watt, 1996). The Long Beach Model Forest (LBMF) Society (www.lbmf.bc.ca/tourism.html) and Rick Mader's Eco Travel in Latin America (www.txinfinet.com/mader/ecotravel/ecotravel.html) are two other good examples of Internet technology being used to create forums for information exchanges.

Integrating Electronic Interactive Media Into Marketing Planning

Taking full advantage of commercial online services, the Web, CD-ROM and hybrid technologies enable travel and tourism marketing organisations to improve product development, communications and promotion, distribution and placement, and return on investment. Incorporating interactive media in a travel organisation's marketing plan can provide much more relevant, in-depth and up-to-date information about any product or destination, and it can be organised in such a way as to encourage travelers to:

- extend visits and pursue special interests;
- dine in a larger variety of restaurants in more diverse locations;
- shop more extensively and purposefully for specific types of products in varied downtown, outlying, outlet, bazaar and street locations;

- time trips to attend more special and cultural events;
- have the information necessary to make advance reservations for theater, concert and other tickets and the means to actually purchase the tickets remotely in advance;
- use the destination as a base for short excursions, day-trips or overnight trips;
- identify unique or unusual sites which normally are not covered in guidebooks;
- use maps that encourage planning self-guided trips and that show itineraries of varying lengths; and
- use public and transportation alternatives for economy and convenience, which also encourages budgeting of longer stays.

Numerous organisations and enterprises involved in the travel industry have now made substantial commitments to using Internet technologies as an integral part of their overall marketing strategy.

Commercial Online Services

Consumer online services and Internet access providers have grown substantially in recent years, and several US providers are launching services overseas. America Online teamed with Bertelsmann AG to launch AOL Europa in Germany in 1995, and plan to expand to France and the United Kingdom this year. UUnet Technologies, an Internet service provider, has established telecommunications links in 21 countries, while CompuServe, Inc. has had a strong presence in Europe for the past 10 years (Swisher, 1995).

Non-US companies aggressively involved in Internet provision include Deutsche Telekom, Luxembourg-based Europe Online, and France's Minitel system, which was the world's first mass-market online system in the 80s. Perhaps most interesting is Sardinia-based Video Online (www.vol.it), which has developed a global network of Internet affiliates which publish in local languages. Most of these online services offer contents specific to travel products or destinations and access to reservation systems. A proliferation of travel resources also exists on the Internet, from websites, discussion areas, chat rooms and electronic mailing lists.

Computerised Reservation Systems (CRS)

Commercial online services such as CompuServe, AOL and Prodigy all provide some type of online reservations booking system to their subscribers. The most diverse is CompuServe, which offers its 4·1 million users access to Easysabre (American Airlines' Sabre System), Worldspan Travel Shopper (Worldspan), United Connection and the Official Airline Guide. AOL offers Easysabre and ExpressNet (American Express) (Faiola, 1996). American Travel Corporation provides Internet direct booking access to Apollo.

Gradually, however, the process of making reservations is moving onto the Web. Internet Travel Network is an Apollo-based system that offers real time, online reservations, but tickets are distributed through local Apollo travel agencies. One of the best examples of commercial development of the Internet is PC Travel (www.pctravel.com) which has successfully offered online air reservations and ticketing, interfaced to the Apollo Reservation System since April 1994. They recently introduced a second site, the 'Web-Net Traveler Club' (www.webnet.pctravel.com/), offering unique discounts through PC Travel not offered anywhere else as well as a comprehensive listing of links to other travel sites categorised by main topics.

More recently, other online travel agencies have emerged. Go Explore (www.goexplore.com) is a digital travel agency with a dynamic site that focuses on the business and frequent traveler market. In addition to accessing real-time airline reservations, users can customise the system and conduct searches to fit their individual needs by completing confidential user profiles. Links to international travel information resources and an interactive map feature that produces detailed street maps for travel companies featured on the site are also provided (Daffron, 1996).

Thompson TravelMart (www.travelmart.no/travelmart/index_eng.html) is the first Norwegian-based electronic agency that focuses on last minute bookings and sales of travel products at discounts of up to 40%. Most of the focus is on accommodations in hotels, apartments, summer homes and yachts. Suppliers fax in their availability and the site is updated every Monday afternoon, payment is made by phone or fax using Visa or directly into the agency's Norwegian bank account (Blikom, 1996).

Travelocity, a 'one-stop shopping' travel site powered by the joint efforts of Worldview Systems Corporation and Sabre Interactive, claims to have the largest collection of integrated and searchable travel information on the Internet. Travelocity has featured airline booking and purchase capabilities since its inception and recently announced the addition of 'GeoEnabled Maps' for US landmarks and attractions described in its 'destinations and interests' department. Vacation packages will also soon be offered online, as well as reservations for more than 50 car rental companies and 31,800 hotel properties worldwide (Quigley, 1996).

Preview Media (www.vacations.com), a leading provider of reservation services and travel-related content on both America Online and the Web, sells both airline reservations and vacation packages (Pernick, 1996).

All of these services tap directly into the CRSs like Apollo or Sabre and are filled with industry jargon (like airport and city codes), so advances are still needed before online booking systems can present easy-to-use options for the average consumer. It is evident, however, that leading CRSs are planning to offer simple point-of-sale services in the near future.

Travel Companies

In 1995, Promus Hotel Corporation (www.promus-hotel.com) was one of the first hotel companies to offer 'real time' on-line bookings on the Web. Hyatt and Best Western have established sites on TravelWeb (www.travelweb.com), an electronic shopping mall maintained by THISCO. Holiday Inn Worldwide has successfully employed virtual reality technology in its Holiday Inn (www.holiday-inn.com) and Crowne Plaza (www.crowneplaza.com) websites, which include virtual tours, electronic brochures and interactive forms for meeting planners. World Hotel (www.worldhotel.com), the largest hotel guide on the Web, provides booking access to over 200,000 properties and special features for travel agents and corporate travel planners. Their site (www.eScope.com) recently introduced 'travel radiusing', which enables users to search for all travel related resources within a 50 mile radius of a given city in the US.

The American Automobile Association (www.aaa.com) and Rand McNally (205.230.66.103/cdrom/tripmake.html) have launched trip itinerary planning systems; Avis Rent a Car (www.avis.com), Alamo Rent a Car (www.freeways.com), VIA Rail Canada (www.viarail.ca) and hundreds of other travel vendors either have pages or are planning to set up pages on the Web.

Most major airlines are establishing a presence online and even offer special tour packages and discounted air fares or seat auctions to Internet travelers. A few airlines have begun to offer direct Internet booking access into their reservations systems. Most recently Japan Airlines went live with booking access for domestic flights; however tickets must be paid for and picked up at a JAL agency (Dingley, 1996).

AMR Corporation, parent company of American Airlines, Sabre and AMR Management Services uses interactivity on its Web site 'AA On Board' (www.amrcorp.com) to develop global focus groups. The company also recently introduced 'AAccess' on American's home page (www.americanair.com) which ties an interactive travel planning network to its frequent flyer program, further enhancing consumer loyalty.

Another leader in innovative online travel marketing is Cathay Pacific (www.cathay-usa.com), which sponsors contests and cyber-auctions of airline tickets, and in the process builds a large mailing list of consumers for their CyberTraveler Digest electronic newsletter. Their approach is designed to foster consumer trust and build relationships by providing an atmosphere of news-sharing that can enhance the user's experience in cyberspace.

Destinations

At the end of 1995, the World Tourism Organisation (www.world-tourism.org) reported that at least 25 governments were directly distributing tourism information online, either through the Web or commercial services such as CompuServe. Fifty governments reported having information available on diskettes, while 25 governments had information available on CD-ROM. A few national tourism associations, such as Argentina and the United Kingdom reported providing information to other services such as Sabre (Wayne, 1995). As of February 1996, Web experts estimated that over 8000 destinations worldwide could be accessed through travel-related sites. One site, City Net (www.city.net) provides information on almost 2500 cities and over 800 other destinations worldwide (Faiola, 1996).

Comprehensive umbrella online destination sites are increasingly popping up on the Web, attempting to provide a sense of organisation to the proliferation of information available. The United States Travel and Tourism Information Network (USTTIN) (www.usttin.org), a collaborative effort of the University of Colorado and the Rural Tourism Foundation, organises travel and tourism information for the entire US, as does the Department of Agriculture's 'OurTOWN' (www.cs.usu.edu/projects/ourtown). The Indian Ocean Tourism Organization (IOTO) (www.bs.ac.cowan.edu.au/IOTO), based in Perth, Australia, serves 25 core destinations and focuses on raising the awareness and identity of the Indian Ocean as a tourism destination. Links are provided to member's sites. The Great Outdoors Recreation Pages (GORP) (www.gorp.com), caters to the adventure traveler with its cartoon-style, rugged design and neatly organises everything you ever wanted to know about outdoor adventure travel. Attractions are organised by destinations or activities; there are resources for guide books and other media; links to environmental organisations, public land agencies and associations; sources of recreation research information; and vendors selling travel gear.

Bermuda Online! (microstate.com/bermuda) is the most comprehensive site on the Web for Bermuda, offering details on virtually every aspect of life, culture, business and tourism in the country. Bali (www.indo.com) has an equally thorough site. The Hong Kong Tourism Association offers an 'Interactive Tour Guide' on its Wonder Net site (www.hkta.org/); Singapore Online (www.singapore.com) is a one-stop link of information that marries business trade with travel; and Nova Scotia has a number of interesting websites that can be accessed via a comprehensive link page (www.whatasite.com/onvacation.html).

Universal Studios Florida (www.usf.com) has developed an attractions-based online marketing presence. Disney World (www.disneyworld.com) has teamed up with Green World Productions (www.green-room.com), specialists in multi-media design and programming for online travel sites, to develop a new site that will feature interactivity, information on all of the Disney parks and facilities, and a national McDonald's promotional tie-in. Destination Florida (www.goflorida.com), a joint venture of Tribune Company and Knight-Ridder, and the Orlando/Orange County Convention and Visitors Bureau (www.goflorida.com/orlando) demonstrates the effectiveness of partnering to combine traditional marketing expertise with online Internet expertise to develop the maximal marketing mix.

Conventions, Meetings and Festivals

A number of convention and visitors bureaux are offering virtual site inspections of their convention centers, including space floorplans, details of available services, listings of hotels and restaurants, event calendars, and descriptions of local attractions (Tesar, 1995). The International Association of Convention and Visitors Bureaux (www.iacvb.org) provides information services to its members as well as links to those who have sites. The Arlington Texas CVB (www.acvb.org/welcome) also links directly to the reservations' sites of its local hotel members. The Dallas CVB (cityview.com/dallas) is a good example of establishing hyperlinks between web sites to attract visitors and develop partnerships. The Philadelphia CVB (www.libertynet.org:80/phila-visitor) has introduced a second site focusing just on the Pennsylvania Convention Center (www.libertynet.org/pcc/index.html).

Meeting Planners International (MPI) established a private bulletin board on CompuServe in 1994 and they now sublease space to others in the meeting and conventions industry, giving smaller businesses the ability to have their own presence on CompuServe. A number of trade shows are using the Web to provide information to potential exhibitors, generate revenue through selling online advertising, and to offer real-time chats with people in sales booths during a show (Tesar, 1995). The Association of Business Travelers (www.abt-travel.com) offers international travelers a hotel reservation service, special rates and information on top-class hotels, restaurants and business office facilities,

as well as a unique lost luggage tracing and forwarding service (Online Airline FAQ, 1996).

The International Festivals and Events Association, (www.ifea.com) provides a wealth of information for its membership of 2000 organisations in over 20 countries. The site offers a conference discussion area for members to exchange ideas and share information, a searchable database of events, links to member's pages, seminar calendars, publications and even educational information such as tips on how to work with the media and develop publicity (Tucker, 1996).

Travel Media Online

The Travel Channel Online Network (www.travelchannel.com) illustrates how broadcast media can be further leveraged with the Internet to enhance travel. This site has won numerous awards and reviews for design and content. New features are constantly being added, such as 'TravelChat', the first frames-based chat room on the Web. Time, Inc. New Media (pathfinder.com) shows how net-based promotion, coupled with interactivity, can increase advertising revenues. This site offers a lot of diversity, from mini foreign language lessons for travelers, to Zagat Restaurant surveys, flight schedules, and 'Planet Surfer' reports – 'real audio' travel accounts from the field.

Travel Weekly (www.traveler.net), an industry trade magazine of the Reed Travel Group, offers news from both its US and UK publications; a searchable database of 6000 hotels online, and brief descriptions of links to more than 1000 travel businesses. Condé Nast Traveler (travel.epicurious.com/travel/g-cnt) offers an interactive 'Great Escapes' program that queries the user about individual travel interests and then produces the ideal dream vacation itinerary. Numerous guide book publishers, such as Lonely Planet (www.lonelyplanet.com) are now available online, offering lots of practical travel information, reports from the field and links to related destination sites.

Other sources of useful travel information include Embassy Page (www.embpage.org) and the US State Department travel warnings (www.stolaf.edu/network/travel-advisories.html), which provide the latest international travel requirements and travel advisories from consular offices of foreign governments worldwide.

Tour Operators, Travel Suppliers and Agencies

In the United States, the National Tour Association has launched NTA Online (www.ntaonline.com), a closed member-network, linking tour operators, travel suppliers and destination management organisations. The site facilitates electronic commerce among members of the leisure-package travel industry. Travel suppliers and travel agent fulfilment centers can increase impressions and sales by partnering to create a unified presence on the Internet. Costa Travel (mmink.cts.com/costa.htm) has established itself as a leader in partnership marketing and uses the Internet to increase sales, expand vendor-preferred relationship, increase performance-override opportunities for agents, and utilise excess inventory, special events and other promotional offerings.

Sabre Travel Information Network has recently partnered with IBM to develop a website called TravelExplorer (www.travelexplorer.com) which will provide Sabre travel agents with the ability to market their services online. Using a set of predesigned Web pages with varying features, Web Marketing by Sabre provides a cost-effective and flexible solution for agencies wanting to develop their own home page, while the TravelExplorer site provides a searchable 'yellow pages' of Sabre agencies for online customers.

Numerous tour operators are establishing websites. Mountain Travel*Sobek (www.mtsobek.com), the oldest adventure travel company in the US, has defined its position in the travel industry by using the latest interactive and multi-media Internet technologies as an integral component of its marketing mix. Presently, the tour operator is updating its site to include live reservations and booking capabilities to its online catalogue. Abercrombie and Kent have teamed up with Green Room to add Java programming, Shockwave and quicktime video to target the upscale online luxury-adventure (Green Room Productions, 1996). International Expeditions (www.snsnet.net/intexp) is combining the use of CD-ROMs, photo CDs and Web pages to market its tours. Thousands of small- and medium-sized tour operators are realising the cost-effective benefits of using the Internet to reach out to millions of potential consumers across the globe.

Digital Travelogues

A proliferation of travel destination information is available on CD-ROMs, but often it is a costly, outdated alternative to the more traditional travel guide books and Web resources. One exception however, is the genre known as 'Electronic Travelogue', whose 'Passage to Vietnam', created by photojournalist Rick Smolan, brings the human reality of experiencing another culture effectively into your home computer (Faiola, 1996).

With 40 years' experience and 148 books under his belt, legendary travel writer Arthur Frommer has released a new generation of travel guides on CD-ROM. The first titles to be released are New York, San Francisco, New Orleans and Boston, with London and Paris to follow. All offer current information on where to stay, locations and full-color pictures of rooms, lobbies and restaurants. By connecting to AOL or the Internet, users of the interactive travel guide can make immediate reservations through their home computers (Crossman, 1996).

Finally, many entrepreneurial travelers have built sites around first-hand accounts of travel tales, on-the-road reports and photo essays. The Russian Chronicles (www.f8.com/FP/Russia/index.html) are an experiment in interactive digital photojournalism by two journalists who traveled across from Russia's Pacific Coast to St Petersburg. Travel chronicles, expanded photo essays and interviews with local Russians were uplinked daily via a laptop, digital camera, and satellite phone and e-mailed to a design group in California where the information was then transferred to the Web (Focal Point, 1996). Numerous travelers with less sophisticated resources are also producing vivid, entertaining accounts of their immersions in foreign cultures. A few other good sites include Nepal Travel Log (www.Solutions.Net/rec-travel/asia/nepal), Virtual Galapagos (www.terraquest.com) and a personal traveler's account of Vanautu at (silk.net/personal/scombs/vanautu.html).

Distributed Database Applications and Multi-Media in Tourism Websites

Green Room Productions (www.green-room. com) specialises in online production and programming for the travel industry, utilising Websites that incorporate the latest technological advances including: Hot Java, VRML, Real Audio, and Shock Wave. Presently, the company is developing a new Website for ITT Sheraton Corporation, that will integrate proprietary databases to help develop online marketing programs and manage the strategic planning process of the worldwide franchise hospitality network (Green Room, 1996).

Carlson Wagonlit Travel (www.travel.carlson. com) collects, measures and manages data from customers in tailoring their travel offerings. Its site has become an 'information intermediary' and anchor site for its franchise locations. It directs potential and existing customers to nearby Carlson agencies, while also providing internal and external communications tools for the various offices and their customers. AMR Corporation (www.amrcorp.com), the parent company of American Airlines, provides interactive research tools through a global focus group which links online research into action activities.

Market Research Applications

Internet and Web technology can be established useful for integrated database market research applications, competitor analyses, market surveys and academic research. CIC Research, Inc., a travel-related marketing and research firm, provides a lot of good information on its Website (www.ten-io.com/cic). The company conducts the regular 'Net Traveler Survey', as well as various analyses and economic studies on the visitor industry market.

In addition, a significant amount of information can be obtained free, for those who want to seek it out. Several applications of Internet technology exist that can aid academic and marketing researchers in the travel and tourism industry. Typical applications include: creating electronic list discussion groups (UseNets and ListServes); accessing online databases at remote computer sites (Telnet); and transferring files of data from one computer to another (FTP) (Williams *et al.*, 1996). Many Internet search engines exist that can facilitate tourism research applications (see earlier paragraph on search engines).

Increasingly, numerous government tourism ministries, industry trade associations, NGOs, and community/special interest stakeholder groups are setting up Web sites to make their holdings of publications, technical reports, case studies, conference proceedings and statistical information available to academic and tourism market researchers (Williams *et al.*, 1996). Some key sites include:

- IOTO (www.bs.ac.cowan.edu.au/IOTO/brief. html);
- PATA Travel Industry Update (www.PATA. org/patanet);
- Singapore Tourism Cybrary (STPB's Tourism Resource Centre) (www.focusasia.com/stc.);
- Tourism Reference Documentation Centre (www.ic.gc.ca/ic-data/industry/tourism/trdc);
- US Travel and Tourism Information Network (www.usttin.org/);
- World Tourism Organization (www.world-tourism.org); and
- World Travel and Tourism Council (www.fleethouse.com/wttc.wttca.htm).

Specialty sites dedicated to ecotourism, heritage, cultural or outdoor tourism include:

- Eco Travel in Latin America (www.txinfinet. com/mader/ecotravel/ecotravel.html);
- ICOMOS (www.icomos.org/Internet_Resource Guide.html);
- Hawaii Ecotourism Association (www.planet-hawaii.com/hea);
- Outdoor Recreation Research (sfbox.vt.edu: 10021/Y/yfleung/recres.html); and
- World Heritage Centre (www.unesco.org/ whc/welcome.htm).

Numerous challenges still exist for investigators conducting secondary research on the Internet. These include lack of a central index of online resources, credibility of information, lack of participation among tourism researchers in Web design and development, and equal accessibility to Internet technologies among all researchers worldwide. Simultaneously, new groupware technologies promise to increase the effectiveness of the Web as a primary research tool involving interactive and real-time collaboration among researchers and focus groups alike. However, the tourism research community must first become actively involved in establishing protocols to ensure the credibility of information and research activities (Williams *et al.*, 1996).

Online Travel Information Guides and List Serves

The sheer quantity of travel resources available on the Internet and Web have created a new genre of travel information directories. For example, Marcus Endicott (mendicott@igc.apc.org) has developed an extensive print directory of tourism information sources named the *Electronic Traveler*. This directory includes a helpful bibliography and a detailed description of Internet/usenet groups and travel-related Web and Gopher sites. It also includes information on travel-related proprietary systems, computer reservation systems, bulletin boards, commercial full text databases and international telephony resources. Fodor's Net Travel is a new book primarily aimed at leisure travelers and designed to be a comprehensive map to travel resources on the Internet and online services. Free updates are available at www.ypn.com. The book includes general travel information sites, magazines, book stores, travel agents, airlines, reservation systems, business travel, theme travel and geographical regions of the world (*Book Review*, 1996).

Several electronic listserves are active providing a global forum of information exchange among tourism professionals, government representatives, academic researchers and community stakeholder groups. Endicott (mendicott@igc.apc.org) moderates two extremely popular industry e-mail lists: Infotec-Travel, which tracks new technology-related events as they occur on both the Internet and proprietary online services; and Green-Travel, a list dedicated to ecotourism and sustainable tourism development. Additionally, TRINET (TRINET-L@UHCCVM.ITS.Hawaii.Edu) serves as a medium of exchange among tourism researchers and scholars.

Furthermore, a good example of a Usenet for tourism research is Mailbase (www.mailbase.ac.uk), the United Kingdom's major electronic mailing list service linking researchers and academics at various institutions of higher education throughout the country. Participants manage their own discussion groups and associated files by topics (such as tourism) and use e-mail to exchange ideas, collaborate on projects, coauthor papers and share research findings (Ascanio, 1996).

Education and Training

New Internet technologies also have the potential to transform the traditional educational process because the world's digital storehouse of learning can be made available to anyone, anytime, anywhere who has the necessary hardware and software to take a roadtrip on the information highway. Even before the Internet, the growth in the diversity and availability of educational software for PCs was transforming the way in which many people could learn.

Now Web technologies have the power to profoundly impact the world of understanding via distance-learning programs for adult learners. Indeed, entirely new universities are building their foundations in the Web. University Online, Inc. (UOL) (www.uol.com), in partnership with Dunn and Bradstreet Information Services, caters to the needs of educational institutions and corporate campuses who wish to establish learning programs online. Using seamless integration into the Web, UOL provides electronic access into a vast library of interactive online courses (UOL Homepage, 1996).

Presently, the International Institute of Tourism Studies at The George Washington University has joined University Online (UOL) to offer its seven-course, certificate Event Management Program (www.uol.com/gwu/esi/em) online. This innovative program, offered through the School of Business and Public Management, allows students to gain critical, up-to-date knowledge in event marketing and management. The distance-learning option allows remote students to complete coursework on their own schedule, while still maintaining essential contact with fellow students and university instructors who are on campus. Web-facilitated distance-learning can be especially important to the tourism industry because workers must constantly upgrade skills to keep pace with the ever-changing technologies that shape the world of travel.

FUTURE CHALLENGES

With insight into the evolution of the Internet and the revolutionary impact of the World Wide Web, it is possible to better understand the nature of the paradigm shift that is taking place in the global marketing of products and services, including travel and tourism. Businesses and organisations worldwide are realizing that marketing on the Web is multi-dimensional content-marketing that requires the following paradigm shifts: from traditional advertising to interactive marketing; and from developing and managing one-way information flows to computer-mediated empowerment of users, consumers and entrepreneurs who will be engaged in electronic commerce in the information age.

However, numerous issues are currently being addressed that must be solved before the Internet will reach its full potential as a global marketing and information medium. Some of these include: security of data transmissions; credibility of information; intellectual property and copyrights; bandwidth limitations; user confusion and dissatisfaction; lack of adequately trained specialists; and equal access and pricing.

The Next Generation of the Internet

What's next? Just as large numbers of computer users are discovering the Internet, rapid commercialisation of the cyberspace is producing a new generation of global electronic malls including department stores, banks, travel agencies and, not least of all, educational systems structured to operate distance-learning programs.

Technology forecasters predict that in coming decades the Web will become a sizable marketplace as technology companies solve online commerce security issues. Intelligent agents will do your bidding, acting as personal assistants and the Web will go mobile via handheld devices similar to cellular phones and pagers, able to transmit and receive data on-the-go. VRML technology will elevate the Web into the world of three-dimensional television 'intercasting' where it will compete with or possibly supplant cable networks. The desktop computer and television will evolve into one 'ubiquitous' high-definition information appliance that will hang on your wall like a painting. We will enter the virtual world of the Web as miniature 'avatars' (realistic graphical representations of ourselves) and we will no longer 'surf' but rather 'hang out' (Schwartz, 1996).

Tourism and Technology in the Year 2000

Battelle Technology forecasters have identified several innovative technology products that will lead us into the next decade (Millet and Kopp, 1996). Adoption of new technologies in the travel and tourism sector have the potential to dramatically impact the travel experience by the year 2000 in the following ways:

- *Digitourism* will emerge as a major growth market. Catering to a new kind of global entrepreneur who cannot afford to have less than full access to his business while traveling, the digitourist will seek out new business opportunities while lounging by the beach with his laptop computer and cellular phone. 'Digitourism' can foster economic development and investment in regions where the global information infrastructure of fiber optics, digiports and direct broadcast satellite technology can be made available to the executive vacationer. Resorts can align themselves with international business centers that offer trade, processing, financial and regional human resources capital to become centers for digitourism, which can stimulate higher paying jobs, new investment and foreign exchange the region (Hanchard and Bleakley, 1996).

- *Tourism marketing and destination management* will be significantly impacted by the Internet, Web and CD-ROM applications due to increased world-wide exposure for relatively little cost. The Internet is especially effective for enhancing yield management and inventory practices through last minute, time-sensitive sales to a wide market. E-mail, electronic surveys and 'intranets', provide new ways of conducting primary and secondary research to maximise marketing efforts.

- Use of *biometrics* will play a key role in tourism applications where security and identity are of key importance. 'Smart cards' that hold an array of personal data will serve as driver's license, car and house keys, passports and medical records all-in-one.

- The development of *electronic cash*, credit-card-sized smart cards that will be used in vending machines, travel kiosks, and online purchases, as well as in international computerised financial transactions, will facilitate a wide variety of travel-related commerce.

- New construction materials with electronic sensors included at the molecular level, known as *Smart Materials*, will be developed that will emit warning signs when they detect excessive stress. For example, warning signals emitted by fuselage skin sensors or cruise ships equipped with hull sensors could further enhance the safety of airline and boat travel.

- Small electronic devices that serve as *personal translators* will assist both business and leisure travelers in communicating around the world, thus making international travel and business more accessible to all.

- 'Getting There' will be decidedly easier with the widespread use of *GPS* (global positioning systems). *Smart Maps* and compasses will collect information from satellites and provide travelers, hikers and boaters with exact geographic position and directions. Navigable systems are already providing dynamic route guidance for in-vehicle, online and PC travel direction.

CONCLUSION

The document-centric paradigm shift will bring both business organisations and educational institutions closer together because of their respective awareness that marketing on the Web is content-marketing and that educational institutions have been developing, accumulating, storing and, only through limited educational channels, distributing valuable intellectual property for centuries without, until recently, really taking advantage of the inherent commercial value of their knowledge bases in an increasingly literate and computer-literate world hungry for knowledge and information.

There will be many new travel marketing applications for these new powerful interactive information technologies, including planning, product development and education. However, the driving force will be the extent to which the Internet as a new medium and utility can be used as an effective marketing strategy. To do this, industry leaders and marketing specialists will need to fully understand interactive media, including reservation systems, security features, electronic payment facilities and customer service, whether delivered through wired or wireless, broad band or narrow band platforms.

This chapter has attempted to describe the state of the Internet and tourism online at a moment in time, with the hope of informing tourism practitioners of both present developments and future opportunities. In order to realise these opportunities, however, it is imperative that industry professionals and academics do not stand by the sidelines as the technology transforms the world around them. The Internet must be taken seriously as an object of management science and market research, and all of the traditional tools developed for disciplines should and must be applied.

REFERENCES

Ascanio, A. (July 12 1996) [aascanio@usb.ve]. Tourism-Internet, private e-mail to Wendy Oden, [wendyo@gwis2.circ.gwu.edu].

Bambon, J. (1995), The NetPC: will it fly?, *Information-Week*, November 17, 14–15.

Bauer, C. J. (1996), Intranets add to demand for Internet expertise, *High Tech Advertising Supplement to The Washington Post*, April 18, 20–23.

Blikom, T. (1996), Last minute booking based on Internet in Norway, Information and Communications Technologies in Tourism, *Proceedings of the International Conference*, Innsbruck, Austria.

Book Review (1996), Unraveling travel on the net, travel marketing decisions, spring/summer, p. 17.

Cash, J. J. (1995), Catching the net wave, *Information-Week*, November 17, 104.

Crossman, C. (1996), CD-ROM review of Frommers interactive travel guides, USA: in *Washington Business*, June, 10, 16, Macmillan Digital.

Daffron, S. C. (1996), The digital travel agent, *Internet Advisor*, July, 44–47.

Dingley, D. (1996) [david_dingley@uk.ibm.com], Your posting to infotec.

Ellis, D. (1995), Internet simplifies communication with customers, *The Denver Business Journal*, October 6–12, p. 8C.

Faiola, A. (1996), Net worth: it's never been easier to click and go, but does travel really compute?, Travel Section, *The Washington Post*, February 11, E1, E6, E7.

Focal Point (1996), *The Russian Chronicles* [www.f8.com/FP/Russia/index.html].

Green Room Productions (1996), *Clients and Projects* [www.green-room.com].

Gross, J. (1996), Long Range Web Planning, *Netguide*, January, pp. 101–102.

Haber, L. (1996), TCP/IP: Is it safe?, *InformationWeek*, April 29, 63, 65.

Hanchard, E. and Bleakley, K. (1996), *Conference on Digi Tourism in the Caribbean*, Washington, DC, June 14.

Hayes, M. (1996), Interactive systems, media circus, *InformationWeek*, January 1, 48–49.

Heyman, K. (1996a), Web 2000, *Netguide*, January, 53–58.

Heyman, K. (1996b), Bridging the gender gap, *Net-guide*, January, 85–88.

Jean-Joyce, A. (1996), [tourism@whatasite.com], Re: Introductions.

Kerr, E. B. and Hiltz, S. R. (1982), *Computer-Mediated Communication Systems: Status and Evaluation*, New York: Academic Press.

Klinghagen, B. (1995), Internet gives ground to virtual marketplace, *The Denver Business Journal*, October 6–12, 3C.

Linstone, H. A. and Turoff, M. (Editors) (1975), *The Delphi Method: Techniques and Applications*, Reading, MA: Addison-Wesley.

Lottor, M. (1996), Internet Domain Survey, at http://www.nw.com.

Martin, M. H. (1996), Why the Web is still a no-shop zone, *Fortune*, February 5, 127–128.

Metzger, P. (1996), The Web nets a commercial success, *Wired*, July, 36.

Millet, S. and Kopp, W. (1996), The top 10 innovative products for 2006, *The Futurist*, July–August, 16–20.

Mills, M. (1996), Final notice: past due, *The Washington Post*, June 22, C1, C4.

Online Airline FAQ (1996), at http://iecc.com/airline update, May 31.

Patel, A. (1996), More data from Websites, *Information-Week*, April 8, 84.

Pernick, R. (1996) [rpernick@previewmedia.com]. US West Media Group Invests in Preview Media, Inc., in *Infotec-Travel List* [infotec-travel@igc.apc.org].

Quigley, K. (1996) [kjg@onramp.net]. Travelocity one-stop travel site announces three-month performance figures, in *Infotec Travel List* [infotec-travel@igc.apc.org].

Resnick, R. (1996), Follow the money, *Internet World*, May, 34–36.

Schwartz, J. (1996), The site-seer's guide to some way-out Internet futures, *The Washington Post*, July 3, A1, A18.

Swisher, K. (1995), Old world, new frontier in cyberspace, *The Washington Post*, December 12, C1, C4.

Swisher, K. (1996a), There's no place like a home page, *The Washington Post*, July 1, A1, A8.

Swisher, K. (1996b), Freeloader thinks it's found a better way to the Web, *Washington Business*, April 1, 11.

Tesar, J. (1995), How to exploit the marketplace of the next millenium using electronic bulletin boards and the World Wide Web, *EXPO*, October, 21–26.

Tittle, E. and Stewart, J. (1996), The intranet means business, *Netguide*, July, 121–127.

Tucker, M. (1996), [mark@ifea.com], IFEA Website, private email to Wendy Oden [wendyo@gwis2.circ.gwu.edu].

University Online (1996), University Online [http://www.uol.com].

Watt, G. (1996), [hkpro.ab@pi.se], Do look at our site!

Wayne, S. (1995), Tourism and technology: the world is just a click away, *WTO News, World Tourism Organization*, October, 16, 17.

Williams, M. (1996), Java is promising, but still a few applets short of a pie in the sky, *Washington Business*, February 19.

Williams, P. W. Bascombe, P., Brenner, N. and Green, D. (1996), Using the Internet for tourism research: information highway or dirt road, *Journal of Travel Research*, Spring, 63–69.

Yastrow, S. (1995), Profile of new consumers: How to market to them, *Travel and Tourism Executive Report*, Volume XVI–#1, pp. 1–4.

Encompassing the Social and Environmental Aspects of Tourism within an Institutional Context: A National Tourist Board Perspective

6

Stephen Wanhill

ABSTRACT

It took some two years for the Wales Tourist Board to produce the final version of *Tourism 2000: A strategy for Wales*. The process of consultation was extensive and the strategy was launched by the Secretary of State for Wales. This chapter explores the nature of the social and environmental issues that were debated in the consultation process and how they emerged in the final strategy document.

INTRODUCTION

Tourism is an established and dominant industry in Wales. It generates, directly and indirectly, more than nine per cent of employment and brings in about £1·5 billion per annum. Tourism in Wales is, however, a fragmented industry, made up largely of small independent operators. Being diffused in this way, tourism needs leadership and partnership in order to thrive. Many public and private sector organisations have a direct or indirect interest in the industry. As the lead agency for tourism, the Wales Tourist Board (WTB) has an important role to play as a catalyst and as a co-ordinator, and because of its separate reporting structure, as shown in Figure 6·1, it has been able to adopt a somewhat different approach to the other tourist boards in Britain.

BACKGROUND

The tourist boards in Britain, the British Tourist Authority (BTA) and the English, Scottish and Wales Tourist Boards (ETB, STB and WTB respectively) owe their present structure, illustrated in Figure 6·1, to an Act of Parliament, the *1969 Development of Tourism Act* (House of Commons, 1969). Under this Act, the boards are classified as Non-Departmental Public Bodies (NDPBs) which keeps them at arm's length from the usual Ministries of State. The dashed lines shown on Figure 6·1 serve to indicate that all the boards

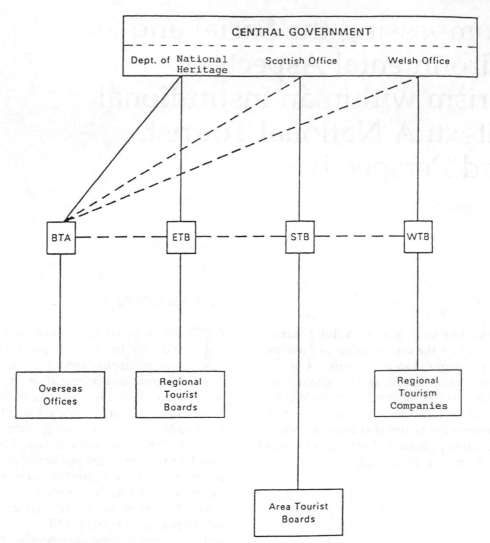

Figure 6·1. The statutory tourist board framework in Britain.

liaise with each other, especially with the BTA, which has prime responsibility for overseas marketing, and in turn, the BTA liaises with the Scottish Office and Welsh Office for policy directives, although its reporting authority is the Department of National Heritage (DNH). The chairmen of the three national boards, ETB, STB and WTB, are also board members of the BTA, though, due to a rationalisation of functions by the Government in the 1980s, the chairman of the BTA and the ETB is one and the same person. Although reasons can be advanced for this that go back to the original 1969 Act, which did not propose an ETB at its inception, the policy making and organisational practicalities of this situation are less than satisfactory.

While the primary role of each of the boards lies in marketing, the 1969 Act also gave them powers to shape the product on the ground by offering financial assistance. Section 4 of the 1969 Act states that:

"4. (1) A Tourist Board shall have power –
         (a) in accordance with arrangements approved by the relevant Minister and the Treasury, to give financial assistance for the carrying out of any project which in the opinion of the Board will provide or improve tourist amenities and facilities in the country for which the Board is responsible:

(b) with the approval of the relevant Minister and the Treasury, to carry out any such project as aforesaid.

(2) Financial assistance under subsection (1) (a) of this section may be given by way of grant or loan or, if the project is being or is to be carried out by a company incorporated in Great Britain, by subscribing for or otherwise acquiring shares or stock in the company, or by any combination of those methods.

(3) In making a grant or loan in accordance with arrangements approved under subsection (1) (a) of this section a Tourist Board may, subject to the arrangements, impose such terms and conditions as it thinks fit, including conditions for the repayment of a grant in specified circumstances; and Schedule 2 to this Act shall have effect for securing compliance with conditions subject to which any such grant is made.

(4) A Tourist Board shall not dispose of any shares or stock acquired by it by virtue of this section except –
(a) after consultation with the company in which the shares or stock are held; and
(b) with the approval of the relevant Minister and the Treasury."

The terms of the Act are fairly general, and so it was left to the individual tourist boards to issue appropriate guidelines. These they agreed with the government body which acted as their reporting authority.

In 1989, Section 4 financial assistance was suspended in England following a government review. The documentation was not made public on the grounds that the consultants' report was directed to the responsible Minister rather than the House of Commons. The act of suspension meant that the Government did not have to change the legislation, which would have been the case if Section 4 was terminated. The political argument for suspension was that the tourism industry in England was now mature and no longer needed government support. This is the 'infant industry' case for public subsidy in the situation where the 'infant' has now grown up. However, this argument is difficult to substantiate, for the majority of tourism establishments in Britain are small in scale, as is true of many other countries. A better explanation can be found in the political climate of the time which favoured a clawback of public expenditure and less intervention so as to give private markets a greater say in resource allocation. In a product as complicated as 'the tourist trip', this is somewhat simplistic when judged against the requirement to develop a balanced range of facilities to meet the demands of tourists in a sustainable way and the possibilities of market failure.

Following a review of tourism support arrangements in Scotland, the STB had its Section 4 activities suspended from the end of June 1993 (Secretary of State for Scotland, 1993). The key recommendation was an adjustment of responsibilities between the STB and other NDPBs. From the beginning of April 1994 responsibility for tourism marketing and for Area Tourist Board support was consolidated in the STB, while business development activities were transferred to the Scottish Enterprise and the Highlands and Islands Enterprise networks. Unlike the situation in England, the effect of this adjustment was designed to be neutral in terms of public expenditure and so the arguments for supporting the tourist industry, namely small scale and market failure still held sway. Thus Section 4 assistance is now only formally available in Wales, although in Scotland it appears in another guise via the enterprise agencies.

TOURISM 2000: A STRATEGY FOR WALES

Section 4 grants and loans provide the foundation for the product development components of the WTB's strategic plans. In 1993, the Board's strategy *Tourism in Wales – Developing the Potential* (WTB, 1988) came to an end, only to be replaced in 1994 by *Tourism 2000: a Strategy for Wales* (WTB, 1994). As is customary *Tourism 2000* was launched by the Secretary of State for Wales, but work on the strategy had begun some two years earlier. Although this might seem an inordinate length of time to develop a strategy, the answer lies in the extensive consultation process as

62

Tourism Development

Table 6·1

DEVELOPING THE WALES TOURIST BOARD'S TOURISM 2000 STRATEGY

START OF STRATEGY PROCESS

Work programme

Initial consultations

Commissioned	Review Research	Prepare Key
Research	Data	Discussion Papers

> CONSULTATION STAGE I <

Seminars

Advisory committees

Regional panels

Written submissions

PREPARE DRAFT STRATEGY

CONSULTATION STAGE II

Written submissions

Advisory committees

Regional panels

PUBLISH FINAL STRATEGY

indicated in Table 6·1. The second consultation stage was particularly helpful in eliciting a wide range of constructive responses; these were critical to refining the strategy. The added bonus from this approach was the opportunity it gave to the various stakeholders in the national tourist product, specifically:

- Central and local government;
- Quasi-public bodies;
- Voluntary organisations and charitable trusts;
- Private commercial sector;
- The host community

to have their say, which created a sense of common ownership (see, for example, Cooper, 1995).

Tourism 2000 is an integrated strategy, embracing product development, marketing, research and organisational matters. The strategy was developed in the knowledge that the power and resources of the WTB are finite and the well-being of the industry must be based on partnership formulation. In an industry made up of so

many different components and founded largely on small businesses, the Board's medium term strategic planning of about five years provides a sense of direction and a focus for action (Kotler *et al.*, 1993). The framework of the strategy was in three parts:

- Review of tourism in Wales drawing on the Board's research and the views of the industry;
- In consultation, setting out strategic principles aimed at fostering tourism development in a sustainable way;
- Establishing policy priorities and programmes in pursuit of these principles.

ENVIRONMENT

A cursory examination of the environmental resources of Wales serves to emphasise the importance of designated landscape areas and historic buildings to the tourist industry. In terms of landscape Wales has:

- One quarter of the land area covered by three National Parks and five Areas of Outstanding National Beauty;
- Two-fifths of the coastline designated as Heritage Coast;
- Additional attractive and fragile landscapes such as Cambrian Mountains and Llyn Peninsula;
- National Nature Reserves and 730 Sites of Special Scientific Interest.

From a tourism perspective, the built environment is quite considerable as well:

- Conservation Areas and 14,000 plus listed buildings;
- Four World Heritage Sites: Caernarfon, Conwy, Beaumaris and Harlech;
- Several historic towns such as Conwy and St. Davids;
- Key resorts such as Llandudno and Tenby;
- Major cities in Cardiff and Swansea.

However, care of the environment is more than just preservation or protection, as the principles laid down during the first consultative stage were able to show. The second consultative paper (out of a series of eight) drew out the key principles that would govern environmental policy for the implementation of *Tourism 2000* (WTB, 1992a):

Table 6·2. Two-way tourism and environmental relationship

Tourism to Environment	Environment to Tourism
Opportunities	Opportunities
Commercial returns for preservation of built and national heritage.	Fine scenery and heritage as visitor attractions.
New use for redundant buildings and land.	Ecotourism based on environmental appreciation.
Increased awareness and support for conservation.	
Threats	Threats
Intrusive development.	Off-painting, drab environments.
Congestion.	Pollution hazards as in water and on beaches.
Disturbance and physical damage.	Intrusive developments by other industries.
Pollution and resource consumption.	

Source: WTB, Tourism 2000, Consultative Paper No.2, 1992.

- A two-way relationship between tourism and the environment;
- Visitor management to reduce pressure;
- Environmental improvement for the benefit of residents and visitors;
- Sensitive development that respects and, if possible, enhances the environment;
- Responsible operation through ecologically sound practice in tourism enterprises and means of travel;
- Consideration through tourism.

The significant feature arising from the various channels used for consultation was the recognition that there is a two-way relationship between tourism and the environment, as illustrated in Table 6·2. Further, the consultation process raised a number of policy areas for the Board (WTB, 1994) that would need careful examination in *Tourism 2000*:

- The Rural and Coastal Environment;
- National Parks;
- Other Rural Areas;
- Clean Beaches;
- Rivers;
- The Built Environment;
- Responsible Operation;
- Paying for Conservation;
- Windfarms.

The detailed policy statements relating to the above, both at the draft and final stage, are listed in Appendix 1. Most of the policy areas were cleared at Stage 1 (see Table 6·1) and were well known, given the breadth of the environmental resources in Wales. For example, in 1978 the WTB and the then Countryside Commission for England and Wales entered into an agreement with regard to tourism in the National Parks, to the effect that conflict between conservation and visitor enjoyment would be resolved in favour of the former. Similarly, there are over 350 beaches in Wales and some sixty per cent of holiday tourists stay on the coast. Also, day visitors include a trip to the seaside as a part of their stay. It follows, therefore, that clean bathing water and litter-free beaches are of great importance. The issue of Rivers and Windfarms was raised during the Stage II consultation process. The National Rivers Authority is embarking on catchment management plans to secure the contribution of rivers to the aesthetics of the landscape and recreational activities. Windfarms are a controversial matter and the Board is opposed to their development in primary designated sites (National Parks, Heritage Coast, etc.).

CULTURE AND COMMUNITY

The consultative paper dealing with tourism and the community (WTB, 1992b) drew out a series of criteria that needed to be evaluated with regard to the establishment of community based tourism, namely:

- Size of the community;
- Socio-cultural profile, particularly in respect of the Welsh language;
- Economic status – rural, industrial and resort areas lagging behind or in decline;
- Existence of 'leaders' or entrepreneurs, both from the private sector and local authorities;
- Availability of financial assistance;
- Organisational or administrative support.

The Welsh language and the cultural traditions it

Table 6·3. Wales Tourist Board: Community Initiatives

Place	Type of Location
Aberaeron	Coastal Town
Bala	Rural with lake resource
Dinefwr	Rural with historic town
Llanberis	Rural with redundant quarrying
Milford Haven	Declining dock area
Pentrefoelas	Sparsely populated rural
Pwllheli	Coastal resort
Tywyn/Aberdyfi	Coastal resort

Source: WTB.

bestows give a 'sense of place' to visitors, especially to those coming from overseas, although some would argue that there are culture costs to this (Pitchford, 1995). The WTB has a clear bilingual policy for its operations, the details of which can be found in Appendix 3. Evidence from resident surveys indicates that the majority of the host population welcomes tourism as a positive force and are more concerned with congestion, over-crowding and environmental damage (WTB, 1981), as shown in Appendix 2 than any socio-cultural impact, though Sheldon and Var (1984) indicate that for North Wales there is more sensitivity to cultural impacts among Welsh speakers than non-Welsh speakers.

In view of the fragmented nature of tourism in Wales, the Board has operated and participated in a wide range of community schemes, which may be appreciated from the following list:

- Small projects ranging from washbasins in bedrooms to cottage craft workshops;
- Small Establishment Loan Funds (SELF);
- Bilingual signs to emphasise cultural distinctiveness and give a 'sense of place';
- Farm Tourism initiatives in response to changes in agricultural support policies;
- Community Local Enterprise and Development programme (LEAD) to provide integrated development on a public/private/community partnership basis;
- Support for the European Union rural development initiative (LEADER);
- Jigso Community Appraisal scheme which is essentially a community SWOT analysis;
- Welsh Village Weekend Breaks.

The emphasis is on job creation, maintaining local businesses, improving infrastructure and raising the status and profile of the community. Tourism is to be seen as one part of a balanced and integrated economy, offering a diverse range of opportunities. The major community programmes are LEAD and LEADER; the latter being sponsored by the European Union.

Table 6·3 lists the Community LEAD projects which have been completed by the Board. Their locations in Wales are shown in Figure 6·2, together with the eight major LEAD schemes covering Resorts, Historic Towns and Tourism Action Areas. Within the overall LEAD programme, community developments had, on average, a far higher percentage of public sector projects than the major LEAD schemes, reflecting the role of the Board in acting as a catalyst and mentor in the implementation of local strategies. There was also a requirement for greater support so that leverage ratios, defined in terms of the proportion of private money to public money, were generally lower than those for projects in the major schemes and job creation costs higher (Wanhill, 1996). However, it is important to remember that community initiatives in tourism, no less than any other area, have to function within a commercial environment. For this reason, all LEAD investments are undertaken on a competitive bidding process to ensure that only serious and realistic proposals are put forward.

LEADER is an initiative that was established by the European Union in 1991 to fund innovative and integrated rural development programmes led by community groups (Wanhill, forthcoming). Across Europe, LEADER initially brought in a network of one hundred local rural development action groups, operating as part of an interactive network by using new communication technologies. In this way, the groups were helped to act as local intermediaries by linking up with database networks providing, among other things, studies of market potential, the establishment of relations with travel agencies, and sales and reservation systems for accommodation such as bed and breakfast. Specific provision was made under this programme for rural tourism. This is shown in the Wales schemes, which were all primarily to do with sparsely populated rural areas where there is a strong identification with the Welsh language and culture, as witnessed by the majority of Welsh names

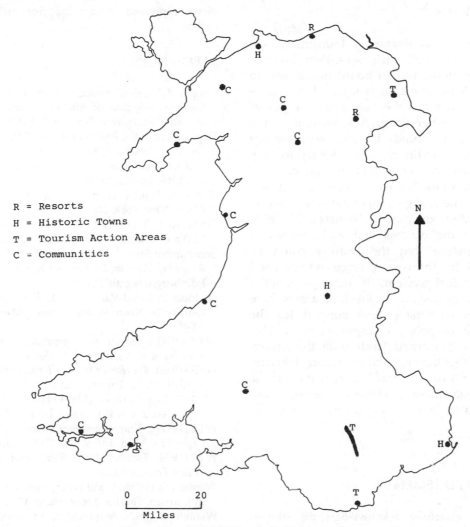

R = Resorts
H = Historic Towns
T = Tourism Action Areas
C = Communities

Figure 6·2. LEAD areas in Wales

attributed to the various LEADER groups: Menter Mon, Cadwyn, South Gwynedd, Menter Powys, Antur Teifi, Menter Preseli, South Pembrokeshire Action for Rural Communities (SPARC) and Antur Cwm Taf.

The broad community policy issues arising from the consultation process were as follows:

- The Welsh Language and Culture;
- Communities and Tourism;
- New Developments.

As before, the details are given in Appendix 1. Clearly, the language and culture of Wales, used in a positive way, are an asset to the tourist product and are viewed by the Board as such. But, more importantly, there is a policy to involve more Welsh speaking people in tourism enterprises, a matter which was raised by Pitchford (1995). On the whole, leadership in Wales has tended to come from the public sector which, in turn, has given prestige to public employment and encouraged the educated Welsh speaker to seek a career in public service to the detriment of the private sector. By its actions the Board has demonstrated its commitment to tourism initiatives based in the community and the policy is for this to continue. The issue of New Development was only raised in Stage II. Here the Board's approach echoes the advice of the Government's planning guidance (Department of the Environment, 1992) which stresses the need to use the flexible technology of tourism to ensure that any new projects fit comfortably into their environmental, cultural and community surroundings.

CONCLUSIONS

In an industry as diverse as tourism, with a proliferation of small businesses, then the existence of a national tourist board that is able to offer a strategic direction is invaluable. This is particularly so when the board has the power to intervene, either through legislation or the provision of project funds. It is also very necessary in areas where conditions for market failure may be found, such as in environmental and community tourism issues. These matters were discussed here against the background of the Wales Tourist Board's strategy document, *Tourism 2000*. Table 6·1 outlined the process that was adopted in order to ensure that the strategy could be accepted by the industry at large and endorsed by the political system. It required lengthy consultation periods to establish an atmosphere of common ownership and support for the detailed list of policy recommendations. This chapter has concerned itself with the underpinnings, either through actions already taken by the Board or through consultation, that led to the final policy statements in respect of the social and environmental aspects of tourism policy in Wales.

ACKNOWLEDGEMENTS

The author gratefully acknowledges the support given by the Wales Tourist Board, especially Paul Loveluck, Elwyn Owen and Jeff Pride. The views expressed remain the responsibility of the author.

REFERENCES

Cooper, C. (1995) Strategic planning for sustainable tourism: the case of offshore islands in the UK, *Journal of Sustainable Tourism*, **3**, 4, 191–209.

Department of the Environment (1992), *Planning Policy Guidance: Tourism (PPG 21)*, London: HMSO.

House of Commons (1969), Development of Tourism Act 1969, London: HMSO.

Kotler, P., Haider, D. H. and Rein, I. (1993), *Marketing Places*, New York: Delmar.

Pitchford, S. R. (1995), Ethnic tourism and nationalism in Wales, *Annals of Tourism Research*, **22**, 1, 35–52.

Secretary of State for Scotland (1993), *Statement on the Review of Tourism Support Arrangements in Scotland*, Edinburgh: Scottish Office.

Sheldon, P. J. and Var, T. (1984), Resident attitudes to tourism in North Wales, *Tourism Management*. **5**, 1, 40–47.

WTB (1981), *Survey of Community Attitudes towards Tourism in Wales*, Cardiff: Wales Tourist Board.

WTB (1988), *Tourism in Wales – Developing the Potential*, Cardiff: Wales Tourist Board.

WTB (1992a), *Tourism and the Environment*, Consultative Paper No. 2, Cardiff: Wales Tourist Board.

WTB (1992b), *Tourism and the Community*, Consultative Paper No. 3, Cardiff: Wales Tourist Board.

WTB (1994), *Tourism 2000: a Strategy for Wales*, Cardiff: Wales Tourist Board.

Wanhill, S. (1996), Local enterprise and development in tourism, *Tourism Management*, **17**, 1, 35–42.

Wanhill, S. (1997), Peripheral area tourism: a European perspective, *Progress in Tourism and Hospitality Research*, **3**, 1, 47–70.

Appendix 1. Wales Tourist Board: Social and Environmental Policy Statements.

PROPOSED FINAL POLICY	DRAFT POLICY	COMMENT
THE RURAL AND COASTAL ENVIRONMENT		
National Parks		
P1 The Board reaffirms its commitment to the Principles for Tourism in National Parks. We will keep the Principles under review, in association with the Countryside Council for Wales and the three National Park authorities, to ensure that they remain relevant to the needs of Wales.	P1 The Board reaffirms its commitment to the Principles for Tourism in National Parks. We will keep the Principles under review. in association with the Countryside Council for Wales and the three National Park authorities, to ensure that they remain relevant to the needs of Wales.	Policy unchanged
P2 The Board will continue to collaborate with the Countryside Council for Wales and the National Park authorities in pursuit of the	P2 The Board will continue to collaborate with the Countryside Council for Wales and the National Park authorities in pursuit of the	Policy unchanged

Appendix 1. Cont.

PROPOSED FINAL POLICY	DRAFT POLICY	COMMENT

National Parks

P2   Principles for Tourism in National Parks. An annual work programme will be agreed, embracing such diverse topics as research, visitor management, interpretation and marketing.

P2   Principles for Tourism in National Parks. An annual work programme will be agreed, embracing such diverse topics as research, visitor management, interpretation and marketing.

Other Rural Areas

P3   The Board will apply the same principles in Areas of Outstanding Natural Beauty and in Heritage Beauty Coasts as in National Parks, recognising that they offer opportunities for appropriate and well managed forms of tourism development. The Board will seek opportunities for joint policy initiatives with other bodies within Areas of Outstanding Natural Beauty and Heritage Coast areas in pursuit of the objectives of this strategy.

P3   The Board will apply the same principles in Areas of Outstanding Natural Beauty and in Heritage Beauty Coasts as in National Parks, recognising that they offer opportunities for appropriate and well managed forms of tourism development.

Policies P3 and P4 amalgamated

P4   The Board will seek opportunities for joint policy initiatives with other bodies within Areas of Outstanding Natural Beauty and Heritage Coast areas in pursuit of the objectives of this strategy.

(See above)

P4   The Board's policy priorities in non-designated rural areas will respect the Principles for Economic, Environmental and Community Sustainability set out within this strategy.

New policy

P5   The Board recognises the importance of nature conservation and archaeological conservation to the tourism prospects of Wales. We welcome and will support measures by the Countryside Council for Wales, Cadw, other agencies and voluntary bodies which enhance such prospects.

P5   The Board recognises the importance of nature conservation and archaeological conservation to the tourism prospects of Wales. We welcome and will support measures by the Countryside Council for Wales, Cadw, other agencies and voluntary bodies which enhance such prospects.

Policy unchanged

Clean Beaches

P6   The Board endorses Dŵr Cymru's strategy aimed at introducing a comprehensive programme of treatment and disinfection around the Welsh coast, eliminating virtually all the traces of bacteria and viruses at its 136 discharge points. The Board would welcome the speedy implementation of this programme, within an overall strategy devised in consultation with the National Rivers Authority.

The Board endorses Dŵr Cymru's strategy aimed at introducing a comprehensive programme of treatment and disinfection around the Welsh coast, eliminating virtually all the traces of bacteria and viruses at its 136 discharge points. The Board recommends the speedy implementation of this strategy and completion of the improvement programme by the year 2000.

Policy modified

P7   The Board encourages and will seek to support initiatives to ensure that the National Rivers Authority Welsh Region is able to monitor regularly on an annual basis all bathing beaches, as identified by local authorities in Wales.

P7   The Board recommends that resources should be made available to ensure that the National Rivers Authority Welsh Region is able to monitor regularly on an annual basis all bathing beaches, as identified by local authorities in Wales.

Policy modified

P8   The Board will encourage local authorities to seek EC designation for further bathing beaches in their areas. We encourage and will seek to support local authorities to participate

P8   The Board will encourage local authorities to seek EC designation for further bathing beaches in their areas. We encourage and will seek to support local authorities to participate

Policy unchanged

Appendix 1. Cont.

PROPOSED FINAL POLICY	DRAFT POLICY	COMMENT
Clean Beaches		
P8 in the European Blue Flag Award and the Seaside Award	P8 in the European Blue Flag Award and the Seaside Award.	
P9 The Board welcomes and will encourage initiatives to provide information to visitors on water quality, in advance of their visit and on-site. We endorse the principle of providing on-site information panels, incorporating standardised multi-lingual wording agreed by the Keep Britain Tidy Group in association with the NRA.	P9 The Board welcomes and will encourage initiatives to provide information to visitors on water quality, in advance of their visit and on-site. We endorse the principle of providing on-site information panels, incorporating standardised bilingual wording agreed by the Keep Britain Tidy Group in association with the NRA.	Policy modified
P10 The Board endorses the efforts of the Department of the Environment to bring into line all monitoring programmes under the EC Directive throughout Europe. We recognise the need for all EC member states to follow the same principles and regulations.	F10 The Board endorses the efforts of the Department of the Environment to bring into line all monitoring programmes under the EC Directive throughout Europe. We recognise the need for all EC member states to follow the same principles and regulations.	Policy unchanged
P11 The Board would welcome the introduction of an European awards scheme for rural beaches, whose criteria are appropriate to such areas.	The Board would welcome the introduction of an European awards scheme for rural beaches.	Policy modified
P12 The Board welcomes and will support initiatives and the Keep Britain Tidy Group for better beach maintenance.	P12 The Board welcomes and will support initiatives by local authorities and Keep Wales Tidy for better beach maintenance.	Policy modified
Rivers		
P13 The Board recognises the potential offered by the rivers of Wales in the context of tourism. We will seek opportunities to collaborate with the National Rivers Authority and other bodies on initiatives which will help to secure the objectives of this strategy.		New policy
THE BUILT ENVIRONMENT		
P14 The Board encourages measures by local authorities, Cadw, the Welsh Development Agency, the Development Board for Rural Wales and voluntary bodies to enhance the appeal of the built environment to tourists and to day visitors. We will seek opportunities to collaborate with those bodies on projects which will help to secure the objectives of this strategy.	P13 The Board encourages measures by local authorities, Cadw, the Welsh Development Agency and voluntary bodies to enhance the appeal of the built environment to tourists and to day visitors. We will seek opportunities to collaborate with those bodies on projects which will help to secure the objectives of this strategy.	Policy modified and re-numbered
P15 The Board welcomes the sensitive conversion of redundant buildings to tourism-related uses, where appropriate and viable.	P14 The Board welcomes the sensitive conversion of redundant buildings to tourism-related uses, where appropriate and viable.	Policy re-numbered without change
RESPONSIBLE OPERATION		
P16 The Board will strive to pursue the Principles of Environmental Sustainability set out in this strategy.	P15 The Board will strive to reflect the Environmental Principles of this strategy.	Policy modified and re-numbered
P17 The Board encourages initiatives by tourism operators to adopt ecologically sound practices and to promote the Principles of Environmental Sustainability set out in this strategy.	P16 The Board encourages initiatives by tourism operators to adopt ecologically sound practices and to promote the Principles of Environmental Sustainability set out in this strategy.	Policy re-numbered without change
P18 The Board will produce and distribute an advisory guide on the subject of environmental responsibility in a tourism context, in association	P17 The Board will produce and distribute an advisory guide on the subject of environmental responsibility, in association with other partners.	Policies P17 and P18 amalgamated, with modification

Appendix 1. Cont.

PROPOSED FINAL POLICY	DRAFT POLICY	COMMENT

RESPONSIBLE OPERATION

with other partners. We will investigate ways of giving formal recognition and incentives to operators who adopt ecologically sound practices.		
	P18 The Board will investigate ways of giving formal recognition and incentives to operators who adopt ecologically sound practices	(See above)

PAYING FOR CONSERVATION

P19 The Board welcomes voluntary initiatives by the tourist industry and environmental bodies aimed at helping to finance conservation projects. We are not in favour of compulsory taxes and levies directed specifically at the tourist, for reasons of principle, equity and practicality.	P19 The Board welcomes voluntary initiatives by the tourist industry and environmental bodies aimed at helping to finance conservation projects.	Policy modified
P20 The Board will investigate with partner bodies ways in which tourists can help to pay towards conservation and environmental improvement. We consider it essential for such mechanisms to be practical, equitable and not prejudicial to Wales' competitiveness.	P20 The Board will investigate with partner bodies ways in which tourists can help to pay towards conservation and environmental improvement. We consider it essential for such mechanisms to be practical, equitable and not prejudicial to Wales' competitiveness.	Policy unchanged

WINDFARMS

P21 The Board supports initiatives by the Government, other public bodies and local authorities to provide clear land use policy guidance on wind turbine power stations.		New policy
P22 The Board endorses the policies of the Countryside Council for Wales which oppose the introduction of commercial wind turbines and wind turbine power stations in primary designated areas. We further consider that elsewhere:- a) proposals for windfarms in close proximity to such areas require very careful considerations. b) the likely effects of windfarm proposals upon the tourist industry should be among the matters for consideration.		New policy

THE WELSH LANGUAGE AND CULTURE

P23 The policies of the Board reflect the fact that Wales is a bilingual nation, with its own cultural identity. We will strive to use the Welsh language positively in our efforts to market Wales, especially overseas.	P21 The policies of the Board reflect the fact that Wales is a bilingual nation, with its own cultural identity. We will strive to use the Welsh language positively in our efforts to market Wales, especially overseas.	Policy re-numbered without change
P24 The Board commends to the tourist industry in Wales the advice available from the Welsh Language Board and we will consult with that body on issues affecting the tourism industry.	P22 The Board commends to the tourist industry in Wales the advice available from the Welsh Language Board and we will consult with that body on issues affecting the tourism industry.	Policy re-numbered without change
P25 The Board welcomes the industry's efforts to provide bilingual services to customers and also to use the Welsh language positively as a means of highlighting the cultural diversity of Wales. Initiatives will be taken to encourage	P23 The Board welcomes the industry's efforts to provide bilingual services to customers and also to use the Welsh language positively as a means of highlighting the cultural diversity of Wales. Initiatives will be taken to encourage	Policy re-numbered without change

Appendix 1. Cont.

PROPOSED FINAL POLICY	DRAFT POLICY	COMMENT
THE WELSH LANGUAGE AND CULTURE		
P25 tourism businesses to introduce specific bilingual schemes in keeping with this strategy.	P23 tourism businesses to introduce specific bilingual schemes in keeping with this strategy.	
P26 The Board commends the work of Menter a Busnes to encourage Welsh speaking people to become more involved in business enterprise. We will continue to work with that body to develop practical initiatives in keeping with the aims of this strategy.	P24 The Board will continue to encourage Welsh speaking people to become more involved in tourism.	Policy modified and re-numbered
P27 The Board will commission further research, as required, aimed at helping to make positive use of the linguistic and cultural traditions of Wales in tourism.	P25 The Board will commission further research aimed at helping to make positive use of the linguistic and cultural traditions of Wales in tourism.	Policy modified and re-numbered
COMMUNITIES AND TOURISM		
P28 The Board commends and will support community based initiatives in tourism, where these:- a) are in keeping with the principles of this strategy; b) are based upon sound marketing principles and are viable.	P26 The Board commends and will support community based initiatives in tourism, where these:- ☐ are in keeping with the principles of this strategy; ☐ are designed to complement the programmes of public agencies and local authorities.	Policy modified and re-numbered
P29 The Board will provide support and advice on tourism matters to community groups. Our aim will be to encourage good practice, without stifling innovation and enterprise.	P27 The Board will provide support and advice on tourism matters to community groups. Our aim will be to encourage good practice, without stifling innovation and enterprise.	Policy re-numbered without change
P30 The Board will continue to support the Jigso Community Appraisal scheme, together with the Countryside Council for Wales, Welsh Development Agency, Development Board for Rural Wales, Tai Cymru, the British Trust for Conservation Volunteers, the Prince of Wales Committee and the Welsh Council for Voluntary Action. We will provide pump priming support to appropriate tourism projects which follow on from Jigso appraisals.	P28 The Board will continue to support the Jigsaw Community Appraisal scheme, together with the Countryside Council for Wales, Welsh Development Agency, Development Board for Rural Wales and Tai Cymru. We will develop schemes to provide pump priming support to appropriate tourism projects which follow on from Jigsaw appraisals.	Policy modified and re-numbered
P31 The Board welcomes enterprise in tourism by the people of Wales. We will encourage tourism businesses to make use of local labour and supplies.	P29 The Board welcomes enterprise in tourism by the people of Wales. We will encourage tourism businesses to make use of local labour and supplies.	Policy re-numbered without change
P32 The Board will encourage tourism operators to develop products which promote constructive links and shared use between visitors and host communities, bringing a better understanding of the importance of the tourism industry.	P30 The Board will encourage tourism operators to develop products which promote constructive links and shared use between visitors and host communities, bringing a better understanding of the importance of the tourism industry.	Policy re-numbered without change
NEW DEVELOPMENTS		
P33 The Board's policies recognise the need for the location, character and scale of new tourism development to respect the environmental, cultural and community related objectives of this strategy.		New policy

Appendix 2. Community Perspectives on Tourism.

WHAT DO YOU THINK ARE THE MAIN ADVANTAGES WHICH THE PRESENCE OF TOURISTS BRINGS TO THIS TOWN/AREA?

RESPONSES	AREA OF RESIDENCE							
	Tenby	Pontypool	Lampeter	Blaenau Ffestiniog	Brecon	Holyhead	Tywyn	Rhyl
	%	%	%	%	%	%	%	%
More jobs for local people	51	1	32	9	8	3	18	15
Brings money into the town/area	81	42	78	62	82	68	77	62
More local facilities as a result of tourism	2	3	2	2	1	1	–	1
Better roads/existing roads kept better	2	–	1	1	–	–	–	–
More/larger car parks	1	1	2	–	–	–	–	–
Better shops/more shops	2	3	3	1	–	1	–	1
Lower rates	2	–	–	–	1	2	–	3
Keeps the town alive/town would not exist but for tourists	9	1	23	4	2	–	–	1
Buildings/public parks/attractions better preserved	1	1	1	1	2	–	–	–
Other reasons (miscellaneous)	2	4	5	8	1	3	–	–
Don't know/no particular advantages	5	44	14	16	9	23	5	18

BASE: All respondents (1077)

WHAT DO YOU THINK ARE THE MAIN DISADVANTAGES TO THE LOCAL PEOPLE OF TOURISM IN THE TOWN/AREA?

RESPONSES	AREA OF RESIDENCE							
	Tenby	Pontypool	Lampeter	Blaenau Ffestiniog	Brecon	Holyhead	Tywyn	Rhyl
	%	%	%	%	%	%	%	%
Noise	5	1	24	2	1	1	18	2
Traffic congestion/difficulty in parking	50	13	57	16	22	18	35	22
Crowded streets/pavements	34	1	36	1	15	5	7	4
Difficulty in shopping	28	–	17	3	4	11	14	10
Higher prices	9	1	14	1	1	9	2	4
Damage to environment	12	1	5	5	1	8	2	27
Higher rates	–	1	–	–	–	–	–	1
Crowded local facilities	1	1	1	1	2	6	–	2
Can't get on buses/taxis	–	–	–	–	1	–	–	3
Poor social life in summer	2	1	–	1	2	1	–	1
Tourists rude – think that town/area belongs to them	2	–	1	3	–	2	–	1
Bad effect on Welsh language	–	1	6	3	–	1	–	–
Brings too many second home owners	2	–	5	7	–	–	–	–
Crowded cafes/restaurants – wait too long for service	–	–	4	1	2	3	1	1
Other disadvantages (miscellaneous)	4	1	1	2	4	3	2	–
Don't know/no particular disadvantages	12	80	27	58	50	33	22	22

BASE: All Respondents (1077)

Appendix 2. Cont.

TAKING EVERYTHING INTO CONSIDERATION ABOUT TOURISM IN YOUR TOWN/AREA, WOULD YOU SAY THAT THE BENEFITS OUTWEIGH THE DISADVANTAGES, OR THE OTHER WAY ROUND?

RESPONSES	AREA OF RESIDENCE							
	Tenby	Pontypool	Lampeter	Blaenau Ffestiniog	Brecon	Holyhead	Tywyn	Rhyl
	%	%	%	%	%	%	%	%
Benefits outweigh disadvantages	78	57	42	69	82	66	71	41
Disadvantages outweigh advantages	4	3	5	7	4	14	11	8
They are both equal	14	21	44	19	10	20	14	31
Don't know	4	19	9	5	4	1	2	20

BASE: All respondents (1077)

Appendix 3. Bilingual Policy of the Wales Tourist Board.

THE BILINGUAL POLICY OF THE WALES TOURIST BOARD

The Wales Tourist Board seeks to develop and market tourism in ways which will yield the optimum economic and social benefit for the people of Wales. Implicit within this objective is the need:

- *to offer high standards of product quality and of service;*
- *to sustain and promote the culture of Wales and the Welsh language;*
- *to safeguard the natural and the built environment.*

In order to achieve its aims, the board works in partnership with statutory agencies, local authorities, the private sector and other bodies.

The activities of the Wales Tourist Board are undertaken within and for the benefit of a bilingual community. This is reflected in the following statement of our bilingual policy.

GENERAL PRINCIPLES

1   The Board's bilingual policy will operate throughout Wales, and will apply to staff employed by the Board at its head office and elsewhere in Wales.
2   The policy is a dynamic one, which will be kept under review in response to developments in society and to legal requirements. In particular, it will be reviewed in the light of the Welsh Language Act 1993, upon receipt of guidance from the Welsh Language Board.

CORPORATE IDENTITY

3   The Board will project a coporate image which is consistent with its bilingual policy. The Board's logo and stationery headings will be fully bilingual. Signage within the Board's offices will be bilingual, as will signage and plaques produced by the Board for use by the tourist industry.

CORRESPONDENCE

4   The Board welcomes correspondence in either Welsh or English, and will respond in the language used by the correspondent.
5   In initiating correspondence the Board will do so in Welsh where the recipient has previously expressed a wish to communicate thus.

TELEPHONE

6   The Board is happy to receive telephone enquiries in either Welsh or English. If the recipient of the call is unable to speak Welsh then we will arrange for another member of staff to deal with the enquiry.

PRESS RELEASES

7   Press releases and other statements by the Board will be produced in Welsh and English.

POLICY DOCUMENTS

8   The Board's Annual Report and other major policy documents will be produced in bilingual form. The preferred approach will be to combine the two languages within the same document, but it may be appropriate to produce separate Welsh and English editions.

Appendix 3. Cont.

THE BILINGUAL POLICY OF THE WALES TOURIST BOARD

FORMS AND CIRCULARS

9   All circular letters issued by the Board will be bilingual. The Board is moving towards a situation where all the forms issued within Wales in the course of its development, marketing, research and other activities will be bilingual. Most of our forms already conform with this principle, and we will seek to extend the practice as expeditiously as possible.

PROMOTIONAL LITERATURE

The Wales Tourist Board produces a wide range of promotional literature. It may be the sole publisher or it may issue joint publications with a variety of public and private sector partners. The Board's publications are targeted at a wide audience, most of whom live outside Wales.

10   The Board will seek wherever possible and appropriate to draw attention to the fact that Wales is a bilingual nation, with its own cultural identity. We will endeavour to use the Welsh language positively in our efforts to market Wales, especially overseas.

11   It is not necessary or practical for all the Board's guides, leaflets and other marketing material to be produced bilingually. However, the Board recognises the importance of producing specific marketing items in Welsh to meet the needs of people within Wales. Similarly, it will produce some items in other languages apart from English, in order to meet the needs of key overseas markets.

12   Where appropriate, the Board will refer to the Welsh language in publications intended primarily to be read outside Wales, in order to create a better awareness and understanding of the fact that Wales is a bilingual society.

MEETINGS

13   Meetings convened by the Board will be conducted bilingually where appropriate. In such instances instant translation services will be provided, enabling participants to use the language of their choice.

STAFFING AND RECRUITMENT

14   It is the policy of the Board to designate certain posts as requiring the ability to speak Welsh or a willingness to gain proficiency in Welsh. These are posts where the facility to communicate bilingually is necessary in order to deliver a service effectively and in a way which commands the confidence of all users.

15   The Board encourages existing and new members of staff to learn Welsh, irrespective of their specific duties. Financial assistance will be given to enable staff to take advantage of approved courses.

16   Advertisements for posts within the Board will indicate clearly whether an ability to speak Welsh is essential or desirable.

THE TOURIST INDUSTRY

17   The WTB commends to the tourist industry in Wales the advice available from the Welsh Language Board and will work with that body where our interests coincide.

18   We support the industry's efforts to provide bilingual services to customers and also to use the Welsh language positively as a means of highlighting the cultural diversity of Wales. Financial assistance may be given by the WTB to operators to assist specific bilingual initiatives.

Tourist Organisations in Catalonia: Regional and Local Structures and Issues

7

Douglas G. Pearce

ABSTRACT

Interorganisational analysis is used to explore the structure and functions of tourist organisations in Catalonia since the region obtained autonomy in 1979. The regional context is outlined, the structure and functions of the regional organisations are discussed and a range of interorganisational issues are analysed before selected sub-regional and local examples are examined, namely those of the Costa Brava Girona, La Selva, Lloret de Mar and Barcelona. One of the most explicit changes in the post-Franco era has been the creation of tourist organisations at the regional level and the subsequent development of regional policies and programmes. The most significant of the Catalonia-wide activities would appear to be that of promotion and marketing. In other domains regional policies are yet to have a major impact. Much of the action still lies at the local level where interesting recent initiatives responding to local circumstances have been taken. Relatively little horizontal interaction occurs and a strong functionally integrated network can scarcely be said to exist as of yet. In contrast to trends in many other parts of the world the degree of public–private sector interaction is rather limited.

INTRODUCTION

Tourist organisations, their structures and functions, have only recently attracted systematic attention from researchers and comparatively little work has been done in examining the institutional frameworks within which tourism develops (Pearce, 1992; 1996a; 1996b; Choy, 1993). The work that has been undertaken so far shows that networks of tourist organisations, from the local to the national scale, exist in many countries and that these exercise a range of functions such as marketing, visitor servicing, development, planning, research and regulation – functions which may influence the nature and extent of tourist development. While common features and patterns may be found, tourist organisations tend to differ in terms of their structure, funding and the number and type of functions they perform, leading this author (Pearce, 1992, p. 200) to conclude, in a comparative study of tourist organisations in six countries, that: 'There is no single best type of [tourist] organisation nor interorganisational network; rather each country must evolve a system which best reflects local, regional and national conditions'.

The relationship between tourist organisations and the context in which they develop and operate is conceptualised in Fig. 7·1, an open-systems model in which a multi-scale network of tourist organisations is set within its broader political economic environment, a sub-environment of which is the tourism environment. Figure 7·1 also gives explicit recognition to questions of spatial scale and temporal change (T_1, T_2, T_3 ...). As exchanges occur between the organisations and their environments, the structure, functions

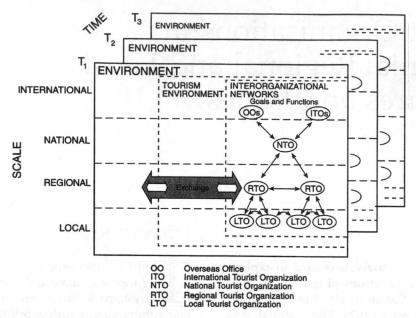

Figure 7·1. A conceptual framework for the interorganisational analysis of tourist organisations. Source: Pearce (1992).

and goals of the network, or of individual organisations, may evolve in response to changing environmental conditions and changes may occur in the nature and strength of interorganisational relationships. Conversely, tourist organisations may seek to change the conditions under which they operate.

Using Fig. 7·1 as a conceptual model and interorganisational analysis as the underlying methodology, this chapter explores the structure and functions of tourist organisations in Catalonia, one of Spain's, and indeed the world's, leading tourist destinations. The chapter forms part of a wider study examining the changing institutional framework for tourism in post-Franco Spain and extends the analysis of the emergence of the new tier of regional tourist organisations and their relationship to Spain's national tourist organisation (Pearce, 1996c; 1997) by focussing in more detail on structures and relationships at the lower end of the hierarchy within a particular region. The regional context is outlined, the structure and functions of the regional organisations are discussed and a range of interorganisational issues are analysed before selected sub-regional and local examples are examined, namely those of the Costa Brava Girona, La Selva, Lloret de Mar and Barcelona. More generally, this Catalan case study may also serve to illustrate further the

need to include local and regional examples in research on tourist organisations (national bodies have received most attention to date), and to incorporate discussion of tourist organisations more fully and explicitly when community issues in tourism are being addressed. The study is based on field visits and in-depth interviews with key personnel in the organisations examined undertaken in mid-1995 and on an analysis of relevant documentation (annual reports, plans, statistics and publicity material).

REGIONAL CONTEXT

Located in north-east Spain, Catalonia is one of the country's wealthiest, most industrialised and populated (six million inhabitants) regions. Possessing a strong and distinct cultural identity and previous history of autonomy, Catalonia was one of the first regions to push for regional self-determination in post-Franco Spain. The Catalonian Statute of Autonomy was approved by referendum in October 1979 and the first Catalonian parliament (Generalitat) since 1932 was elected early the following year (Elazar, 1991). As elsewhere, tourism was amongst the powers transferred to the new autonomous community of Catalonia; others included agriculture, culture, economic development, land use and building, public works and transport, in so far as these matters fall exclusively within regional boundaries. With regard to tourism, the latter is a significant qualification, with central government having reserved the right to promote Spain as a whole abroad, a situation which has not gone uncontested (Pearce, 1997).

Administratively, tourism in Catalonia is handled as a directorate general within the Department of Commerce, Consumer Affairs and Tourism. A separate agency for tourism marketing, the Catalonia Tourist Board (Consorci de Promoció Turística de Catalunya) was established in 1986. Regional tourism policy was initially outlined in a 1983 white paper on tourism (Miguelsanz, 1983). Catalonia's tourist competitiveness was subsequently addressed in a report undertaken by Professor Porter's Monitor Company (Departament de Commerç, Consum i Turisme, 1992), with major Catalan tourism strategies being outlined in a policy

document which appeared later that year (Alegre i Selga, 1992). Other sub-regional and local tourist organisations have also emerged.

This situation contrasts markedly with that which prevailed during the boom years of the 1960s and 70s when national tourism policy under Franco consisted primarily in encouraging demand-led growth of international tourism in coastal areas, with scant concern for regional and local interests and consequences (Cals, 1974; Torres Bernier, 1985; Jurdao, 1990), nor any public sector intervention at a regional scale (information offices did exist in each of the 50 provinces, and provincial offices administered hotel and other regulations). As Morris and Dickinson (1987, p. 19) point out, national boosterism and the lack of regional powers and policies were compounded by the administrative fragmentation of Catalonia's Costa Brava – 22 municipalities occupy this stretch of the coastline – with the result that:

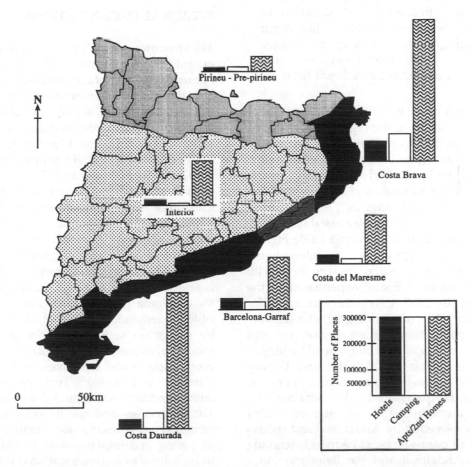

Figure 7·2. Distribution of accommodation in Catalonia, 1993. Data source: ACTT (1995).

Figure 7·3. Evolution of foreign visitors to Catalonia, 1981–1993. Source: after ACTT (1995).

land use planning passed very largely into the hands of municipalities which guided it in different directions according to dominant local interests – those of major landowners, or more frequently those of mayors and other municipal officers who were also proprietors and perhaps owned construction companies. The law was flouted openly in many ways, but the point is that local government held the strings and could control also the level and direction of corruption. Some municipalities, like Begur and Palafrugell, developed on a restricted basis... Others welcomed massive new construction, as did Lloret and Rosas from the late 1960s.

In these and other ways, much of the present structure of tourism in the region was inherited from the Franco era (Priestley, 1995), with other factors also having an influence in recent years, for example the increasingly competitive nature of Mediterranean tourism and Barcelona's hosting of the Olympic Games in 1992. Figure 7·2 illustrates well the continuing coastal concentration of tourism plant in Catalonia while Fig. 7·3 highlights the stagnation in international demand which the region, in common with many other parts of Spain, experienced in the early 1990s. In 1993 Catalonia accounted for approximately 25% of all foreign visitor destinations in Spain (the leading region on this measure), and 14% of all foreign hotel bednights (third ranked, after the Balearic and Canary Islands). The region is also an important domestic destination, particularly for intra-regional travellers, attracting 15% of domestic trips (marginally exceeded by Andalusia) and receiving 13% of all domestic hotel bednights (coming third after Andalusia and the Balearics). As a result, tourism is one of Catalonia's leading

economic sectors, accounting for around 13% of the region's gross domestic product and a similar share of direct employment (Alegre i Selga, 1992). Other estimates show revenue generated by tourism in Catalonia in 1989 exceeded that of such countries as Portugal, Turkey and Greece (Departament de Commerç, Consum i Turisme, 1992).

REGIONAL ORGANISATIONS

The structure and policies of the regional tourist organisations provide a first measure of the nature and extent of sub-regional considerations and the degree of interaction with lower level organisations. Here, significant differences occur between the main administrative organ of tourism in Catalonia, the Directorate General for Tourism (DGT), and its promotional arm, the Catalonia Tourist Board (CTB).

As a part of the Department of Commerce, Consumer Affairs and Tourism, the DGT, located in Barcelona, is responsible for tourism throughout the whole of Catalonia and has as its basic tasks the improvement, promotion and commercialisation of the region's tourist product; that is, it is primarily concerned with the supply-side while the Catalonia Tourist Board is essentially responsible for demand. The DGT's tasks are undertaken by two main sections, one for businesses and tourist activities and the other for planning, programming and incentives, while the Agència Catalana de Tecnologia Turística acts as a think tank providing technical advice and expertise. The businesses and tourist activities section is primarily responsible for regulatory matters, preparing and implementing legislation relating to such areas as accommodation classification and the activities of travel agencies, though much of

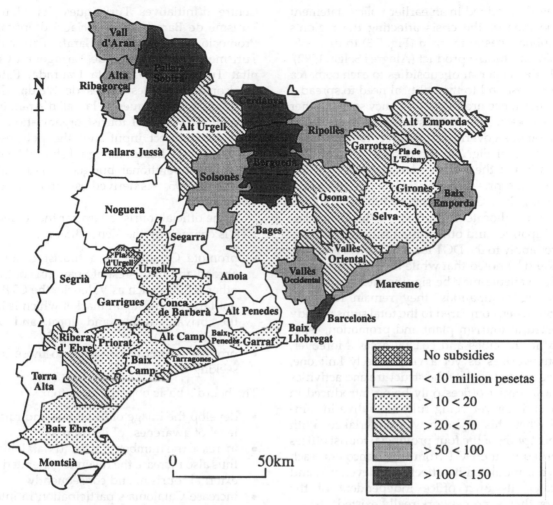

Figure 7·4. Distribution of tourism subsidies in Catalonia, 1994. Data source: Departament de Comerç, Consum i Turisme (1995).

the day-to-day work here may be undertaken in the decentralised territorial services located in each province which are better placed geographically to deal with inspections and complaints. This section is also responsible for overseeing human resource development and professional training and qualifications. Various activities are undertaken by the section for planning, programming and incentives. According to the department's 1994 annual report (Departament de Comerç Consum i Turisme, 1995), planning that year largely consisted of a tourist signage plan for Catalonia aimed at improving road signs throughout the region, a good example of an activity in which region-wide consistency is desirable. Advice was also given to various other departments on tourism-related projects. In addition, financial assistance was made

available under a variety of programmes, for example those to foster rural tourism, skiing, the development of new tourist routes and specialised tourist products. Promotional subsidies went to a range of organisations at the local, county (comarca) and other levels, as well as to non-profit organisations and businesses.

Total assistance from these different schemes amounted to 1469 million pesetas in 1994. Figure 7·4 reveals that subsidies that year were directed in particular to some of the mountainous counties in north-western Catalonia (Cerdanya, 9·8%; Pallars Sobira, 7·9%; Berguedà, 6·8%) and also to Barcelonès (8·9%) but every comarca except Pla d'Urgell received some assistance under one or more programmes. The pattern shown in Fig. 7·4 might be interpreted in different ways; the concentration as reflecting the need identified in an earlier policy statement at the time of the crisis affecting the region's traditional coastal tourism (Fig. 7·3) to diversify Catalonia's tourist product (Alegre i Selga, 1992), while the dispersal of subsidies to each comarca may correspond to the political need to spread a little assistance around, a tendency seen in other regions keen to demonstrate the benefits of autonomous government (Pearce, 1996c).

In terms of Fig. 7·1, the relationship between the DGT and the lower order organisations and private enterprises is essentially a top-down one, reflecting the DGT's regulatory functions and its ability to allocate resources — the comarcas, municipalities and other organisations and businesses apply to the DGT for assistance. However, it should be noted that while the subsidies being made available may be significant to small and emerging destinations, they remain relatively limited when compared to the total sums already invested in tourism plant and promotion, especially in the cities and coastal areas. Moreover, the network is as yet a very loosely knit one, legislation to regulate the structure and activities of local tourist offices only being introduced in 1994 and not yet being fully operative in mid-1995 when this research was undertaken. With the exception of the four provincial tourist offices inherited by the DGT from the Franco era, each resort or municipality effectively developed and operated its own office independent of the others; that is, no network really existed.

In contrast to the traditional bureaucratic structure of the DGT, the Catalonia Tourist Board was established in 1986 as a much more flexible body, capable of responding more quickly and effectively to the commercial realities of tourism promotion and marketing, activities up until then undertaken by the DGT. A similar separate marketing agency had been set up the year before in Valencia (Institut Turistic de Valencia) and others followed later in the Balearics, Galicia and Andalusia (Pearce, 1996c). In the case of Catalonia, membership of the new board included not only the Generalitat, via the DGT, and representatives of the private sector, through the trade associations, but also representatives of key local and zonal tourist organisations. Some variation in the latter group has occurred from time to time, but in 1995 the following destinations were represented: Patronat de Turisme Costa Brava-Girona;

Centre d'Initiatives Turístiques del Maresme; Turisme de Barcelona; Associació d'Entitats de Promoció Turística del Garaf; Patronat de Turisme de la Diputació de Tarragona i Comunitat Turistica de la Costa Daurada; Patronat Intercomarcal de les Terres de Lleida, Centre d'Initiatives Turístiques de la Vall d'Aran. In this way, the lower level tourist organisations thus have some direct input into the policies and activities of the board, though it should be noted the CTB's operational budget — 1100 million pesetas in 1995 — is derived essentially from the Generalitat.

As the official tourist board for the region, the CTB is charged by the Generalitat to:

- promote Catalonia as a tourist destination abroad and to the rest of Spain (in contrast to other regions such as Valencia, the CTB does not target the Catalan market which is left to the private sector and local and zonal organisations);
- provide technical assistance to those bodies seeking it.

The board's basic objectives are to:

- develop the image of Catalonia and raise the level of awareness of its product;
- increase the number of trips to Catalonia and thus also increase the revenue generated from external tourism; and consequently
- increase Catalonia's participation in international tourism and individual markets.

To this end the CTB, with a staff of 29 plus the services of a series of overseas 'promotors', undertakes a variety of activities including market research, providing advice on matching supply and demand, marketing directly to the consumer and indirect marketing (participation in fairs and workshops, hosting familiarisation trips, press and public relations and working through the various commercial channels such as the carriers, tour operators and wholesalers). Working with the latter group is particularly important given the amount of package tourism to Catalonia and the more direct control operators have over large segments of the market. Some success has been achieved in having the name Catalonia appear in certain catalogues, rather than those of particular zones (notably the Costa Brava), but often it is more a question of maintaining contact with the tour operators and monitoring trends. Developing the image of Catalonia also has broader implications beyond the realm of tourism promotion in this strongly nationalist autonomous community, as was most evident in the series of 'In which country is Barcelona? In Catalonia' advertisements which appeared in the international media at the time of the 1992 Olympic Games.

INTERORGANISATIONAL ISSUES

On closer inspection, the division of responsibilities between the DGT and the Catalonia Tourist Board is not as clear-cut as it might first appear, generating the need for close coordination to avoid mismatches or duplication. The brochures and other publicity material distributed by the board are not produced by them, nor indeed by the DGT; rather they are published by the information, documentation and publications service of the department's General Secretariat. Likewise, the board has no input into the promotional subsidies given out by the DGT to the lower-order tourist organisations, making development of a concerted, coherent promotional strategy for all of Catalonia difficult. Nor would the board appear to be well-placed to promote all of the new forms of tourism being encouraged by the development incentives. Much of the rural tourism product, for example, is not yet of a sufficient calibre to promote abroad, nor indeed to other parts of Spain, which in any event are developing their own rural tourism programmes. The demand for rural tourism in Catalonia essentially comes from within the region itself, but, as noted above, promotion to the home market lies outside the domain of the Catalonia Tourist Board.

Where more than one tier of organisation exists or where different agencies at the same level have separate but inter-related functions, clear and explicit policies setting out the roles and responsibilites of each are needed in order to avoid gaps and duplication and for the set of organisations as a whole to function as effectively and efficiently as possible. Such guidelines are not very evident in the 1992 report and policy document which form the most explicit recent statements on the direction of tourism in Catalonia.

The 1992 report undertaken by Professor Porter's Monitor Company (Departament de Commerç, Consum i Turisme, 1992) was commissioned at a time of stagnating demand (Fig. 7·3) and, following the strategic analysis of defined clusters, elaborated a plan for the competitiveness of the tourist sector in Catalonia in which eight priority programmes were outlined:

- differentiation of accommodation;
- environmental protection;
- human resource development;
- modernisation of systems of business financing;
- updating information on tourist needs and desires;
- promotion of complementary tourism services;
- selecting promotional campaign objectives;
- strengthening segment diversification.

However, few explicit recommendations are given as to who should do what even though the plan's principal objective was 'to increase awareness among all the economic sectors involved, public as well as private, of the repercussions of their actions on the competitiveness of tourism'. In the penultimate section of the report the DGT is urged to put in place any necessary legislation and regulations. On the very last page the role of the local authorities and business associations is recognised as being 'crucial' to the plan and the Generalitat's role is defined as being: 'the catalyst for local and county initiatives through the creation of mixed working groups for "clusters" that integrate all the economic agents of each "cluster" with a single objective: the reinforcement of the competitive advantage of the "cluster".' Clusters had earlier been defined in a 'multidimensional and iterative' process based on the criteria of geography, commercial linkages and strategic typologies incorporating elements of both supply and demand. Emphasis in the report is given to 'sun' segment clusters (Costa Brava Nord, Roses, Costa Brava Centre, Costa Brava Sud, Maresme Nord and Costa Daurada Centre) and to nature-based clusters, those of Cerdanya and the Vall d'Aran getting the most attention. It is unclear whether these clusters are meant to be comprehensive, a priority set or only illustrative, but some major gaps occur, notably Barcelona. In any event, although the clusters may have formed a logical and functional territorial basis for the creation of sub-regional tourist organisations, nothing further appears to have come of them.

In following up the Porter report, the Catalan *Conseller* for Commerce, Consumer Affairs and Tourism, Lluis Alegre i Selga (1992), announced in November 1992 the strategies which were to constitute the new Catalan Conception of Tourism, namely:

- creation of a special body, the Agència Catalana de Ordenació de l'Oferta Turística, to regulate the growth of tourism in saturated areas;
- preparation of a Pla Horitzontal de Turisme to coordinate public sector management of environmental matters;
- implantation of a new model of tourist urbanisation;
- diversification of tourist businesses through development of natural resources, promotion of touring and encouragement of greater activity abroad by Catalan businesses to develop their potential in emerging markets;
- elaboration of a series of 'marketing' initiatives.

While some institutional change is alluded to in order to operationalise these strategies, there is no longer mention of territorial clusters or indeed of any sub-regional organisations. Three years later only variable progress could be determined in the implementation of the new concept. The regulatory agency had not been established and such matters seem in any case to lie outside the jurisdiction of the tourism directorate. However, a series of carrying capacity studies had been undertaken and it remains to be seen what political will exists to address the implications of these. Likewise, no coordinating plan has materialised nor is any new general model of tourist urbanisation evident. It should be noted that responsibility for physical planning and development essentially remains the domain of the municipalities, some of which have taken steps to redress some of these problems, for example Lloret de Mar with its Lloret Prestigi programme (see below). As has already been noted, limited financial assistance is being made available for product diversification and modernisation and diversified if not wholly coordinated coverage is given to the region. One direct outcome of the 1992 report was the creation in 1993 of the Agència Catalana de Tecnologia Turística (ACTT) whose role is 'to give the Catalan tourist sector the capacity to identify future scenarios, develop solutions and create an ongoing network for communication between the private sector and government agencies in an attempt to create more competitive tourist enterprises'. Activities of the ACTT to date include research (surveys on Catalan vacations and on Spanish visitors to the region) and promoting the introduction of new technologies to the tourist industry.

Other related organisational and scale issues also arise with regard to marketing and promotion, for although the Generalitat is primarily concerned with promoting Catalonia, functionally tourism in the region has developed in terms of smaller territorial units whose boundaries and nomenclature have evolved over the past three decades (Anon, n.d.). In the mid-1960s the central Ministry of Information and Tourism had created a register of 'geotouristic' names to avoid confusion in the areas of promotion and marketing, for example the same name being given to two different areas. In Catalonia the term Costa Brava was reserved for the littoral of the province of Gerona while the name Costa Daurada applied to the littoral of the provinces of Barcelona and Tarragona. While the former has been widely used and is now well known, the latter has had a more complex history. Through their local organisation (the Centre d'Initiatives Turístiques del Maresme), hoteliers along the coast north of Barcelona sought to disassociate themselves from the term Costa Daurada in favour of the Maresme itself. Likewise, the city of Barcelona and the comarcas of the Garraf have seen little benefit in being associated with the name Costa Daurada. At the same time, the Provincial Deputació of Tarragona has been keen to appropriate the name for its exclusive use, creating the Comunitat Turistica de la Costa Daurada. With the exception of the Vall d'Aran, known for its skiing, the interior of Catalonia had few established tourist names or images, the Patronat de Turisme Terres de Lleida, being a recent creation in the province of Lerida (Lleida).

While the denomination of these smaller geotouristic units has had no formal basis under Catalan law, the organisations which represent them are members of the Catalonia Tourist Board (listed above). For practical purposes, official statistics of supply and

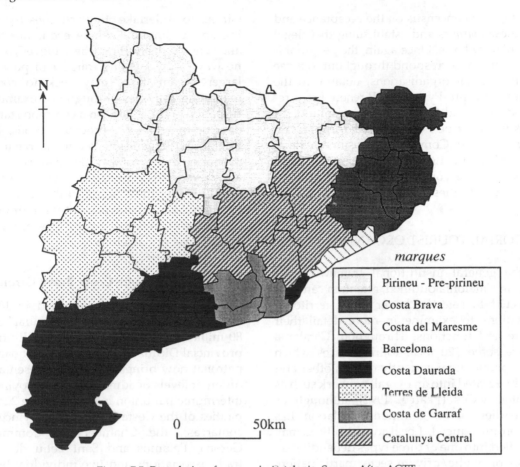

marques

Pirineu - Pre-pirineu
Costa Brava
Costa del Maresme
Barcelona
Costa Daurada
Terres de Lleida
Costa de Garraf
Catalunya Central

0   50km

Figure 7·5. Boundaries of *marques* in Catalonia. Source: After ACTT.

demand have been presented on a zonal basis, implying at least some formal differentiation. The boundaries of these have evolved since the first subzones were used in the 1983 white paper. Figure 7·2, for example, depicts the distribution of accommodation in 1993 using the prevailing six zone classification. One disadvantage of this system is that several comarcas are split between different zones, for example Pla de l'Estany. Another is that the six zones do not correspond to those of the seven territorial tourist organisations represented on the Catalonia Tourist Board.

Further changes were set in train in 1994 when the transfer of credit to the DGT to the Catalonia Tourist Board was accompanied by the directive that more generic promotion be carried out in terms of *marques* ('marchlands'), not exceeding eight in number. Spatially, the boundaries of the eight *marques* subsequently identified by the ACTT respect the comarca divisions (Fig. 7·5),

but their integrity rests primarily on a set of defined characteristics. The Costa Brava, for example is defined in the following terms:

(1) a brand with a long-lasting tradition, occupying the maritime fringe of the northeastern coast of Catalonia, stretching from the Cap de Creus peninsula to the Tordera River mouth;

(2) a deeply dissected coast, in which abrupt cliffs and hidden coves alternate with sandy sections such as the G of Roses or Pals;

(3) the Aiguamolls de l'Empordà Natural Park where the fauna is of interest;

(4) enchanting and picturesque fishing villages frequented traditionally by artists and writers who have brought international prestige;

(5) inland, the attractive cities of Gerona and Figures, Lake Banyoles and a section of Montseny;

(6) renowned gastronomy and cuisine.

However, there remains the more difficult task

of arriving at a consensus on the acceptance and use of these *marques* and establishing their legal and regulatory basis. Once again, the geographical limits do not correspond throughout to those of existing zonal organisations, notably in the Pyrenees and pre-Pyrenees (Pireneu–Pre-pireneu) and in central Catalonia, and resolution of these issues may be no easy matter. Moreover, the Department of Commerce, Consumer Affairs and Tourism in its annual report of 1994 continued to use comarca boundaries in summarising its activities (see for example Fig. 7·4).

TERRITORIAL TOURIST ORGANISATIONS

With the general institutional framework for tourism in Catalonia outlined, attention can now be directed to selected lower order territorial organisations to examine in more detail their structure and functions. Throughout Catalonia there are some 120 local tourist offices which largely operate independently of each other and are not integrated into an overall network such as the Dutch VVVs (Pearce, 1992), although as noted earlier, some common legislation has now been introduced. Local tourist offices may be classified into one of three types depending on the basis of public/private sector participation. Municipal Tourist Offices (Oficines Municipals de Turisme) are operated by a municipality with no direct participation from local businesses and act mainly to provide visitor information services and to coordinate the tourist-related services of the council. Centres d'Iniciatives Turìstiques, on the other hand have been established by local businesses to provide visitor information services and coordinate activities for them, as well as perhaps acting as a lobby group. Some may now receive part of their funding from the municipality. Patronats de Turisme, the third group, consist of a partnership between the public and private sectors, with representatives of each group on the board and share capital usually divided equally, though the operational budget is normally derived from the municipal coffers. The general tendency would appear to be towards this third type, the partnership offering greater operational flexibility. Local tourist offices may combine as members of some larger entity, for example a zonal tourist organisation such as the Patronat de Turisme Costa Brava

Girona, to undertake other activities, e.g. marketing and promotion, where economies of scale and synergy of effort may be achieved, but this in no way represents any transfer of power. Such larger organisations may seek to coordinate marketing activities, through, for example, participation at trade fairs on a common stand or by developing common brochure types, but the local tourist organisations remain free to participate or go their own way. Some tourist activity is also starting to occur at the level of the comarca, usually under the auspices of the county administration. Examples of each of these drawn from Gerona will now be given, together with the special case of Barcelona.

Patronat de Turisme Costa Brava Girona

This partnership was established in 1977 and today has a staff of four and an annual budget of 80 million pesetas, derived essentially from the provincial Diputació de Girona. The board of the patronat now brings together representatives of different levels of administration (provincial, the intermunicipal union made up of the 22 municipalities of the Costa Brava, the province's eight comarcas), the Chambers of Commerce of Gerona, Palamos and Sant Feliu de Guixols, trade associations and five individual businessmen. Originally established to develop and promote a common image of the Costa Brava, the patronat now incorporates the rest of the province, emphasising in particular the Pyrenees of Gerona, with attempts being made to sell the coast with the interior and vice versa. The patronat sees itself as a bridge between supply and demand and much of its activity is centred on the coordinated promotion of the region through participation in trade fairs and workshops, usually under the umbrella of the Catalonia Tourist Board. With the recent growth in interest from the developing Russian market, for instance, the patronat has been putting Russian tour operators in touch with local tourist offices, but the operators from such well-established markets as the United Kingdom and Germany have long had their own incoming agents and, in the words of the director, many of the visitors 'are the clientele of the tour operator, not of the zone'. Although it relies on external intelligence to monitor trends in the market place, the patronat regularly commissions its own visitor surveys and other research in order to analyse developments in the region. This research includes some original complementary measures of seasonal demand such as the consumption of potable water, treatment of waste water and telephone usage (Patronat de Turisme Costa Brava Girona, 1993).

Consell Comarcal de La Selva

As a relatively new administrative unit with incipient but non-specific interests in tourism, the county council of La Selva contrasts with the more established special purpose tourist organisations, but is perhaps nonetheless typical of many recent ventures at this level in Catalonia. The comarca is a peculiarly Catalan unit of administration, first established under the Second Republic, abolished under Franco, with councils being reintroduced at this level by the Generalitat in 1988. Their current raison d'etre is still uncertain. The councils have few of their own resources, being largely dependent on targeted grants from the Generalitat and the municipalities to carry out designated functions, for example the delivery of some social services. The comarca of La Selva extends over 26 municipalities, three on the coast and 23 in the interior, including Santa Coloma de Farners where the council is located. As tourism in the coast municipalities, consisting of three of the largest resorts on the Costa Brava – Tossa de Mar, Lloret de Mar and Blanes – is distinctive and well developed, the county council has directed its attention to fostering tourism in the inland areas. In 1992 a grant was obtained to commission a feasibility study of tourist potential in the comarca. The study recommended a series of modest short- and long-term initiatives and promotion of La Selva under the theme of 'County of Water' – the area has some small spas, rivers and is known for its mineral waters. With a grant from the DGT the council has also produced a county tourist brochure and is planning to open a county tourist office on the motorway at Maçanet with the intent of trying to inform and capture some of the many holiday-makers who traverse the region. With limited resources, however, much of the council's role is that of a facilitator of rural tourism, offering advice to the rural councils, putting farmers in touch with specialists in the field and informing them about grants and other sources of financing.

Patronat Municipal de Turisme de Lloret de Mar

A mature mass destination, a product of the 1960s boosterism outlined in the introduction, Lloret de Mar lies at the opposite end of the resort life cycle to inland La Selva. These differences are reflected in the concerns and activities of the local tourist organisation, the Patronat Municipal de Turisme de Lloret de Mar. The patronat was established as a public–private sector partnership in the mid-1980s, replacing the municipal tourist office. However, the budget of 130 million pesetas (larger then that of the Patronat de Turisme Costa Brava Girona) continues to be derived solely from the city council with no private sector payments. Up until recently the patronat has concentrated on promotion, providing visitor information services and some signage. Faced with the stagnating conditions of the late 1980s–early 1990s (Fig. 7·2), conditions in which returns decreased more rapidly than visitor numbers as many hoteliers responded to competition by dropping prices further, the patronat became more interventionist and developed a new strategy termed Lloret Prestigi. The new strategy, introduced in 1992, emphasises quality, the defence of tourists as consumers and above all seeks to change attitudes away from that based solely on increasing numbers through lowering prices. Selected hotels with guarantees of quality and service are marketed under the Lloret Prestigi name. Begun as a local initiative, some financial assistance for this project was subsequently obtained from the national tourist office through grants from the Plan FUTURES (Pearce, 1997). By 1995 22 hotels from a total of more than 200 in Lloret de Mar were included in this programme. It should be recalled that the municipality itself has no direct control over quality, hotel classification being the responsibility of the DGT. Selected promotion of this type is thus one means of inducing improvements. Supporters of Lloret Prestigi are also aware of the need not to focus solely on accommodation. To this end the patronat is seeking to broaden the range of activities on offer in what has been a typical sol y playa (sun sand sea) resort and is actively intervening to

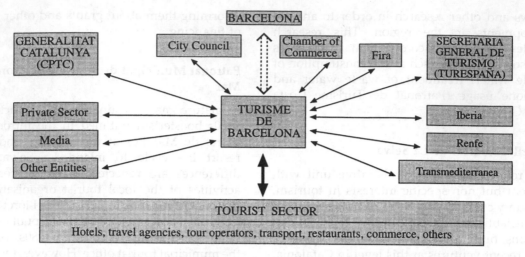

Figure 7·6. Model of Turisme de Barcelona's relationships. Source: after Fontana (1994).

organise day trips, for example to Barcelona and to inland areas. It is also supportive of the city council's efforts at urban regeneration and infrastructural improvements. Clearly the attitudes, images, practices and built environment developed over several decades will not be changed overnight, but at least a start has been made and an alternative model more adapted to the conditions of the 1990s and beyond has now been put forward.

Turisme de Barcelona

Recent changes in the organisation of tourism in Barcelona, Catalonia's capital and largest city, in large part reflect changing local circumstances resulting from the staging of the Olympic Games there in 1992 (Fontana, 1994). Turisme de Barcelona was set up as a consortium on 8 September 1993 by the city council and Chamber of Commerce in conjunction with the Foundation for the International Promotion of Barcelona. The new organisation replaced Barcelona's Patronat de Turisme, which was effectively an organ of the city council although it did have some private sector representatives on its board. The new consortium marked a formal bringing together of city council and Chamber of Commerce interests in tourism in a process which had begun in 1989 when the two bodies had jointly sponsored preparation of a Tourist Marketing Plan for Barcelona. Following the successful completion of the games, attention turned to

the implementation of the plan and identified the need to create a more dynamic and flexible tourist organisation in which city businesses, through the Chamber of Commerce, could play a more direct role. In this respect Barcelona's institutional restructuring to achieve this end contrasts with the absence of measures to implement the new Catalan strategies outlined above.

Clearly the holding of the Olympic Games added impetus and urgency to this process in Barcelona. On the one hand the city had invested heavily in major infrastructural improvements, facilities and urban redevelopment projects, especially on the waterfront. On the other hand, large sums had been spent by the private sector on new hotel construction, especially on four- and five-star hotels. The total number of hotel rooms in the city increased from 10,265 in 1990 to 13,352 in 1992, with a further 1500 rooms being added by the end of 1994. Over this period (1990–94) total room capacity increased by 44·5%, but room occupancy rates declined by 23·2% (Turisme de Barcelona, 1995). In this situation both the municipal authorities and the private sector wanted to capitalise on the international exposure which the games had brought to the city to sustain and increase visitor numbers. The Chamber of Commerce's interest is also tied to the nature of Barcelona's tourist traffic – almost half of all visitors to the city in 1994 were on business, 10% were attending fairs or congresses while vacationers constituted 31% (up from 23% in 1990). Turisme de Barcelona, however, portrays itself not just as a consortium of the city council and Chamber of Commerce, but also as an organisation having close links with other tourism bodies (Turespaña and the Catalonia Tourist Board) and a wide range of industry partners (Fig. 7·6).

The basic aims of Turisme de Barcelona are:

- to consolidate the tourism which the city already attracts;
- to attract new tourism; and
- to boost and make cost effective the commercial potential of Barcelona.

These aims are being pursued by implementing the different strategies contained in the tourist marketing plan, for example fostering short breaks, conferences and incentives, cultural tourism and educational visits. More explicit links are also being developed with other parts of the region, for example creating an image of Barcelona as the city associated with the major new theme park of Port Aventura, 110 km away. The consortium's two main activities are promotion and visitor servicing. The consortium had a budget in 1994 of almost 700 million pesetas, of which around two-thirds came from institutional contributions and about a third from self-generated revenue and other sources. This represents more than a doubling of the Patronat de Turisme's 1992 budget. It is too early yet to evaluate the impact of the new organisation, but the creation of Turisme de Barcelona would seem to mark an important step forward in a city where the role of tourism had previously been rather neglected.

CONCLUSIONS

In the decade and a half since autonomy was obtained, a new institutional framework for tourism in Catalonia has gradually emerged. One of the most explicit changes has been the creation of tourist organisations at the regional level, notably the Directorate General of Tourism and the Catalonia Tourist Board, and the subsequent development of regional policies and programmes, none of which existed in the Franco era. However, the strength and effectiveness of these should not be overestimated. The most significant of the Catalonia-wide activities

would appear to be that of promotion, an activity for which a specific organisation has been created, having a sub-regional membership. In other domains regional policies are yet to have a major impact. The call to diversify Catalonia's tourist product, for example, would appear to be moving rather slowly and little has been put in place to tackle the problems of the mature coastal strip. Much of the action still lies at the local level where interesting recent initiatives responding to local circumstances have been taken, for example in Lloret de Mar and Barcelona. Although some zonal tourist organisations have emerged in the field of promotion and marketing, relatively little horizontal interaction occurs and a strong functionally integrated network can scarcely be said to exist yet. Some vertical interaction occurs, especially in the field of promotion and marketing, but in other domains, such as development grants, the relationship is basically a dependent one. In contrast to trends in many other parts of the world the degree of public–private sector interaction is rather limited. Partnerships do exist in which both sectors are formally represented, but without joint funding the degree of commitment and effective input from the private sector is likely to remain restrained.

ACKNOWLEDGEMENTS

Research on which this paper is based was undertaken during a period of study leave from the University of Canterbury in 1995. Field work in Spain was supported by a grant from the Spanish Ministry of Education and Science whose assistance is gratefully acknowledged. Thanks go also to the host institution, the Department of Geography, Universitat Autònoma de Barcelona and particularly to Gerda Priestley, for her hospitality, advice, assistance and logistical support. The assistance of Jose Antonio Donaire in setting up several meetings is also acknowledged, together with that of the individuals interviewed at the tourist organisations examined. The maps and figures were drawn by Michelle Rogan in the Department of Geography, University of Canterbury.

REFERENCES

ACTT (1995), *La Catalunya Turística en Números 1994*, Barcelona: Agència Catalana de Tecnologia Turística.

Alegre i Selga, L. (1992), *Debat de Política Turística*, Barcelona: Departament de Comerç Consum i Turisme, Generalitat de Catalunya.

Anon (n.d.), *Denominaciones Geoturístiques*, Barcelona: Agència Catalana de Tecnologia Turística (mimeo).

Cals, J. (1974), *Turismo y Política Turística en España: una Aproximación*, Barcelona: Ariel.

Choy, D. (1993), Alternative roles of national tourism organizations. *Tourism Management*, **14**, 5, 357–365.

Departament de Comerç, Consum i Turisme (1992), *Reforçament de l'Avantage Competitiu del Sector Turístic a Catalunya*, Barcelona: Generalitat de Catalunya.

Departament de Comerç, Consum i Turisme (1995) *Memòria del Departament de Comerç, Consum i Turisme 1994*, Barcelona: Generalitat de Catalunya, Barcelona.

Elazar, D. J., Editor (1991), *Federal Systems of the World*, Harlow: Longman.

Fontana, P. (1994), Turisme de Barcelona: una nova etapa en la promoció turística de la ciutat, *Revista Barcelona Economia*, **21**, 9–14.

Jurdao, F. (1990) *España en Venta*, 2nd edn, Madrid: Endymion.

Miguelsanz, A., Editor. (1983), *Libre Blanc del Turisme a Catalunya, Generalitat de Catalunya*, Barcelona: Departament de la Presidència.

Morris, A., and Dickinson, G. (1987), Tourist development in Spain: growth versus conservation on the Costa Brava. *Geography*, **72**, 1, 16–25.

Patronat de Turisme Costa Brava Girona (1993), *Estudis Estadístics Informàtics de l'Index Ocupacional de la Costa Brava 1987-88-89-90-91-92*, Gerona: Patronat de Turisme Costa Brava Girona.

Pearce, D. G. (1992), *Tourist Organizations*, Harlow, Longman.

Pearce, D. G. (1996a), Federalism and the organization of tourism in Belgium, *European Urban and Regional Studies*, **3**, 3 189–204.

Pearce, D. G. (1996b), Tourist organizations in Sweden, *Tourism Management* 413–424.

Pearce, D. G. (1996c), Regional tourist organizations in Spain: emergence, policies and consequences, *Tourism Economics*, **2**, 2, 119–136.

Pearce, D. G. (1997), Tourism and the Autonomous Communities in Spain, *Annals of Tourism Research* **21**, 1, 156–177.

Priestley, G. (1995), Evolution of tourism on the Spanish coast, in Ashworth, G. J., and Dietvorst, A. G. J. (Editors), *Tourism and Spatial Transformations: Implications for Policy and Planning*, Wallingord: CAB International, 37–54.

Torres Bernier, E. (1985), La construcción de una política turística para Andalucía, *Información Comercial Española*, **619**, 109–117.

Turisme de Barcelona (1995), *Turisme de Barcelona Memòria 1994*, Barcelona: Turisme de Barcelona.

Environmental
Issues

Greenspeak: An Analysis of the Language of Eco-tourism

8

Graham M. S. Dann

ABSTRACT

One of the registers of the language of tourism is 'Greenspeak', a promotional discourse which focuses on the environment and the corresponding motivations of the new green tourist. Like the language of tourism itself, Greenspeak is also multi-layered. This chapter, while acknowledging that such a language is both pictorial and verbal, concentrates on the latter component. The first outer covering or surface layer sees the advertiser luring the eco-tourist through a series of captions or headlines, some of which are accompanied by brief explanatory messages. A perusal of a number of print media advertisements demonstrates an attempt to woo the client by contrasting the simplicity of the destination area with the complexities of an alienated urban existence in the consumer. Travel thus becomes a liberating escape with limitless possibilities. The second layer witnesses Greenspeak's attempt to associate itself with various principles of eco-tourism. At a covert level, however, the eco-explicitness of the message hides the agenda of the promoter, i.e. the exploitation of the periphery by the centre and the appropriation of rural patrimony by outsiders. The third layer shows how Greenspeak tries to convert the themes of conventional mass tourism ('sun', 'sea', 'sand' and 'sex') to those of eco-tourism ('nature', 'nostalgia' and 'nirvana'), the latter being separately examined with several examples. However, closer inspection reveals that 'nature', instead of being presented in its pristine form, is offered as a 'cooked' version of 'raw nature' – a cultural production of the 'natural'. Furthermore, the sexual imagery it seeks to replace is still present in a discourse of narcissism. Similarly, 'nostalgia' is based on a romantic socially constructed version of reality, one that is underpinned by eco-fundamentalism. Finally, 'nirvana', which is a Greenspeak substitute for 'paradise', completes the trilogy. Yet even here, blissful union with nature is largely a flattened and contrived experience.

INTRODUCTION

Increasingly there has been an emerging consensus among researchers (e.g. Boyer and Viallon, 1994; Dann, 1996; Febas Borra, 1978; Hollinshead, 1992; Moeran, 1983; Selwyn, 1993) that tourism has a language of its own. Furthermore, whatever the medium of communication (whether brochures, travelogues, guidebooks, videos, etc.), such a discourse is one of persuasion, or even social control, in which the goals of the promoter are merged with the attributed need satisfaction of the consumer. Therefore in order to disentangle these two components it is necessary to peel off the various layers of expedited messages, thereby exposing their connotative or ideological framework.

Once a linguistic paradigm for tourism is accepted, it follows that the type of language it employs will vary according to the object of promotion and the corresponding needs which it attempts to fulfil. One can therefore expect to encounter within the overall language of tourism a number of registers arising out of differences in topic and their related motivational appeal. One of these registers, and the focus of the current presentation, is 'Greenspeak' – the language of eco-tourism. It exists not only on account of its subject matter (the environment), but also through the myriad ways it addresses the associated 'green concerns' of its clients.

Stripping off the layers of this multi-faceted discourse via a series of readings and interpretations, one first comes across a surface layer. This comprises slogans and accompanying brief lure pieces through which Greenspeak tries to capture the attention of targeted groups. Second, by identifying with a number of eco-principles, Greenspeak sends several explicit messages to the receiver. Third, via a process of conversion, it seeks to transform the symbols of conventional mass tourism to those more closely associated with alternative environmental tourism.

Although Greenspeak is both a pictorial and verbal register, here only the latter is examined. Since its vocabulary is a social construction of reality operating at the level of myth, a content analysis of its messages should reveal more about the hidden agenda of tour operators than the places they seek to promote.

THE FIRST LAYER OF GREENSPEAK: CAPTURE THROUGH CAPTIONS

A random perusal of a number of advertising headlines taken from Britain's Independent on Sunday (1994) includes such captions as:

> English Country Cottages, Specialist Greece, Simply Ionian, Simply Crete, Individual Traveller's Spain, Simply Turkey and Hello Italy.

It also features the following slogans:

> Encounter Overland – Discover the Real Africa. Casas Cantabricas – Escape to the Green North of Spain. High Places – Not One of the Crowd, 100 Treks, Walks and Climbs. Vacanze in Italia – The Art of Living in Tuscany. Sherpa Expeditions – Walking Holidays Worldwide.

The first point to emerge from this brief, though typical, listing is the designation of the destination as 'simple'. Here an unstated contrast is made between the complexities of urban existence (attributed to the target audience) and the bucolic, pristine and uncomplicated life of the vacation area. One can 'simply' convert the

former into the latter by taking a 'simple' holiday to a 'simple' place inhabited by 'simple' people (Cazes, 1976; Tresse, 1990).

Second, the liberating act of travel is described as one of 'escape' – 'Escape to the Green North of Spain', for example. Not only is a familiar motivational appeal established by supplying a getaway *from* the alienating forces of postmodernity, but an escape route is also provided. Additionally, the potential traveller can escape *from* the environmentally degraded Costas of Spanish mass tourism by escaping *to* an unspoiled Cantabrica Verde. The standardised package hotel is also exchanged for a more intimate 'casa' or home. In escaping, the tourist replaces a normal state of homelessness by returning to a true home.

Third, by replacing a mere house with a 'home', the tourist is afforded the opportunity for 'real living', as for example in a little Tuscan farmhouse where such living is described as an 'art'. No longer is life a tedious nine to five daily grind. Rather, it is a sophisticated existence, something cultural and refined, analogous to the possession of an oil painting where status is conferred on the owner (Berger, 1983). Consequently, the tourist can also identify with the image of a little cottage in Tuscany.

Fourth, the escape *to* the simple life, the green green grass of a new 'home', and the gentle art of living, collectively emphasise the need to *distance oneself from others* – the golden hordes of mass tourism (Turner and Ash, 1975). Hence the slogan for High Places stresses that the eco-tourist is no longer one of a rabble. Instead, a person who engages in trekking, walking and climbing, somehow ascends from the multitude, and in the process becomes transfigured into a divine-like being.

Fifth, in the act of locating the individual far from the madding crowd, the whole world is preserved as an infinite domain with limitless possibilities. Thus Sherpa Expeditions are 'worldwide'. The trail into the unknown is portrayed as an active journey undertaken by a genuine traveller, as a counterpoint to a trip to a fixed destination which is passively experienced by the stationary tourist (Fussell, 1979).

Sixth, this odyssey becomes analogous to a pilgrimage with the realisation that it is a voyage of discovery and a quest for the authentic. One can therefore 'Discover the *Real* Africa'. At the same time, by encountering the Other, one also discovers onself.

Some of the other offerings of the Independent (1994) are more detailed. Thus, for example, the advertisement for 'Vacances en Campagne' is accompanied by the following body copy:

> We have a feeling for France. The Loire Valley is a land of infinite variety. Fields of golden corn contrast with cool green woodlands. And everywhere, there are vines of noble pedigree. Our simple stone cottage is set beside a lake with glorious views ... What better holiday base from which to find a true feeling for France.

Here, several of the foregoing themes are presented in a single message. There is a 'land of infinite variety', 'simplicity' and a 'true feeling for France', all of which are intimately transferred from the tour operator to the client. Our feeling becomes your experience of authenticity. Our cottage too can be your home. There are no other people – just you, the fields, the lake and the *cool green* woodlands. The juxtaposition of the italicised epithets indicates that being 'green' is to be 'cool' or trendy, someone discerning, not one of the ignorant undifferentiated masses.

An excerpt from an advertisement featuring Laskarina Holidays reads as follows:

> Which unspoilt Greek island?
> Lipsi. Sandy coves, gentle hills and far from the madding crowds. Skyros. The wilder shores of Greece. Unspoilt. Remote. Lovely. Tilos. Remote, tranquil, serene beauty. Where time stands still.

Now, with Greece connoted as the whole planet Earth, there are limitless possibilities. This is an unspoilt world where the knowledgeable tourist is spoilt for choice. Again, there is a distancing into remoteness and separation from the common herd. On this occasion, however, the experience is not only out-of-place, it is also out-of-time. Unlike the ubiquitous pressure of the clock in the tourist generating environment, here time 'stands still' as in eternity. The bliss ('lovely', 'tranquil', 'serene') is heavenly (Greece as home of the gods), as one eternal Olympic moment in the present.

Finally, the eco-tourist is wooed by the prestigious programme of Earthwatch:

> Give two weeks to save the earth.
> Excavate Mexican mammoths.

> Aid sea turtles of Bahia, Brazil.
> Assist Kew botanists in the Cameroon.
> Study Pacific Ring of fire volcanoes, New Zealand.

Here the eco-tourist is called upon to make the supreme sacrifice – the surrendering of self via the paid participation in environmental projects. One now *gives* to an illustrious environmental organisation in order to *save* the Earth. Touristic salvation is wrought, not by faith alone (learning about nature), but by good works (aiding, assisting, excavating). Interestingly, the mammoth mining in Mexico can be interpreted as a digging into the past in order to come to terms with the present.

THE HIDDEN AGENDA OF FIRST LAYER MESSAGES

From the foregoing slogans and accompanying brief commentaries, we have already reached the point where a hidden agenda is discernible and the aims of the operator begin to poke out of the captions designed to attract the attention of the eco-tourist. Such an infiltration of the message is hardly surprising when one appreciates that the profit motive of the tour company lies behind a Greenspeak, which, ostensibly and through promotion, seeks to match the needs of the consumer with a supposedly ever-abundant supply of green destinations. However, this hidden agenda becomes more evident when the messages are exposed to a further reading. Thus, while agreeing with Nöth (1990, p. 479) that publicity rarely refers to its own vested financial interests, preferring instead to promote enjoyment of the product, we nevertheless may be able to discern covert or indirect instances of the former.

For instance, we earlier noted a series of advertisements which sold the idea of a limitless planet ripe for worldwide expeditions and adventure. Implied in this discourse was the suggestion that the further one travels, and the more remote the location – the more enjoyable the experience. However, apart from the obvious inference that greater distances signify more expense for the consumer (and hence higher profits for the producer), there is another much more significant issue, namely: who proclaims such an unbounded universe, and where exactly is it to be found?

A closer inspection of the allied publicity material reveals that, for the most part, such definitions emanate from the centre (First World tour companies) and that they mainly refer to the periphery (Third World countries). Moreover, in spite of the evident ecological reality that the world has very finite natural resources, the message, apparently unaware of its self-contradiction, indicates that somehow such resources are still abundant in those societies waiting to be discovered. Johnston (1990, p. 2) puts her finger on the anomaly by way of a rhetorical question when she asks 'Can tourism, an industry that inherently creates dependency relationships, truly be tailored in a socially responsible and environmentally viable fashion?' English (1986, p. 48) makes a parallel observation when he notes that 'North–South tourism injects the behaviour of a wasteful society in the midst of a society of want'.

The same sort of promotional strategy seems to be employed whenever a whole continent is defined as ready for exploration, e.g. 'Discover the Real Africa', regardless of the many individual nation states which comprise that land mass, and in spite of the realisation that these various territories face very different environmental problems. Daltabuit and Pi-Sunyer (1990, pp. 10–11) refer to this process as one of appropriation, wherein societies deliberately defined as undifferentiated become re-defined as global patrimony, and where the environment is taken over by outsiders chiefly to satisfy their own needs. Seen in this light, the environment becomes a fantasy commodity for post-modern seekers of authenticity, in which there is often a greater concern shown towards trees than for indigenous peoples.

THE SECOND LAYER OF GREENSPEAK: ECO-EXPLICIT MESSAGES

So far we have examined a number of captions, slogans and other brief advertising messages in order to highlight their relationship to the environment, and how these in turn may be understood in terms of the receiver (motivational appeal) and sender (ideology). However, none of these expressions has been sufficiently explicit as

to provide direct links between tourism and the principles of sustainable development (Bramwell and Lane, 1993, p. 2). This section analyses some examples where such a connection is made. In so doing, it moves from the stage of initial capturing of attention (first layer) to that of maximising green appeal in the client (second layer).

The first principle of eco-tourism is that it should be *sustainable*. In other words, for natural attractions to endure essential ecological processes must be *preserved*. Thus in a recent publicity pamphlet on Poland (Polish Tourist Information Center, n.d., p. 18) one is told, for example, that:

> The Białowieza Wilderness is the largest single forest complex in the Central European plain. A portion of this wilderness has been *set aside* as the *Białowieza National Park*. The conditions inside are primeval: virgin backwoods, marshes, swamps and ranges. Moose is also prevalent here (emphasis added).

Here a portion of the wilderness has been 'set aside' in the form of a 'national park'. The discourse implies that, had this step not been taken, the virgin backwoods, marshes and swamps contained therein would somehow have been violated. Moreover, the gentle free ranging moose, without protection, would otherwise, via the hunter's gun, have made its way on to the already ample game menus of fashionable restaurants in Warsaw and Krakow. The imagery is both sexual and moralistic. The honour associated with preserving virginity is metaphorically linked to an untamed, soft, dark and liquid feminine interior of innocent primeval delights, and ultimately with the national duty of protecting the environment from (male) assault.

The second principle of eco-tourism states that *the environment should be preserved for future generations*. Thus, in the brochure promoting the Alpes d'Azur (Comité Régional du Tourisme Riviera – Côte d'Azur, n.d., pp. 5–6), visitors are informed about Le Parc National du Mercantour and its 'verdure à l'état pur ... où prospèrent en liberté une flora et une faune remarquables'. However, the connection between greenness and natural freedom is deemed to be insufficiently explicit since the script writer feels the obligation to spell out the very concept of a national park, as follows:

Un Parc National est un espace exceptionnel; crée quand un ensemble écologique paysages – flora – faune représente à l'échelle d'un pays un véritable patrimoine-nature. A préserver à tout prix, pour notre bien-être et celui des générations futures.

Here the National Park is treated with utmost reverence. Capital letters are assigned to the expression. It is said to be a very special place linked to the divine act of creation. Furthermore, this patrimony of nature bestowed upon a country calls forth a corresponding patriotic duty in its citizens to preserve it at all costs, since it is on natural heritage that quality of life ultimately depends, both now and in the years ahead.

The third principle of sustainable tourism relates to *the maintenance of bio-diversity*. Hence, instead of depleting natural resources to the point of exhaustion and irreplacement, touristic diversification of natural attractions can help spread the ecological load, just as diversification in agriculture can represent a viable alternative to reliance on a mono-crop. Seen in this light, Greenspeak becomes a language of choice promoting individual alternatives to the enclave ghetto of the mass tourism resort. Thus Crawshaw (1994) refers to pigeonniers, windmills, barns, gypsy caravans and even lighthouses as suitable alternative locales for tourist accommodation. Similarly, Max von Sydow (1990, p. 1), in his testimonial introduction to the Swedish Tourist Board's pamphlet, extends freedom of choice to environmentally friendly touristic activities, as follows:

It is in the Swedish countryside that I find rest and refreshment for body and soul. The country covers such a vast area that you will have no problem in finding plenty of wide open spaces. Sweden has Europe's largest and most accessible wilderness; forests to wander in; mountains to climb; lakes and rivers in which to swim or fish; and long coastlines with spectacular archipelagos to explore by boat.

The fourth principle of sustainable eco-tourism is that of *holistic planning and implementation*. In this connection, one finds an eco-explicit reference to the Hawaiian Mauna Lari resort (Islands, 1990) in the following advertisement:

AIR. Take a deep breath. And look around. It can't get much better. Completely master-planned well into the 21st century for environmental integrity.

On this occasion it is an international hotel chain that has taken the environmental initiative. In its Greenspeak, the company addresses the urban smog-filled client in terms of the simple quest for fresh air. No longer are there references to artificial air conditioning in every room – once the hallmark of a mass tourism five-star hotel. Instead, a careful appointing of the establishment maximises the forces of natural sunshine and sea-borne breezes. All site positioning has been holistically 'master planned' 'for environmental integrity' now and in the future.

Fifthly, there is the principle of *carrying capacity* which requires limits to touristic development in order to ensure quality experiences for both host and guest. Thus, in 'Simply Caribbean' (1989), where the merits of various islands are extolled in terms of the happiness they provide, one reads the following eco-explicit extract:

Nature gave Bermuda one of the kindest climates imaginable, and the *Bermudans have so controlled the growth of tourism* as to leave their island unspoilt and charming (emphasis added).

Here the accent is on 'control' and the fact that, unlike many territories in the Caribbean where growth at all costs seems to be the only tourism policy in operation, the inhabitants of Bermuda have apparently taken a conscious decision to opt for quality over quantity, even though such a preference might yield lower rates of return in terms of foreign exchange. Furthermore, the effect of this deliberate choice is said to be beneficial to the natural environment. However, implied in this line of argument is also the point made by McElroy and de Albuquerque (1993): controls aimed at enhancing the environment do not necessarily result in decreased earnings, since higher spending (quality) tourists tend to be attracted to quality destinations.

Interestingly, this is also the first time we have encountered a direct reference to *decision-taking by local residents*, the final and arguably the most important principle of sustainable tourism (de Kadt, 1992). What is even more interesting is the fact that such participatory democracy has been articulated in Greenspeak, at least in its eco-explicit second-layer messages.

THE HIDDEN AGENDA OF ECO-EXPLICIT MESSAGES

Since Greenspeak is a form of advertising, even when it explicitly addresses environmental matters, it still does so in terms of the attributed needs of the client. At the same time, underpinning the overt messages are the latent interests of the operator.

Thus, when Greenspeak refers to special wilderness areas being *set aside* (as in the case of Białowieza, for instance), or to the designation of a region as a 'national park' (e.g. Mercantour), in order to detect the covert message one has to ask exactly who is responsible for such environmental labelling. The language of publicity deliberately avoids this issue by employing the passive voice. Yet Tovey (1993) reckons that rural areas are appropriated by urban dwellers, and that tourism interests on behalf of the latter define 'rural' as 'nature' in a language of appropriation. An ideological conflict therefore arises between the official conservation movement of the urban middle class and an alternative environmentalism of the local rural community. Needless to say, reference to such a tension is significantly omitted in promotional material.

Another characteristic that was observed in passing is the proclivity of Greenspeak to address its customers as if they were exclusively male. The adventurer, the explorer, the mountain climber, the trekker – is generally assumed to be a man, and, the object of his quest – discovery and conquest – is usually referred to in feminine terms. The male is active. The female is passive and supine.

Yet why should this sexist bias be introduced in relation to the environment, and why do the voices of women go largely unheard? According to the Women and Development Unit of the University of the West Indies (1994), the answer to these questions resides in the fact that women experience environmental degradation to a greater extent than men, especially in developing countries. There women must find the food, fuel and water to meet the survival needs of their families. In the Third World, women are expected to care for the sick whose illness has resulted from environmental pollution, and, as bearers of children, they pass on the effects of such pollution to the next generation. Greenspeak neatly sidesteps this issue since it is quite at odds with the ideology of its (First World) operator dominated goals. Consequently it omits it in favour of a discourse which asymmetrically targets the male money earner.

However, the question of empowerment of destination people goes beyond considerations of gender, since in some cases (Bermuda, for instance) decision-taking is said to reside with locals, who are portrayed as having no problem in imposing limits on the growth of the tourism industry. Here the operator seemingly endorses this form of participatory democracy and apparently sides with the environmentally sound preference for quality over quantity.

Yet the authors of Greenspeak make no mention of the conflict experienced by Third World people, who, in opting for reduced numbers of visitors, may well see a diminution in their standard of living. Nor do they refer to the virtual impossibility of placing limits on carrying capacity, since they well know that Bermuda's arrivals (along with those for similar destinations) will soon rise again. They are also sure that no political directorate in a developing country devoid of realistic economic alternatives to tourism is going to risk its own power base by suicidally placing environmental issues before the basic needs of food and shelter. Similarly, a discourse which stresses preservation for future generations has little or no place in the thinking of dependent micro-states where today looms far larger than tomorrow, and where short-term considerations outweigh any long-term vision. The hidden agenda of Greenspeak is fully aware of this scenario, but obviously cannot transmit such a message to its receivers. It therefore addresses the topic in environmentally friendly terms, knowing for certain that any limits to growth will be imposed by the tourists themselves. They will be the ones who will bring about a reduction in the number of arrivals, and all that will be necessary then will be the provision of alternative destinations accompanied by the same rhetoric. Plog (1994, p. 45) sums up the situation well when he observes:

> Just when everything seemed so rosy to local travel providers – uninterrupted growth

had been going on for years – tourists begin casting votes on the changes in the only manner they know how – with their feet. They gradually select other places to visit, as the word spreads year after year. They do not like what they see now when they visit. The destination has lost its charm written about in travel brochures and tourism books. Crowds of people have replaced once deserted streets, the 'natives' no longer seem as friendly and relaxed, and the environment shows obvious signs of abuse and misuse. In short, it is not as nice as it used to be, so why not go somewhere else?

This last point emphasises another previously noted quality of Greenspeak – that it is a discourse of *choice* – whether it is talking about a variety of destinations or types of accommodation. The accent is on alternatives, and 'alternative tourism' (AT) is promoted as being more eco-friendly than conventional mass tourism (CMT).

However, as Butler (1992) has recently noted, AT may turn out to be more socially and culturally disruptive than CMT. While villages and environmentally sensitive areas are invaded by ever increasing numbers of eco-tourists, the traditional luxury enclave resort at least had the merit of spatially restricting its clients. Moreover, initially AT might be subject to local control and provide financial benefits in small communities. Yet, once these alternative areas are 'discovered' and the good news of Greenspeak is spread, such rewards accrue to the operator rather than the visited. Thus the choice offered is a pseudo choice since it is predicated on limitlessness and abundance in a world that is finite and ever-decreasing in size and distance.

THE THIRD LAYER OF GREENSPEAK: CONVERTING THEMES

After capturing the attention of the eco-tourist through first-layer captions, and after the enticement stage of second-layer eco-explicit messages, there remains a third layer of discourse through which the traditional themes of mass tourism ('sun', 'sand', 'sea' and 'sex') are converted by Greenspeak into the new themes of environmental tourism ('nature', 'nostalgia' and

'nirvana'). This final strategy, like the other two, also contains a hidden agenda.

Nature

The following examples provide typical instances of the use of 'nature' as a lure to travel:

(a) Discover Dominica. Nature island of the Caribbean. The Caribbean the way it used to be ... unspoilt ... undisturbed ... natural. (Division of Tourism, National Development Corporation of Dominica, 1993)

(b) I ♡ NY. Discover beautiful leaves as far as the eye can see, pick apples fresh from the tree or help us make wine at one of our annual grape festivals. (New York magazine, 1989)

(c) Everybody enjoys our natural beauty. So discover the unspoilt beauty of Austria's lush green pastures against the backdrop of stunning mountains and crystal clear lakes. There's always a warm welcome whether you're looking for tranquillity or adventure. (Sunday Times magazine, 1991)

In two of the advertisements – (a) and (c) – the words 'nature' or 'natural' are employed. The first of these requires an act of discovery, not so much in order to find a new country, but rather a new life, in the same sort of way that upper-middle class conservationists were once attracted to 'Hawaii naturally' and 'California naturally' (Thurot, 1989). At the same time, the advertisement calls for an act of rejection of nearby competitors, since Dominica, unlike many other unmentioned islands in the Caribbean which have opted for mass tourism, is still at the first stage of the resort cycle (Butler, 1980). Dominica is thus *comparatively* unspoilt (by high rise hotels, chain restaurants, polluted waters, etc.), and *relatively* undisturbed (by wide-bodied jet aircraft, tourist buses, noise and other symbols of metropolitan urban existence). It is 'natural' – true to itself, pure and unaffected. As a 'nature' island, Dominica supplies all that nature itself offers (mountains, streams, lakes and volcanoes) – a tourism that is environmentally friendly.

In the Austrian advertisement (c), 'nature' has been replaced by the 'natural'. Its new referent is 'beauty', a quality which is extended outwards to include lush *green* pastures, stunning mountains and crystal clear lakes. The eco-alternatives on offer are passive (isolation, contemplation, tranquillity) or active (mountain climbing, adventure, camaraderie).

In (b), the symbolism of the logo 'I ♡ NY' is clearly meant to stretch beyond the confines of New York City to the rural bliss of New York State. Moreover, the message in New York magazine is targeted at the urban dweller, someone who is apparently unaccustomed to seeing leaves, picking apples or treading grapes. The New Yorker lives an entirely artificial existence where wine and apple pie are supplied by the supermarket. Yet apple pie is a symbol of Americanness, something which requires discovery and re-discovery. By going back to 'nature' and actually picking real apples from a tree, the New Yorker can enjoy a national roots experience.

Nostalgia

Underpinning the discovery of unspoilt nature is the notion that there are few remaining *places* where this can be found and that their attraction resides precisely in the realisation that they constitute the *last* of their kind (MacCannell, 1976, p. 88). Furthermore, since many post-modern tourist generating societies are environmentally degraded, the search for the pristine necessarily involves a step *back in time*. The attempt to capture this bygone era is a nostalgic quest.

Here are some examples in which Greenspeak hankers after the golden age of yesteryear:

(a) Gozo is a world of its own. A place to take a breather from the hectic world of today ... Even the Gozitans, the friendliest of people, sometimes feel that they could do with a little less 'tomorrow'. Gozo, they feel, should stay as it was or as it is now. Up to the present time and even today work has to be done with the hoe and scythe and donkey cart ... Even more astonishing is the result of that hard work: the visitor to Gozo finds many more green fields and flowering plants and wild flowers than he does in Malta. (Malta National Tourist Office, 1988)

(b) Chiloe ... is like stepping back in time. The quaint fishing town Anend ... appears much like a New England

fishing town must have looked a century ago. Colorful wood-shingled houses are scattered on the hills overlooking the bay, while German-style church steeples ... stand out above the roof tops. Horse-drawn carts transport goods from one side of the town to the other, and the fish market and docks are quaint. (South American, Eastern's Easy Tour Guide, 1983)

(c) The Algarve ... Foothills dotted with orange groves, almond trees and small farming communities run down from the mountains to the sea ... Atlantic breakers crashing against rocky headlands, long stretches of sandy beaches, sheltered coves and picturesque fishing villages ... small white houses and tiled churches, the countryside, the wine and the atmosphere is very special. (Cosmos Travel, 1983/4)

In the first advertisement – (a) – the promoter preys upon the anxiety of potential clients who are treated as being unable to come to terms with the rapid pace of change in a post-industrial era. Living in a 'risk society' (of Chernobyl, oil spills, toxic waste and other human-generated disasters), and ever fearful of the future, they experience the need to return to the warmth and safety of the 'good old days' (Mol and Spaargaren, 1993). Gozo provides such an opportunity since its inhabitants have apparently resolved the trauma associated with 'tomorrow' by continuing to live in the past. Gozo is also favourably contrasted with its parent island – Malta – as a haven and a breathing space, where, above all, the people are friendly. Just as the Gozitans can enjoy the fruits of their labour, so too the tourist need not experience guilt in relaxing after equally hard work. The natural happy environment provides just the right milieu for that well-earned rest.

Chiloe, located off the Chilean coast, is said to be *like* stepping back in time rather than a literal experience. As an island, it can physically and psychologically distance itself from the frenetic mainland. Chiloe is described as 'quaint'; even the docks are 'quaint.' North American visitors, the target of the airline's publicity, are asked to imagine Chiloe as a New England fishing town a century ago, complete with horse-drawn carts and Bavarian churches. The introduction of 'old time religion' as a contrast to metropolitan secularisation completes the circle of nostalgia.

Finally, in the Algarve, there is no direct reference to time. Yet the 'atmosphere' stands as a surrogate for the timelessness associated with nature (fruit, farming and fishing). Part of this nostalgic mood relies on smallness – the idea of the little community and tiny white (pure) houses. As with Chiloe, religion is brought into play. On this occasion, however, wine is added to the equation, a symbol not only of the sacred, but also of the good life made wholesome by nature. Another Christian symbol – the 'fish' – is introduced with reference to picturesque fishing villages.

Nirvana

The connection between nature and nostalgia and the ways in which they tend to feed off each other in Greenspeak become completed with the emergence of a third analytic category in the trilogy – that of nirvana. In spite of the fact that this term is rarely encountered in travel advertising, its oblique referencing seems somehow richer in imagery than the flattened 'paradise' theme of mass tourism (Cohen, 1982) which it seeks to supplant. Although 'nirvana' is a Buddhist concept, its acceptance into English as signifying a state of beatitude, a dissolving of the individual and one-ness with nature, makes it quite appropriate for the promotion of eco-tourism. Here are some examples of nirvana in tourism publicity:

(a) Katherine Gorge isn't a gorge at all. It's thirteen gorges separated by rapids. Fish jump. Birds sing. Silence reigns. It's heaven. (Northern Territory Tourist Commission, 1993)

(b) The Grenadines – The few islanders are fishermen or simple farmers, living in close friendly communities, hardly realising that God has given them possibly the most beautiful islands on earth. (Simply Caribbean, 1989)

(c) Kona Village – Somehow, in that remote emerald cove, dotted with thatched hales lulled by tranquil lagoons, the diversions of civilization no longer seemed to matter. For this was the Hawaii I thought was lost for ever. As I looked for my lanai, there was nothing but a stretch of sand between me and the turquoise sea. Following the curve of the bay to my own private beach, I was completely alone in the world. Perhaps it was the seclusion of the place. Perhaps it was the absence of all pressures, or the attentions of people who had my happiness at heart. But gradually I felt myself returning to a time when man was at one with the universe. (Islands, 1989)

The first case is a remote and desolate place in the outback of Australia's Northern Territory. Katherine Gorge is a wilderness with complete absence of persons. Here there are only fish and birds, and, even though the latter sing, there is said to be silence.

In the Grenadines there is no reference to heaven as such. Nevertheless, the inhabitants are portrayed as leading simple blissful lives in close friendly communities amid the most beautiful surroundings on earth. So complete is their lack of sophistication that they are reckoned to overlook the obvious fact that all this contentment is God-given. Tourists naturally know better.

Finally, in Hawaii, there is again an absence of people, as the tourist, by way of testimonial, finds in the remote emerald cove the perfect opportunity for self-discovery. Here 'nature' (the cove, the lagoons, the sea) is linked with 'nostalgia' ('returning to a time', 'this was the Hawaii I thought was lost'), and ultimately to 'nirvana' (absence of diversion and pressure) – being at one with the universe.

THE HIDDEN AGENDA OF CONVERTING THEMES

Williamson (1983, pp. 103–137) observes that in advertising very rarely is *nature in the raw* offered to the client. Rather, it is a *cooked version of nature* which is presented, one worked over by science and culture to yield 'the natural'.

Extending her argument to travel promotion, one can easily see the disadvantages of including the raw nature elements of exotic tropical destinations (torrential rain, hurricanes, cockroaches, poisonous snakes, etc). For this reason such unpleasant elements are omitted and nature instead is presented as an abstract description of an island. As the nature island of the Caribbean, Dominica becomes natural.

In the Austrian advertisement, nature has been similarly 'hollowed out' and replaced by the natural. Barthes (1984, p. 74), in an often quoted essay on the Blue Guide, refers to such language as 'myth'. There, as here, it is the old Alpine myth of Helvetico–Protestant morality which is being exploited, a Puritanism which encourages a cult of nature, a morality based on effort and solitude, a rejuvenation through pure air, the imbibing of moral ideas at the sight of mountain tops, the portrayal of summit climbing as a virtue, and an exclusive focus on a world dominated by mountains, plains, gorges and torrents. According to Barthes (1984, pp. 109–110, pp. 124–125), anything can be a myth provided it is conveyed by discourse. Myth is a type of speech chosen by history, a metalanguage with its own imperatives in which the natural replaces history. Dufour (1978) adds that all leisure activity is couched in myth, beginning with Mother Earth and extending to the Fountain of Youth, Horn of Plenty, and so on. Seen in this light, Greenspeak is also a vehicle of myth. In relation to Austria, the promoter can now tell the client without fear of contradiction that 'everybody enjoys our natural beauty.' You too should enjoy the natural. To do otherwise would be quite unnatural and somehow deviant.

In the New York advertisement, the moral duty of pursuing the natural becomes an affair of the heart. In being placed at one with simple bucolic delights, New Yorkers are told to love their home state. 'I love New York' feeds off the old narcissistic theme of mass tourism. By loving myself, I love my natural peripheral surroundings. The latter, in turn, are equated with a rural environment, appropriated by outsiders and defined as natural for urban consumption.

The ideological component of *nostalgia* becomes evident in its identification with eco-fundamentalism and with the concomitant realisation that 'tourism as the nostalgia industry of the future' represents enormous possibilities for commercial exploitation (Dann, 1994).

Thus in Gozo, greenness is associated with agrarian societies. In an idyllic 'first wave' setting, the eco-theologue nostalgically defines

consumption as sinful and the devil is represented by technology (Toffler, 1990, pp. 369–373). The Protestant work ethic is upheld by an unstated reference to the familiar words of Genesis 'in the sweat of thy brow thou shalt eat bread'. The tourist can identify with the Gozitans who obey this biblical injunction, and, in so doing, experience the friendliness of the Other. Nature is thus extended in the Gozo advertisement in order to include people whose lifestyles are made to correspond with a yearning for simplicity in the tourist. As MacCannell (1976, p. 82) appropriately observes:

> Modern society, only partly disengaged from industrial structures, is especially vulnerable to overthrow from within through nostalgia, sentimentality and other tendencies to regress to a previous state, a 'golden age' which retrospectively always appears to have been more orderly and normal.

In Chiloe, the moral tone is rendered more explicit with the introduction of religion. The German-style church steeples are referred to as belonging to another era, albeit one in which the Reformers ensured that signs of predestination were sought through hard work (horse-drawn carts, fishing, the docks).

Finally, in the Algarve, the religious symbols of wine and fish connote an identification with the early Christian community and its accent on caring and sharing. There is no reference to the packed beaches and resort enclaves of the other more profane and polluted Algarve coast where time-sharing rather than timelessness is the norm. The conversion from the sinful hedonism of 'sea', 'sun', 'sand' and 'sex' is thus seemingly accomplished. Instant gratification of the present has apparently yielded to a selective and easy paced reminiscence of all that is morally good from the past.

However, and in spite of the high sounding rhetoric, the underlying *romanticism* of nostalgia prevails. Deep down, surely the tourist knows that there are pleasures to be had in Gozo (where the flowers are wild). In the Algarve there is a similar sexual innuendo associated with mountains, Atlantic breakers and rocky headlands, while in Chiloe all is simile and fantasy.

Under *nirvana* there is an attempt to replace the unbridled hedonism of an earthly paradise with the more sublime beatitude of oneness with nature. Yet in many senses it is an attempt which fails to live up to its promises.

In Katherine Gorge, for example, 'heaven' is described in terms of a total absence of people. There is no mention of tour guides, those associated with 'transporting' the tourist to the remote place, or even of fellow passengers. In fact, this wilderness seems to approximate destinations like Melanesia which are deliberately promoted as a 'green hell' (Cohen, 1982, p. 14), or adventure trips up the Amazon (A. E. Travel Corporation, 1990) which emphasise pain and travail. Yet the operator is fully aware that much money can be made from the adventure dimension of eco-tourism, the other side of paradise.

In Hawaii, too, there are at first sight no local people to disturb the experience of union with nature. And yet, amid the loneliness of it all, there are still sexual references to the 'curve of the bay', to '*man* being at one with the universe' and the 'attentions of people who had my happiness at heart'. Even in the secluded cove, it would appear, nirvana finds difficulty in replacing paradise.

And when one reaches the Grenadines, it is now no longer possible to exclude the friendly natives. However, on this occasion the advertiser makes them a collective object of envy. In desiring the happiness and abandonment of these simple folk, tourists are offered the chance to change places with them – to achieve beatitude by appropriating paradise from the Other.

CONCLUSION

Silverstein (1991) quotes a director of Thomson Holidays as saying that 75% of vacationers today choose their holidays 'with environmental concerns in mind', and that 'unless tour operators respond to the demands of the green tourist, they are going to be left behind.'

Another commentator makes a related observation when she refers to tourism *capitalizing* on 'the media fix on the earth crisis.'

According to Johnston (1990, p. 2):

> Environmentalism has apparently moved beyond doomsday prophesying to promoting a quick fix that promises social justice and a healthy environment. 'Sustainable development' appears to be that fix.

Moreover, she adds:

> Decisions prove to meet the interests of the tourism industry first and a resident society second.

This presentation has attempted to show that, ever aware of the potential and actual demand for eco-tourism, operators have sought to maximise their profits from this up-market source. Through a promotional discourse dubbed as 'Greenspeak', they have built upon or created such a demand, while concealing their own material goals from the client. Via this multi-layered language they have managed to capture and convert the consumer from a low-spending mass tourist to a high-spending green tourist.

Yet, in spite of their employing a seemingly environmentally friendly vocabulary, it has been seen that much of this promotional hype simply reinforces the old myths of paradise and unspoiled nature:

> of idyllic settings, friendly people, great food and fabulous accommodations [which] can lull even local planners to sleep. (Plog, 1994, p. 43)

With touristic utopia being defined as unending economic growth and limitless consumption of goods and services, we may soon reach the stage where eco-tourists will spend most of their time trying 'to lose the binocular-draped hordes of *other* eco-tourists' (Shnayerson, 1993, p. 64).

ACKNOWLEDGEMENT

Gratitude is expressed to Virginia Potter and Paul Wilkinson for respectively supplying material from The Independent and Globe & Mail.

REFERENCES

A. E. Travel Corporation (1990), Safaris for beginners, *International Travel News*, April, 17.

Barthes, R. (1984), *Mythologies*, London: Paladin.

Berger, J. (1983), *Ways of Seeing*, London: BBC and Penguin.

Boyer, M. and Viallon, P. (1994), *La Communication Touristique*, Paris: Presses Universitaires de France.

Bramwell, B. and Lane, B. (1993), Sustainable tourism: an evolving global approach, *Journal of Sustainable Tourism*, **1** (1), 1–5.

Butler, R. (1980), The concept of a tourism area cycle of evolution: implications for the management of resources, *Canadian Geographer*, **24**, 5–12.

Butler, R. (1992), Alternative tourism: the thin edge of the wedge, in V. Smith, and W. Eadington (Editors), *Tourism Alternatives. Potentials and Problems in the Development of Tourism*, Philadelphia, PA: University of Pennsylvania Press, 31–46.

Cazes, G. (1976), Le Tiers-Monde vu par les publicités touristiques: une image géographique mystifiante, *Cahiers du Tourisme*, série C, no. 33.

Cohen, E. (1982), The Pacific islands from utopian myth to consumer product: the disenchantment of paradise, *Cahiers du Tourisme*, série B, no. 27.

Comité Régional du Tourisme Riviera – Côte d'Azur (n.d.), *Alpes d'Azur. Mille sommets pour une star*. Nice: Comité Régional du Tourisme Riviera: Côte d'Azur.

Cosmos Travel (1983/4), *Cosmos Winter Sun 1983/4*. Algarve advertisement, 86.

Crawshaw, J. (1994), Make the choice your own. *The Independent on Sunday*, January 2, 43–49.

Daltabuit, M. and Pi-Sunyer, O. (1990), Tourism development in Quintana Roo, Mexico. *Cultural Survival Quarterly*, **14** (1), 9–13.

Dann, G. (1994), Tourism: the nostalgia industry of the future, in W. Theobald (Editor) *Global Tourism. The Next Decade*, London: Butterworth-Heinemann, 55–67.

Dann, G. (1996), *The Language of Tourism*, Wallingford: CAB International.

de Kadt, E. (1992), Making the alternative sustainable: lessons from development for tourism, in V. Smith, and W. Eadington (Editors) *Tourism Alternatives. Potentials and Problems in the Development of Tourism*, Philadelphia, PA: University of Pennsylvania Press, 47–75.

Division of Tourism – National Development Corporation of Dominica (1993), Discover Dominica advertisement. *Barbados Advocate, Dominica 15th Independence Supplement*, November 3.

Dufour, R. (1978), Des mythes du loisir/tourisme weekend. Aliénation ou libération? *Cahiers du Tourisme*, série C, no. 47.

English, E. (1986), *The Great Escape. An Examination of North–South Tourism*. Ottawa: North–South Institute.

Febas Borra, J. (1978), Semiologia del lenguaje turistico, *Estudios Turisticos*, **57/58**, 17–203.

Fussell, P. (1979), The stationary tourist, *Harpers*, April, 31–38.

Hollinshead, K. (1992), The truth about Texas. Unpublished Ph.D. dissertation, Texas: A and M University.

Independent on Sunday (1994), Travel Section, January 2.

Islands (1989), Kona Village Resort, Hawaii, advertisement, October, 7.

Islands (1990), Mauna Lari Resort advertisement, February, 43.

Johnston, B. (1990), Breaking out of the tourist trap. *Cultural Survival Quarterly*, **14** (1), 2–5.

MacCannell, D. (1976), *The Tourist. A New Theory of the Leisure Class*, London: Macmillan.

Malta National Tourist Office (1988), *Gozo. Island of Calm and Relaxation*, Valletta: Malta National Tourist Office.

McElroy, J. and de Albuquerque, K. (1993), Sustainable alternatives to insular mass tourism: recent theory and practice. *Paper presented to the International Conference on Sustainable Tourism in Islands and Small States*. Foundation for International Studies, Valletta, Malta, November 18–20.

Moeran, B. (1983), The language of Japanese tourism, *Annals of Tourism Research*, **10**, 93–108.

Mol, A. and Spaargaren, G. (1993), Environment, modernity and the risk society: the apocalyptic horizon of environmental reform, *International Sociology*, **8** (4), 431–459.

New York Magazine (1989), I love New York (advertisement), September 11, 117.

Northern Territory Tourist Commission (1993), *Australia's Northern Territory*, Alice Springs: Northern Territory Tourist Commission.

Nöth, W. (1990), *Handbook of Semiotics*, Bloomington: Indiana University Press.

Plog, S. (1994), Leisure travel: an extraordinary industry faces superordinary problems, in W. Theobald (Editor) *Global Tourism. The Next Decade*. London: Butterworth-Heinemann, 40–54.

Polish Tourist Information Center (n.d.), *Poland Invites*, Warsaw: Polish Tourist Information Center.

Selwyn, T. (1993), Peter Pan in South East Asia. Views from the brochures, in M. Hitchcock, V. King, and M. Parnwell (Editors) *Tourism in South East Asia*, London: Routledge, pp. 117–137.

Shnayerson, M. (1993), What price paradise? *Condé Nast Traveler*, July, 62–71, 121–126.

Silverstein, T. (1991), The emergence of the green tourist. *Globe and Mail*, April 22.

Simply Caribbean (1989), Grenadines advertisement, December '88–'89, 10, Harrogate: Happiness Islands Ltd.

South America – Eastern's Easy Tour Guide (1983), Chiloe advertisement, 11.

Sunday Times Magazine (1991), Servus in Austria (advertisement), March 24, 21.

Thurot, J. (1989), Psychologie du loisir touristique. *Cahiers du Tourisme*, série C, no. 23.

Toffler, A. (1990), *Powershift*, New York: Bantam Books.

Tovey, R. (1993), Environmentalism in Ireland: two

versions of development and modernity. *International Sociology*, **8** (4), 413–430.

Tresse, P. (1990), L'Image des civilisations Africaines à travers des publications des services officiels du tourisme des pays d'Afrique Francophone. *Cahiers du Tourisme*, série C, no. 11.

Turner, L. and Ash, J. (1975), *The Golden Hordes. International Tourism and the Pleasure Periphery*, London: Constable.

von Sydow, M. (1990), *Sweden*, Stockholm: Swedish Tourist Board.

Williamson, J. (1983), *Decoding Advertisements. Ideology and Meaning in Advertising*, London: Marion Boyars.

Women and Development Unit, University of the West Indies (1994), It's Vital for Women to be Heard, *Sunday Sun*, March 3.

Deontology of Tourism

Krzysztof Przeclawski

9

ABSTRACT

The importance of ethics in the contemporary world is discussed, with fundamental values as the basis of ethics. Ethical issues are raised concerning the behaviour of the tourists, the inhabitants of the visited localities and 'the brokers'/tourism administration, tour-operators, hotel staff and tourist information. Finally a proposal of the Declaration on Ethics in Tourism is attached.

TOURISM IN THE CONTEMPORARY WORLD

Tourism, in its broad sense, is the sum of the phenomena pertaining to spatial mobility, connected with a voluntary, temporary change of place, the rhythm of life and its environment, and involving a personal contact with the visited environment (natural, and/or cultural and/or social).

Contemporary tourism is a social fact and a social process. It is simply a 'way of life' of the contemporary man. Up until modern times, the basic social ties were the function of the spatial proximity. Local communities with local cultural milieux sharing basic fundamental values made it easier for individuals to define their identity and gave the sense of support in the social group. Social ties were generally stable.

The urbanisation process led us to a substantial change. Mass migrations from the rural regions to cities and the intensive development of towns brought about the disintegration of traditional local communities and the decay of neighbourly relations. In a big city the distance between a family and a nation, or between a family and a large religious community, is marked by a vacuum and only partly filled with professional or associational ties. In the 'mass culture society' all the values are intermingled, which leads to the isolation of an individual in the 'lonely crowd'.

At this point we proceed to the third stage, the stage of touristification of the world. The process encompasses various parts of the world. It mainly concerns well-developed countries and regions, but gradually spreads throughout the whole world.

Tourism is, first of all, a form of man's behaviour. Man is the essential subject of tourism. Tourism can not be explained unless we understand man, the human being.

Tourism is at present a form of man's life, a way to materialise various values. Tourism is not only a way of spending free time (although it is true that most tourist's trips are closely connected with leisure activities), but tourism is also a means of reaching certain other goals. Hence, apart from the recreation-oriented tourism, there are also other forms like conference tourism, pilgrimage tourism and so on.

Tourism is, therefore, a form of learning and experiencing the world. It becomes a way of life of the contemporary man.

This process in itself is not 'good' or 'bad', 'positive' or 'negative'. Yet its effects – its consequences related to different fields of life – can be, from a given point of view, evaluated as 'good' or 'bad', 'positive' or 'negative'. Those effects depend on the behaviour of persons involved in the process of 'touristification', of tourists, of inhabitants of the localities visited by tourists and of so called 'brokers'. Those effects depend on the relation of the behaviour of these people to the ethical norms.

THE NEED FOR ETHICS IN TOURISM

For many years the tourism phenomenon has become the subject of interest of various sciences: beginning first with economy, but gradually becoming part of such sciences as management, marketing, regional planning, geography, anthropology, sociology, psychology, law and even philosophy.

However, in recent years it has become more and more evident that ethics should also be interested in the process of tourism development. For instance the AIEST Congress (held in Paris in 1992, AIEST 1992) proposed the creation of a special commission dealing with the ethical problems of tourism.

One has to distinguish tourism as a phenomenon and its consequences; its effects and its functions. The functions of tourism can be analysed with regard to:

- nature (minerals, fauna and flora);
- culture (man's achievements); and
- man and human relations.

The functions with regard to man will be, first of all, connected with the tourist. The functions with regard to human relations are first connected not only with the interrelations between the tourists and the inhabitants of the visited

localities, but also between tourists and brokers and between brokers and inhabitants. All these functions can be evaluated from the ethical point of view as 'positive' or 'negative' ones.

Let us take some examples. While quoting a number of authors, Dogan wrote:

> A majority of the scientists writing on this subject have thought that the effects of tourism on the whole have been negative. Among the major negative consequences of tourism are decline in traditions, materialism, increase in crime rates, social conflicts, crowding, environmental deterioration and dependency on the industrial countries. (Dogan 1989, pp. 217–218).

Tourism is very often connected with some concepts of the 'neocolonialism' (Laine, 1980, and others). The negative economic, social, spiritual and cultural consequences of tourism are also expressed by the Oecumenical Coalition on Third World Tourism in Bangkok (Contours, 1991).

The presence of tourists can lead (in some cases) to social conflicts between the local population, to the commercialisation and decline of the local authentic culture.

As regards the behaviour of the tourist, the misuse of freedom connected with the touristic trip may lead to excessive drinking, use of drugs, devastation of the natural environment, sexual exploitation and so on.

The real 'roots' of many various consequences of the development of tourism, of those mentioned above and other negative ones, can be found in the behaviour of people connected with the tourism activity; in their behaviour contradictory to the ethical norms.

Incidentally, it is a paradox that the real profits of tourism (the economic profits and of course the social and cultural ones) could be greater and not smaller if ethical norms could be more observed and realised.

Speaking about 'people connected with the tourism activity' we have considered three categories of tourism 'actors'.

First of all there is of course the tourists. Without them the phenomenon of tourism can not exist. Tourism is the activity of man, of human beings. The behaviour of the tourist can be – from the ethical point of view – analysed from three sides: the behaviour related to the tourist himself; the behaviour related to other tourists; and the behaviour related to the inhabitants of the localities visited by tourists.

The second 'actor' is the inhabitant, the local population. Their behaviour can be evaluated as the one related to the tourists and of that related to their own environment.

The third category are the 'brokers'. One can analyse their behaviour concerning the tourists and, in contrast, the inhabitants.

Let us now try, as a proposal made for broader discussion, to formulate some suggestions concerning the ethical evaluation of the behaviour of those three categories of people involved in tourism mentioned above. It is possible that this would be the first attempt to elaborate on the 'deontology of tourism'.

THE BEHAVIOUR OF PEOPLE INVOLVED IN TOURISM

The Tourists

What could be said from the ethical point of view about the behaviour of the tourist concerning himself?

First, the tourist trip gives the possibility to become acquainted with people, their culture and social relations, and also with the nature. It gives also the possibility to know ourselves better ('decouverte de soi-meme'). The tourist can make some effort in order to visit and know first of all what is really important, in order to understand better the visited people and its culture, its way of living and thinking. She/he should avoid following only that which is suggested by publicity, which often only concentrates on some 'tourist attractions' and gives us a false image of the visited locality or visited country. This effort of the tourist to get acquainted and to understand could be seen as a moral obligation. It requires also, of course, some prior preparation to the travel arrangements.

The second remark is connected with the concept of freedom. Freedom has always been associated with tourism. A tourist: is free from professional or family duties; can travel in any direction; can do what he feels like doing; can experience various adventures; is independent of his habits; can also feel free from the obligations to follow moral norms which regulate our

everyday life; and can follow his fancies, impulses and imitate other people. Such freedom is the freedom 'from' something and not the freedom 'for'. On the other hand, as tourists we may observe the same values which we follow in our everyday life; we can decide against being temporarily exempted, for instance, from the duty to be true to persons we love. We are perceived by the inhabitants and by other tourists as, in some sense, 'representatives' of a given country. We have to be conscious that we are bearing testimony to our country. It requires responsibility for our words and acts.

Thirdly, one of the main goals of the tourist trip (as regards leisure tourism) is to take rest, to regenerate our physical or mental forces. We can do it reasonably, or we can spend our holidays in such a manner (drinking, smoking, playing cards and so on) that finally we become ill and we need the next working year in order to prepare ourselves to the heavy task of our future holidays (J Krippendorf (1987) wrote about such 'holiday diseases'). The culture of leisure is not neutral from the ethical point of view.

Let us add that the tourist trip can be an occasion either to develop the so-called 'consumer attitude' or an occasion to realise the so-called 'creative tourism'. Unfortunately we do not have enough room in this chapter to develop further this question.

Finally, the ethical problems related to leisure tourism are also connected with family tourism. The family trip can either help to integrate the family and become better acquainted with all the family members, or this chance can be lost through the various minor conflicts.

What could be said about the tourist's behaviour related to other tourists? One has to first mention here the necessity of the attitude of tolerance – the respect towards the fact that they may differ from us. We have to be ready for dialogue and to help where necessary. We do not have to instigate them to do something against the ethical norms, but we shall also not follow their behaviour when it does not correspond to our beliefs. During the common trip it is important not to disturb others with our behaviour and not to steal their time by arriving late for the departure.

Finally, what can be said about the behaviour towards the inhabitants of the visited localities and towards the natural and cultural milieu?

The inhabitants of the visited localities should first of all be treated as subjects, as persons and not as objects. Regardless of their level of education or colour of skin, it is forbidden to manipulate, humiliate or take unfair advantage of them.

The attitude of a tourist towards the inhabitants ought to be the attitude of tolerance. She/he should accept the various differences, the race difference, the cultural and educational difference, the religious difference and so on. It is very important to respect the values which are significant for the inhabitants, to respect that which means sacrum for them. Unfortunately there are tourists who believe that they do not need to behave in a special way in the places of religious cults. What's more, some of them think that their subjective right for freedom entitles them to behave freely. They enter the mosque with their shoes on or the Catholic church with the pipe in the mouth.

Another problem is connected with the fact that arriving as tourists, and especially as leisure tourists, we meet people simply working, and working also because we are there as tourists. We must respect this fact. We have not to forget also that the average tourist spends during his holidays more money than usually he does at home. The inhabitants, especially the young ones, do not always understand this fact. This is especially in the Third-World countries, where there are many poor and simply hungry people around.

The Oecumenical Coalition on Third-World tourism formulates the opinion that tourism causes harm to Third-World countries: spiritual, political, economic and cultural harm. The spiritual harm is connected first of all with the transmission of some behaviour patterns and also with the direct offering of alcohol and drugs to the local people, and infecting them with the AIDS virus. It seems to us that the tourist must be also responsible for the formation of the attitudes of the visited population, especially the young.

The tourist has the opportunity during his stay in a given locality of either protecting the natural and cultural milieu, or destroying it, and in turn destroying the natural environment and the local culture as well.

We have mentioned only some examples of the tourist's behaviour towards himself and towards the inhabitants connected with the ethical norms.

Let us now reflect on the behaviour of inhabitants of the visited localities.

The Inhabitants

The attitude of the inhabitants of the visited localities towards tourists should be the attitude of hospitality and goodwill, and not the attitude of illwill or even hostility.

The tourist has the right to be well informed and to enjoy various services at reasonable prices. It is against moral ethics to swindle, to take the tourist in, or to steal. Contracts should be respected.

If the main motive for the local people is to gain money from tourists, very often the authentic cultural local values become 'commercialised', become values 'for sale' only or simply are replaced by forgeries.

The access to the cultural values ought to be facilitated, with the means of transport secured.

The tourist has the right to medical aid, to satisfactory public hygiene and to a high quality of services. However, it does not mean that every kind of service should be secured. The services against the ethical norms of the local community and against the dignity of the inhabitants should be excluded.

The security of tourists ought to be guaranteed. The tourists have also the right to practise their own religion and use facilities for that purpose.

From the ethical point of view it is not allowed to discriminate any category of tourists either for the reason of race, nor for nationality, beliefs, sex, etc.

Disabled persons should have the same access to 'tourist attractions' as able-bodied people.

Ideally, the inhabitants should learn something about the incoming tourists; their culture and habits.

This main motive of taking profit also leads the inhabitants to act sometimes against their environment (natural, cultural and social).

Instead, tourism should become an essential element not only of the economic, but also of cultural and social development of the locality. It can create the possibilities of employment. It can broaden the horizons of thinking of the inhabitants – become 'an open window' to the world, a factor of education, of formation of attitudes of tolerance, but it should not be a factor of moral relativism. The inhabitants shall take care of the traditional values, be against its commercialisation, still have respect for their sacrum and take care of their national and cultural identity.

The inhabitants, especially the youth, should not follow the behaviour of tourists, their 'depense ostentatoire'.

It is very important to meet everyday obligations irrespective of the presence of tourists. Some special problems arise as regards the holy days. Because of the open shops and of the functioning services, they lose their festive character.

Against the ethical norms are such phenomena as prostitution (including child prostitution), expansion of pornography, cultivation of the opium poppy and of the drug *Cannabis indica*.

The Brokers

By 'brokers' we mean those who are involved in the preparation of the travel, in the transportation, those who organise the stay, the sojourn of the tourists, and also those who create the conditions for tourism development on the level of the countries, regions and localities.

In the broad sense the brokers are:

- the central and local tourism administration, as well as the local self-governments' officers ('ADM');
- tour-operators and guides ('OPR');
- hotel staff as well as hostels and camping staff, and carriers ('HOT');
- tourist information and advertising staff ('INF').

We have to distinguish their behaviour relating to: (a) the tourists; and (b) the inhabitants of the visited localities.

The Behaviour Related to Tourists

ADM – the tourism administration as well as the self-governments are responsible for tourism policy and planning and for creating the necessary conditions for the development of tourism. From the ethical point of view it is especially important they take into consideration not only the economic, but also the social, cultural and educational consequences of it.

They should create the conditions facilitating the arrival of tourists as well as the access to the

regions, localities and objects, which represent an essential value for tourists. Therefore the building of the infrastructure, which creates a system giving suitable information as well as the high quality of services, is needed. Their policy should be also favourable for the departures of the inhabitants of their country, region or locality. They are also responsible for education and training of the tourism staff.

OPR – the most important duties of this category of persons are first of all:

- to supply convenient and safe transportation;
- to ensure convenient and hygienic conditions for the stay;
- to ensure the safety of the tourists and protection of their rights; and
- to adhere to the contracts.

Many of the tour operators are primarily looking for profit. In most cases, the programmes of the trips take into consideration the so-called 'tourist attractions' rather than the authentic values of the visited country or community. Such programmes should be elaborated in a much deeper way and correspond to the needs and desires of different categories of tourists. They should be addressed not only to the 'tourist-consumer', but also to the 'active tourist'.

According to the 'Tourism Bill of Rights and Tourist Code' adopted in Sofia in 1984:

tourists should be able to benefit from:

(a) objective, precise and complete information on conditions and facilities provided during their travel and sojourn by official tourism bodies and suppliers of tourism services, ...
(f) the practice of their own religion and the use of existing facilities for that purpose.

The guides interact closely with tourists. They are responsible not only for giving precise and complete information, but also for the adjustment of the form of information to the level of education and to the profession and age of the tourist.

Disabled persons have the same right to travel. One has to give them the use of easy means of transport, with access to different places and their accommodation. The profession of the 'tourist social assistant' should be created.

Family tourism is very important for the integration of family members. Such forms of tourism should be promoted and the conditions for it ensured.

From the ethical point of view the organised prostitution of women, adolescents and children is absolutely inadmissible. The same must be said about the illegal traffic of drugs.

HOT − the basic task of the hotel, hostel and camping staff is to ensure the safety of the tourists, the appropriate comfort, the necessary level of hygiene, night silence and a high quality of service. They must also have in mind the special needs of disabled persons. The principles of ethics require them to be honest and not to exploit the guests.

The tourist should be well informed. He has also the right to be informed about the places of religious worship and to find in the hotel the holy book corresponding to his religion. The hotel staff should not facilitiate sexual contacts with the inhabitants of the locality.

INF − the tourist wants to have confidence in the supplied information and advertising. He does not want to be lied to or misinformed. The information should be objective and not dependent on either politics or economic profit. The information on the locality and on some 'tourist attractions' must be honest and not create a false image of places and objects. It is also very important to give information about the local culture, customs of the inhabitants and their religion and ethics, in order to facilitate the possibility of mutual understanding and dialogue. One has to inform the tourist about the necessity and means of protection concerning the natural and cultural environment. Finally it is desirable to inform the tourists about the different possibilities of active as well as more relaxing forms of leisure pursuits.

Another very specific but very important category of brokers are school teachers and lecturers who are responsible for organising tourist trips and excursions for pupils and older children. It is their task and responsibility − especially when the family is not involved − to help in the 'tourist initiation' and to use tourism as a means of education.

In order to do that, they must first of all like tourism, know its ins and outs and know how to practise the subject correctly.

The Behaviour Related to Inhabitants
The most important problems seem to be connected with the relations between the brokers and inhabitants of the visited (natural, social, cultural) environment.

These kinds of problems were first raised by the Oecumenical Coalition on Third-World Tourism, in Bangkok, when speaking about the spiritual, cultural, economic and political damages related to tourism (Contours, 1991).

ADM − the tourism administration and the local government should promote first of all humanistic tourism, i.e. a kind of tourism which is not only a source of income, but where social, cultural and educational effects are also 'positive'. The rights of inhabitants and their interests should be taken into account in this case. This type of tourism may consolidate the national identity of the people and does not damage the natural and cultural environment.

They should create the ideal conditions for the economic development of the touristic regions and localities and for the reduction of unemployment. The development of tourism should be included, as an essential element, into the general programme of development of the region and of the community. All the inhabitants have the same rights to take profit from this development.

ADM should take care of the protection of the local, cultural, social and natural values.

It is also very important that the local people be better prepared for contact with the tourist. Therefore it seems necessary to inform the inhabitants about the culture, customs and behaviour of tourists coming from different countries. On the other hand one ought to help the inhabitants in developing an attitude of hospitality and tolerance.

From the ethical point of view it is also suggested authentic local values are promoted at the tourist attraction to act against the impact of foreign cultures through tourism.

Finally the tourism policy should take care of the possibilities of travelling as regards the local population: first of all the younger generation and also the disabled people.

OPR − the investors and the tour operators organising the physical planning for the purposes of tourism development and also the trips must take into account the rights and interests of the local population, i.e. not to destroy their cultural heritage and the natural environment. They must have respect for local values, ethical norms and religious beliefs. They ought to create for them the possibilities for work in tourism and they should not exploit the local population. The values of the local culture should be protected and not commercialised. If possible, the everyday life of the inhabitants and their customs should not be disturbed by the presence of tourists.

HOT — the rights and interests of the local population should be also respected under the construction of new hotels. As mentioned earlier, one ought to create the possibilities of employment for them.

The exploitation of the hotels should not aggravate daily living conditions of the local population.

INF — it is the duty of those who are responsible for marketing and information to tell the inhabitants about the tourists, the countries they come from, their customs and way of life.

It is also necessary to give information about the possibilities of employment connected with the development of tourism in the region and on the possibilities of education and training in tourism.

The inhabitants also ought to be informed about the various possible consequences of the development of tourism.

CONCLUSIONS

In conclusion I would like to suggest the Declaration on Ethics in Tourism:

At the end of the 20 Century humanity is entering into a new stage — the stage of touristification of the world. The process mainly concerns the developed countries, but gradually spreads throughout the whole world. Tourism becomes a way of life of contemporary man.

The effects of this process can be positive or negative. It depends on the behaviour of people involved in tourism, on the behaviour of tourists, of inhabitants of the localities visited by tourists and on the behaviour of brokers. It depends on their attitude towards the norms of ethics. The real profits of tourism could be greater if the ethical norms were observed.

There is now a need to create the foundations of the deontology of tourism. We are convinced that tourists, inhabitants and brokers should respect fundamental values such as:

- human life and dignity;
- natural and cultural environment;
- family;
- holidays and holy places;
- real and suitable information;
- private property;
- freedom (while respecting the rights of others);

and observe the ethical norms connected with them.

REFERENCES

AIEST (Ed.) (1992), La liberté de voyager en l'An 2000, St. Gall, volume 34.
Contours (1991), The quarterly newsletter of the Coalition on Third World Tourism, vol 5, no. 4, Bangkok.
Dogan, H. Z. (1989), Forms of adjustment. Socio-cultural impact of tourism, *Annals of Tourism Research*, **2**, 216–236.
Krippendorf, J. (1987), The Holiday People, London: William Heinemann.
Laine, P. (1980) *Liberons le Tourisme*, Paris: Fayolles.
Tourism Bill of Rights and Tourist Code (1984), Adopted in Sofia. In: Edgell, D. L, Sr. (1990), *International Tourism Policy*, New York: Van Nostrand.

Development of an Eco-tourism Strategy for Texas

Turgut Var

10

ABSTRACT

This chapter deals with the development of a nature tourism strategy for Texas. As opposed to many states and countries Texas is unique in terms of private land ownership. In fact 97 percent of land belongs to private sector owners leaving 3 percent to the public domain. Private ownership makes it very difficult to maneuver in developing a strategy. This chapter gives the history and methodology that was used in developing a nature tourism strategy. The process involved a number of private and public interests and focused on the obstacles that make it difficult for tourism development.

BACKGROUND

Texas occupies about 7 percent of the total water and land area of the United States. According to the revised U.S. Bureau of Census, Texas has a land and water area of 266,807 square miles as compared with Alaska's 591,004 square miles. The State of Texas is as large as all of New England, New York, Pennsylvania, Ohio and Illinois combined. From east to west it is approximately 800 miles and contain two time zones. The distance from north to south is also close to 800 miles. Though most of Texas is located on flat plains or rolling prairies, there are substantial mountains (over 8,000 ft) in the Trans-Pecos region of far West Texas (Dallas Morning News, 1991, p. 74).

Texas has many native animals and birds, plus species introduced on game preserves. More than 540 species of birds – about three fourths of all different species found in the United States. Varied vegetation, altitudes from sea level to over 8,000 feet, rainfall from less than ten inches annually to more than 55 inches, and a strategic position on the North American continent, combine to provide Texas' diversity of avian habitats. In addition, Texas' resident bird population is augmented by multitudes of migratory birds including extremely endangered whooping cranes. Canadian and Siberian geese together with a number of other birds migrate to the Texas coast (over 624 miles) during Fall and go back at the beginning of Spring. There are some 142 species of animals, including opossum, the only marsupial of North America. In addition to bird and animal life Texas is the home of over 250 different species of fish and over 5,000 wild flowers (Department of Transportation, 1994, pp. 250–254).

Compared to other states and countries the amount of publicly owned land per capita in Texas is low (97 percent of Texas land is privately held). Thus, developing a close working relationship with landowners, and providing more recreational land for Texas, are critical. The objective of this chapter is to show the process that is followed in developing a nature tourism strategy for Texas.

TOURISM PLANNING IN TEXAS

The history of tourism planning in Texas is relatively new and limited to coordination of state activities as they relate to tourism. In the early 1980s Texas was at the end of an accelerated 10-year growth period. From 1972 to 1983 Texas Gross State Product grew over 300 percent (State of Texas, 1992 p.iii). Much of the growth may be attributed to steadily rising gas and oil prices during that period. During this rapid growth the population of Texas increased 34 percent, adding another 4 million people. The real estate values soared in the metropolitan centers as more businesses and people moved into the state. Rural land values also increased as oil and gas prospecting were at record levels. But the Texas boom was short lived and the boom economy did not sustain. Beginning in 1983 with the drastic decline in oil and gas prices, the Texas economy – which was largely based upon oil and real estate – began to falter. Most economists agree that the Texas economic recession reached bottom in 1987 when the Gross State Product dipped near the 1984 level (State of Texas, 1992, p. iii).

In contrast, the U.S. travel industry continued to grow throughout the '80s. Unfortunately Texas was not keeping pace with national trends. Between 1982 and 1988, Texas lost national market share for travel spending. In 1985 the total travel expenditures in Texas was $12·9 billion which represented 6·2 percent of the total U.S. market share. In 1988, although total travel expenditures increased to $14·5 billion its market share dropped to 5·6 percent ranking behind California, Florida and New York. Recognizing the need to diversify Texas' economy, the Texas legislature in 1987 dedicated one-twelfth of state hotel/motel tax revenues to tourism marketing and Texas

State Agency Tourism Council was formed. The purpose of this council is to stimulate the development of travel and tourism in Texas and to establish an interagency system for coordinating state-level tourism efforts. The specific mission of this Agency, which is comprised of nine state agencies, is:

'The travel and tourism mission of the State of Texas is to provide promotional, informational, educational and developmental programs, services and facilities designed to maintain and increase Texas' standing as a premier U.S. and international destination, to fulfill and enrich travelers' experiences within the state, and to sustain travel and tourism as major contributor and catalyst for state economic development, while protecting distinctive Texan lifestyles, cultures and environments. (State of Texas, 1992, p. ii)

Under the leadership of the Texas Department of Commerce, Tourism Division, Texas State Agency Tourism Council produced its first *Strategic Travel and Tourism Plan* in 1988. Every two years a new plan which contained new and revised goals and accomplishments was prepared. In addition to the improving coordination and cooperation among state agencies, federal agency cooperation has progressed significantly. In 1989, the Texas Federal/State Agency Tourism Coordinating Committee was formed as a Council initiative. This committee has evolved to the 1994 formation of the Texas Federal Agency Tourism Council. Its Memorandum of Understanding parallels the Texas State Agency Tourism Council's memorandum of understanding and includes: the National Park Service, Southwest Region; United States Fish and Wildlife Service; National Forests and Grasslands of Texas, United States Forest Service, Southeast Region; and the U.S. Army Corps of Engineers, Southwestern Division (State of Texas, 1994, pp. 87–88).

As a result of improved marketing and promotional activities based on research and development, Texas' share in U.S. total domestic travel expenditure has increased steadily and rose to 6·2 percent in 1992, tying with New York (State of Texas, 1994, pp. viii–ix).

One of the goals of the first Strategic Travel and Tourism Plan for the State of Texas (State of

Texas, 1988, p. i) was to increase the Texas share to 8·5 percent by year 2000. In line with this general objective six important goals were stated:

1. Attract more U.S. and international visitors and increase their length of stay in Texas.
2. Encourage Texans to travel within their own state.
3. Improve the perceptions of Texas by potential visitors to Texas.
4. Enhance the quality and international prestige of tourism education in Texas.
5. Support and encourage new and improved visitor facilities and attractions.
6. Preserve and enhance Texas natural, cultural and historic resources.

The 1988 strategic plan also stipulated that a strategy to conduct and coordinate research to enhance the development, management and conservation of Texas' natural, cultural and historical resources (State of Texas, 1988, p. 14). The 1990 strategic plan added another strategy that was related to determine the optimum environmental impacts of recreation and tourism development and use of Texas' natural, cultural, and social resources (State of Texas, 1990 p.7). It should be noted that the objective of developing, managing, preserving, and promoting public use of Texas' natural, cultural, and historical resources, has gained more prominence in the last three strategic plans. As a part of supporting public and private-sector tourism initiatives to improve the quality and quantity of Texas attractions and services, the 1994 Strategic Tourism Plan recommended that nature tourism should be emphasized in order to expand Texas tourism markets (State of Texas, 1994 pp. 21–23).

DEVELOPMENT OF A STRATEGY FOR NATURE TOURISM

Given the above background, a special State Task Force appointed by the governor convened in Austin in late 1993, to develop a report on the economic opportunities on natural tourism in Texas. The membership of the committee included a broad range of Texas interests, reflecting the viewpoint of urban areas, rural communities, the tourism industry, private

landholders, state agencies, non-profit and educational institutions, various ethnic groups, businesses and conservationists (State Task Force, 1995, pp. 3–7). The results of these investigations and discussions were incorporated in a report *Nature Tourism in the Lone Star State*. The report critically evaluated the current nature tourism and made recommendations in four categories: Conservation, Education, Legislation, and Promotion. A brief description of these recommendations are as follows:

Conservation:
1. Provide incentives to private landowners to preserve natural habitats.
2. Manage public land, such as state parks and wildlife management areas, for the enrichment and continuance of wildlife diversity.
3. Acquire additional recreational lands with unique nature tourism elements, but only from willing sellers.
4. Develop resource conservation programs to restore diminished resources such as native grasslands and reintroduce native fauna such as bighorn sheep, pronghorn antelope and bison that attract nature tourists.
5. Identify and categorize existing and potential nature tourism resources, and assess and monitor the impacts of nature tourism.

Education:
1. Create a training program for rural community leaders, tourism-related business managers and prospective business persons.
2. Develop a nature tourism handbook for communities and landowners.
3. Facilitate the development of local tourism infrastructures to support consumer needs.
4. Communicate the importance of preserving and managing Texas' natural resources to communities, landowners and the public and inform them, of the state's programs to conserve wildlife and habitat.

Legislation:
1. Seek legislation, a joint resolution or a constitutional amendment to allow rural landowners to manage their property solely for wildlife without losing their agricultural exemption from ad valorem taxation.
2. Amend Texas transportation laws so that

chauffeur and bus companies transporting tourists to and from rural Texas communities can operate as common carriers and broker freight to increase profitability and efficiencies.

3. Support probate relief for landowners who obligate themselves to manage their land as wildlife habitat. As an example, explore federal probate tax credits in exchange for conservation easements.

4. Develop an insurance program for landowners who are interested in providing for nature tourism on their lands.

5. Landowners presently are granted a limitation from liability regarding recreational activities as long as revenues received do not exceed twice the previous calendar year's ad valorem tax. Remove this cap.

Promotion: In case of promotion the committee recommended establishment of a non-profit industry organization, the Texas Nature Tourism Association (TNTA), with membership to include landowners, tourism managers, regulatory agencies, tour operators, guides, conservation groups, chambers of commerce, convention and visitors' bureaus and service providers. The TNTA would:

1. Develop voluntary guidelines for nature tourism sites and providers.

2. Assist in promotion of nature tourism in Texas.

3. Assist in developing and coordinating an overall marketing strategy and individual marketing elements for nature tourism in Texas.

4. Establish a Texas Nature Tourism Information Center to provide centralized access to those seeking nature tourism and travel information.

5. Conduct demonstration programs in various regions of the state to show the benefits of nature tourism.

CONCLUSION

In terms of land ownership Texas represents a unique case. Almost 97 percent of the total land belongs to private landholders. Consequently development of a nature tourism strategy necessarily requires a fine balance among public and private interests. For this reason, tourism planning activities in Texas has been limited to the public sector's catalytic role. Development of a nature tourism strategy has relied on participation of all interested parties. The recommendations that are made in the areas of conservation, education, legislation, and promotion would require a careful coordination of the public agencies and private interest groups. In conclusion, it will take the combined talents, creativity and resources of government, landowners, representatives of cities and rural areas, the travel industry, the conservation community and other interested parties to position Texas to take advantage of the growing demand in nature tourism (State Task Force, 1995).

REFERENCES

Dallas Morning News (1991), *1992–1993 Texas Almanac*, Houston: Gulf Publishing Company.

State of Texas (1988), *Strategic Travel and Tourism Plan for the State of Texas*, Austin, Texas, December.

State of Texas (1990), *Strategic Travel and Tourism Plan for the State of Texas*, Austin, Texas, November.

State of Texas (1992), *Strategic Travel and Tourism Plan for the State of Texas*, Austin, Texas, November.

State of Texas (1994), *Strategic Travel and Tourism Plan for the State of Texas*, Austin, Texas, November.

State Task Force on Texas Nature Tourism (1995), *Nature Tourism in the Lone Star State*, Texas Parks and Wildlife Department, Austin, Texas.

Texas Department of Transportation (1994), *Texas State Travel Guide*, Austin, Texas, Travel Information Division.

Best Practice Environmental Management and the Tourism Industry

11

John J. Pigram

ABSTRACT

Best practice is now widely accepted and promoted in manufacturing industry as a means of achieving quality management. When linked to environmental performance, the broader concept of best practice environmental management is of direct relevance to tourism. There is growing evidence that the tourism industry is prepared to foster environmental excellence through the adoption of best practice environmental management, and the implementation of self-regulatory auditing procedures to monitor compliance with environmental standards. This trend, which is strongest at the international corporate level of the tourism industry, is being reflected in the 'greening' of major elements of Australian tourism. The challenge is to raise concern for the environment among the many smaller, disparate tourism operations, and to promote best practice environmental management at all levels of the tourism industry.

INTRODUCTION

Environmental issues are becoming increasingly important to the tourism industry and resolution of these issues will demand far-reaching changes in the way tourism operates. Enhanced environmental performance will come first from a concerted commitment to ecologically sustainable forms of tourism development and secondly from the development and application of a coherent framework for positive change. Such an approach must be structured to conform with the special features which characterise tourism and, in particular, be capable of adoption and implementation of the various scales of operation which typify the industry. The concept of 'best practice environmental management' offers a meaningful framework within which to achieve environmental excellence in tourism.

BEST PRACTICE

The term 'best practice' has had a mixed reception in the world of business. To some it remains merely jargon or a buzz-word, popular with management consultants. To others, best practice represents the essential direction which firms need to take to become and remain competitive internationally. The growing globalisation of world economies has imposed pressing demands on business for technological sophistication, flexibility, quality assurance and new forms of organisation. Best practice is now seen as 'the way in which leading edge companies are able to manage and organise their operations – to delivery world class standards of performance' (Department of Industrial Relations, 1992, p. 3).

Best practice originated in business organisation theory and in the world of transnational corporate planning and management. It has found its strongest expression in manufacturing industry, but is also being promoted in the services sector and in natural resources management, including forestry, rangeland management and water quality management.

Put simply, best practice is the best way of doing things relative to levels of performance in comparable firms and operations. Some general principles can be identified which are associated with best practice organisation. These include:

- a commitment to change and continuous improvement and learning, with a highly skilled and flexible workforce and leaner, team-based organisational structures;
- the pursuit of innovation in technology, products and processes;
- a focus on customers and improved communication and consultation inside and beyond the organisation;
- the use of performance measurement systems and benchmarking; and
- the integration of environmental management into all operations of the business.

This last point links best practice directly with environmental performance. For some time now, leading edge businesses worldwide have been responding to the demand for higher environmental standards. In part, this 'greening' of industry reflects a markedly tighter regulatory regime, bolstered by growing community awareness and agitation over environmental concerns. However, it also demonstrates a proactive commitment to the environment which transcends regulatory requirements and permits.

This response translates and extends best practice into 'best practice environmental management' as a means of achieving sustainable growth in a competitive world. Best practice environmental management calls for radically different organisational structures and attitudes designed to bring about continuous improvement in a firm's environmental performance. Environmental excellence is fostered by enlightened management practices which incorporate new, cleaner technologies, and an emphasis on

resource conservation, recycling, reuse and recovery, in progress towards sustainability.

BEST PRACTICE ENVIRONMENTAL MANAGEMENT

The elements inherent in best practice environmental management and the changes needed to implement the concept can best be explained using a framework for organisational analysis (Table 11.1). The framework is based on the idea that organisational effectiveness stems from the interaction of seven elements. Table 11.1 depicts the shift necessary from the existing approach to environmental management to one based on best practice. Clearly, the changes are more than cosmetic. Key elements are:

- a significantly different management style, demonstrating a strong commitment to environmental excellence;
- a more flexible structure involving a devolution of environmental responsibility to all levels of the organisation;
- a proactive strategy or action plan which recognises the link between environmental excellence and competitiveness;
- adoption of environmentally inclusive systems of organisation incorporating environmental indicators and audit processes;
- acquisition of an environmental skill base and focus with an emphasis on an innovative, creative approach to problem solving; and
- staff support and accountability for environmental excellence, and involvement in the process of change required to achieve it.

Since the Earth Summit held in Rio de Janeiro in 1992 and the adoption of Agenda 21, nations of the industrialised world are vigorously promoting best practice environmental management. A range of manufacturing firms in North America, Europe and Australia have adopted a proactive approach to environmental management with best practice as a major corporate goal. The service sector has also benefited from this trend, in particular, tertiary education and telecommunications. Concern for sustainability, and for the environmental management processes which contribute to it, is now also emerging strongly in the tourism sector.

Table 11.1. The best practice environmental management paradigm shift.

Superordinate goal	Efficiency	Excellence
	Old	New
Style	Formal: • command and control; • environmental low priority priority of CEO.	Committed: • CEO vision, personal commitment and leadership; • demonstrated priority for senior management.
Structure	Rigid: • steeply hierarchical; • weak or no links between OH & S, environmental and production management.	Flexible: • devolution of environmental responsibility; • flatter, team oriented; • integration of OH & S, environmental and production management.
Strategy	Reactive: • meet regulations, focus on end-of-pipe; • no specific environmental policy; • closed door to community.	Proactive: • link between environmental excellence and competitiveness; • emphasis on continuous improvement; • 'open door' to community.
Systems	Environmentally exclusive: • minimum required to meet regulations.	Environmentally inclusive: • comprehensive environmental management plan; • formalised communication links with community.
Staff	Directed: • performance measured by cost; • no sense of ownership.	Empowered: • environmental criteria in performance appraisal; • pride in activities in the firm.
Skills	Functional: • production and waste control.	Problem-solving: • integrated approach to improvement; • innovation, problem solving skills highly regarded.

Source: *The Environmental Challenge: Best Practice Environmental Management* (1992), Australian Manufacturing Council.

BEST PRACTICE ENVIRONMENTAL MANAGEMENT AND TOURISM

Since the 1980s, the tourism industry has shown commendable preparedness to apply the principles of best practice environmental management to its activities. As with manufacturing industry, the scale of operations appears to have a decided influence on the type and extent of initiatives undertaken.

Large firms often have more sophisticated systems, bureaucracies and expertise in dealing with public policy issues. Further, the greater public visibility of large firms necessitates a prompt response to environmental

problems. (Australian Manufacturing Council, 1992, p. 6)

Transnational corporate linkages also mean that firms with international connections feel the pressure to respond to the environmental challenge earlier than their smaller and locally based counterparts. This point has significant implications for the tourism industry and these are discussed further below.

On the international scene, a growing number of large hotel corporations have implemented a variety of effective environmental measures. Moves in this direction began initially in 1991 when the Inter-Continental Hotels Group put together an environmental reference manual cataloguing guidelines and instructions for internal environmental management of hotel operations. The aim was to increase awareness of environmental concerns and to encourage greater environmental sensitivity among staff.

The initiative was taken up in Britain by the Prince of Wales Business Leaders Forum, which, together with leading hotel chains, produced a joint operations manual. The International Hotels Environment Initiative followed and, in 1992, produced a revised manual – *Environmental Management for Hotels: the Industry Guide to Best Practice*. The manual is seen as a voluntary code of conduct and offers a useful reference and blueprint for upgrading environmental procedures in areas such as waste management, energy consumption, noise and congestion, purchasing policy and staff training. It is intended that the initiative be promoted among other major hotel groups and tourism operators. Already the larger hotel corporations in the Southeast Asia region (Peninsular, Mandarin, Oriental, etc) have endorsed the move towards higher environmental standards.

Elsewhere, other tourism companies and groups have produced their own environmental management manuals. Canadian Pacific Hotels and Resorts, for example, have undertaken the development of an environmental programme called *The Green Partnership Guide* for all of its hotels in Canada (Troyer, 1992). The main objective of the programme is to institute the highest possible standards of environmental responsibility throughout the hotel chain in order to identify environmental improvements which, at the same time, could result in lower operating costs. The corporation also undertook a programme to identify those areas of hotel operations which could be changed to induce more environmentally benign practices and products, and to determine the level of support for environmental initiatives among its employees (Checkley, 1992).

Another example of self-monitoring is British Airways' internal environmental auditing programme in which the main aims are to make the airline 'a good neighbour', concerned for the community and the environment (British Airways, 1992). The airline places the emphasis of its monitoring programme on noise, emissions and fuel efficiency, waste water, energy, materials

and congestion. It also recognises the importance of sponsorship, recycling, staff training and environmental responsibility. Through these activities the airline has increased its awareness of the importance of identifying and ensuring compliance with environmental regulations affecting the environment.

The moves reflect a global trend towards the 'greening' of tourism reported to the Globe 92 International Conference on Business and the environment (Hawkes and Williams, 1993). The tourism industry appears to be accepting that future prosperity relies heavily on the maintenance of the environmental qualities on which it depends. Moreover, in a more environmentally aware world, green tourism not only offers new experiences and opportunities, but makes economic good sense in terms of reduced waste and lower operating costs.

THE GREENING OF AUSTRALIAN TOURISM

Tourism is of great economic and social benefit to Australia and a source of a substantial part of income and employment in many regions of the country. However, in common with other parts of the industrialised world, concern has been expressed about environmental problems associated with tourism, and pressure is growing to ensure ecologically sustainable forms of tourism development.

Against this background, Australian tourism developers and operators are demonstrating increased understanding of environmental concerns and the Australian Tourism Industry Association has drawn up an Environmental Code of Practice in consultation with conservation groups, industry bodies and planning authorities. The code reflects many of the elements of best practice environmental management and is being applied at a number of sites along the east coast of Australia. Some of these are fully integrated resorts offering five-star hotel accommodation, linked to luxurious residential properties, and a range of world class recreation facilities. Several resorts have been designed and constructed on ecologically sensitive principles and operate on environmentally responsible lines.

THE GREAT BARRIER REEF

Some of the best examples of the 'greening' of Australian tourism are to be found at resorts in the Great Barrier Reef Region of northern Queensland. Two exclusive resorts on Bedarra Island off the Queensland coast are among Australia's most environmentally friendly tourism developments. The structures represent a different approach to resort architecture, using local materials and nature-responsive design. The intention is to offer visitors the chance to retreat from the outside world and recharge themselves through close contact with the surrounding island landscape and rainforest.

Further north, Green Island near Cairns is being developed in keeping with best practice environmental management, with attention to siting, design, materials, sources of supplies and disposal of wastes. Said to be Australia's first five-star 'eco-tourist resort', Green Island is built on a coral cay and offers luxurious accommodation under the rainforest canopy, with structures suspended to protect the delicate ecology of the forest floor.

The redevelopment of Green Island in 1994 was subject to strict controls imposed by Cairns City Council and the Queensland Department of Environment and Heritage regarding:

- the layout of the resort;
- design details including materials and finishes;
- waste disposal; and
- construction methods.

A Code of Environmental Practice was drawn up by the developers and given to site staff and contractors to convey an environmental conservation philosophy to all those involved in development and construction of the resort. The code explains the fragile nature of the island and provides practical advice on:

- avoidance of the spread of weeds, exotic plants and diseases;
- maintenance of ecosystems, fauna and flora;
- the importance of the groundwater aquifer to survival of native rainforest;
- cultural heritage, both European and Aboriginal;
- national parks and marine parks; and
- tourists, visitors and other leaseholders on the island.

Table 11·2 sets out an extract from the code of the explanatory information and instructions prepared by the developers regarding the island's environment. This approach has now been carried over into the implementation of best practice operational procedures for the day-to-day running of the resort. Green Island represents an impressive (and expensive) approach to resort development in harmony with nature and the beauty of the tropical island setting. It provides further evidence of the commitment of developers and operators of tourism facilities in Australia to endorse and apply best practice principles to management of resort environments.

Australian Resorts Pty Ltd, which operates resort facilities at several locations off the North Queensland coast, is another example of an enlightened approach to tourism development in Australia (Australian Trade Commission, 1992). The company's best practice philosophy integrates the resort's structures and processes with the attitudes and skills and staff to support a guest-focused and shared organisational culture. The aim is to build the basis for increased profitability on productivity, efficiency and quality service, linked to environmental responsibility.

A further example is Ramada Reef Resort, on the mainland. The resort is implementing many of the environmental initiatives currently being undertaken by Ramada hotels and resorts throughout the world. From its inception, the Reef Resort was built on ecologically sensitive design principles, with buildings and facilities harmoniously integrated into the surrounding natural environment. Extra precautions have been taken to ensure that individual trees are fully protected, even to the extent of a unique, free-form swimming pool created around the root systems of rainforest trees. The Ramada Reef Resort is rapidly earning a reputation as one of the most environmentally responsible hotel developments along the Australian coast (Kelleher, 1993).

Despite these examples, proposals for further resort development on the Queensland coast continue to encounter strong resistance from 'environmental' groups, intent on protecting and reserving the coastal zone. In 1994, the planned Port Hinchinbrook resort development at Cardwell, south of Cairns, was delayed because of fears that it would affect nearby World Heritage areas. Despite approval by the Queensland State

Table 11·2. Extract from Code of Environmental Practice – Green Island Resort

Introduction	Weeds, exotic plants and diseases
Green Island is a coral cay approximately 27 kilometres northeast of Cairns. It has achieved renown over several decades as an accessible and attractive example of the natural beauty of the Great Barrier Reef. While the island and its reef appear hardy and have survived a long history of human occupation and use, they remain in many respects a fragile system. Daikyo, in its plans to redevelop the tourism lease on the island, asks that you and all the workers on the island carry out your work in a manner which is consistent with the island's character and its special environment. This booklet addresses six important concerns and provides the do's and don'ts which will help you protect the island and reef.	The island has developed a long period in isolation from the mainland with the major source of seed being those carried to the island by birds and fruit bats. The spread of noxious and/or exotic plants and diseases could upset the balance of nature on Green Island. *Do not* Do not bring plant material to the island, unless it is material approved by the Department of Environment and Heritage. *Do* Do ensure that all material brought to the island is free of plants and seeds. Do ensure that all equipment brought to the island is washed down prior to arrival on the island.
Ecosystems, flora and fauna	Ecosystems, flora and fauna
The range of trees and plants on Green Island have been selected by nature and only those suitable to the environment of Green Island remain. These trees and plants virtually hold Green Island together. The animal life is also limited and has adapted to the island. Feral cats, rodents and the like, could very quickly destroy the native animal life, so their introduction is a serious concern for authorities.	Daikyo and the Department of Environment and Heritage have carried out detailed surveys of all the trees and plants within the leased area. All the trees that have been approved for removal have been removed. Specific groupings of plants (ecosytems) have been fenced. *Do not* Do not remove or damage any plants or trees on the island. Do not move fences from around ecosystems. *Do* Do respect the importance of the flora and fauna on the island. Do make certain that there is no way you could introduce a feral animal to the island. Check equipment and storage containers before leaving the mainland. Do take extra care when using machinery near trees.

Source: Daikyo and Thiess (1992), *Code of Environmental Practice and General Safety Instructions*.

Government, federal authorities intervened after initial site clearing had begun. The multi-million dollar project may now only proceed following further environmental assessment, and amendments to the scale and operations of the resort.

THE COFFS HARBOUR REGION

Further south, the Coffs Harbour region, on the New South Wales coast north of Sydney, has seen rapid expansion of tourism in recent years. The region is an established focus for tourism on Australia's east coast and has a remarkable diversity of scenic attractions, ranging from pristine sandy beaches to spectacular rainforest a few kilometres inland. The climate is rated among the best in Australia, with a mean summer temperature of 28°C and 22°C in winter. Visitors can choose from a variety of activities including surfing, sailing, ocean and estuary fishing, whitewater rafting, ballooning and following nature trails on foot or horseback. A wide choice of accommodation styles is also available to tourists visiting Coffs Harbour. The area has long been an attractive location for second homes, but short-term visitors can utilise apartments, motels, caravan parks and camp-grounds.

In 1990, a conference was organised at Coffs Harbour around the theme of 'The Green Resort'. The purpose was to examine and formulate design principles for resort developments along the Australian coastline. Concepts such as environmentally compatible methods of waste disposal, more energy-efficient design and operations, including solar power, and sensitive and aesthetically pleasing resort architecture, were discussed (Oppenheim, 1990).

The scheduling of the conference at Coffs Harbour was no coincidence; rather it comple-mented an emerging trend towards environ-mental responsibility in tourism development in the region. In recent years, a number of sophis-ticated resorts have been created along the coastline north and south of the city. These offer international style facilities with a full range of sporting and recreational activities, entertain-ment, beach access and a setting compatible with the natural environment. In many respects, these establishments reflect the 'greening' of beach resorts along Australia's coast. Typical of this trend is Aanuka Beach Resort.

AANUKA BEACH RESORT

Located six minutes from the centre of Coffs Harbour City, Aanuka Beach Resort is set in four hectares of landscaped grounds on the beach front. Aanuka is a relatively small, secluded resort created in a natural rainforest setting with direct access to a safe surfing beach. It has won awards for the best resort in Australia and best resort design, which features a setting reminis-cent of a island in the South Pacific. The emphasis is on the attractions of native fauna and flora in a sub-tropical environment. The developer boasts that just six trees had to be removed to create the resort, but 20,000 trees have since been planted on the site. Furthermore, construction companies were required to agree to a bond of A$3000 for any tree seriously damaged during development of the resort.

Construction materials, architectural design and landscaping are in keeping with the inherent appeal of the site and no expense has been spared in fitting out the resort for the comfort of

guests. A large outdoor rock pool has been created with waterfalls, a cave with jacuzzi and a swim-up bar. The 48 suites are designed as buré style, low rise units in harmony with the natural environment, and offering complete seclusion and privacy. Each suite is fully equipped with luxury facilities and a two-person spa and atrium. Open space, low density, environmental sensitivity and a casual social setting set the tone for the resort.

Some of the best facilities offered to tourists in Australia are available at Aanuka Beach Resort. However, the beachfront site does present some disadvantages. Maintenance costs are high with corrosion of metal fittings, repeated cleaning of external surfaces, constraints on plant types, and heavy demands on upkeep of grounds. The resort is also exposed to occasional strong winds, and infrequent cyclonic disturbances and storm surge.

Great care has been taken to keep Aanuka compatible with, and yet buffered from, sur-rounding land uses. An important development in this respect is the construction of Aanuka Beach Village adjacent to the resort. Once again, the intention is to maintain the integrity of the setting and provide harmony between architec-ture and nature. Beachside residential villas are offered for sale or investment for longer term visitors, to complement the resort itself and underpin its commercial viability.

Operation of Aanuka Beach Resort incorporates many features of best practice environmental management in the tourism industry. Compre-hensive programmes for recycling and manage-ment of wastes, energy and water conservation, and protection of the natural environment, are features of resort operations. Advertising pro-grammes feature the 'greenness' of the resort and its management. The success of Aanuka Beach resort is perhaps a good indication of the marketing advantage to be gained from envir-onmentally sensitive tourism development. More-over, the demonstration effect of the successful appeal to tourists of a nature-based resort is being reflected in the promotion of neighbouring 'green' beach resorts in the Coffs Harbour region.

ENVIRONMENTAL AUDITING

Aanuka also provides convincing evidence of

the benefits of monitoring environmental performance and the role of self-regulation and environmental auditing. The concept of environmental audits is still relatively new in tourism and there are many interpretations of exactly what is meant by the term (Buckley, 1991). In its common form, environmental auditing is a process whereby operations of an organisation are monitored to determine whether they are in compliance with regulatory requirements and environmental policies and standards. The essential purposes of environmental auditing programmes are: to ensure compliance with environmental management planning; that commitments made are implemented and environmental standards are met; and that relevant procedures are in place and are being followed (Australian Tourism Industry Association, 1990). In this sense, environmental auditing is, or should be, a necessary part of best practice environmental management for the tourism industry.

In the context of sustainable tourism, the principal objectives of environmental auditing are to identify and document the environmental compliance status of tourism developments and operations, and to provide an effective means of monitoring environmental performance. Environmental audits provide a useful picture of the environmental status of a tourism facility and a ready means of self-regulation of its operations.

A well-conducted environmental auditing programme could be expected to:

- increase the overall level of environmental awareness in the tourism industry;
- assist tourism management to improve environmental standards through 'benchmarking' against proven performance;
- identify opportunities to reinforce positive environmental interactions; and
- accelerate the achievement of best practice environmental management in the industry.

Aanuka Beach Resort, for example, has detailed auditing procedures in place for detecting and correcting any environmental impacts which occur, and for checking on levels of compliance with operational procedures. Although the primary responsibility for sustainable management of tourism development presumably rests with regulatory authorities and planning agencies, an important component of environmental

monitoring programmes should also be provision for this type of self-regulation.

The adoption of in-house auditing procedures to monitor the setting and observance of appropriate standards of environmental excellence, as is the case at Aanuka Beach Resort, serves as a useful benchmark for other tourism developments. The approach adopted at Aanuka and similar resorts is important, because experience of large scale international corporations (mentioned earlier) may not translate readily to the level of individual resorts. The challenge is to devise an effective, user-friendly environmental auditing system for tourism undertakings and demonstrate its benefits for specific sectors of the industry at defined scales of operation. Development of such a process is the objective of research focused on beach resorts in the Coffs Harbour region, and reported in Ding and Pigram (1997). This work complements other steps being taken to endorse and implement best practice environmental management in the Australian tourism industry.

IMPLEMENTATION OF BEST PRACTICE ENVIRONMENTAL MANAGEMENT

At a recent conference on ecotourism in Australia, the case was argued for the development of environmental management plans, incorporating monitoring mechanisms, as part of a broad environmental management system for tourism resorts (Anderson, 1994). This reflects a global trend towards environmental stewardship, a key element of which is environmental auditing, and the perceived benefits to be gained from the application of best practice to tourism management (Cornwall and Burns, 1992). These benefits include:

- cost saving, through reduced reliance on raw materials, elimination of wasteful practices, and avoidance or minimisation of legal liabilities for breaches of regulations;
- enhanced public image from consistent environmental performance and demonstrated sound corporate citizenship;
- incremental improvements in operational practices emanating from routine auditing procedures; and
- enhanced environmental awareness within and beyond the workplace.

Despite these benefits, implementation of an industry-wide system of environmental best practice may not be easy because of barriers or impediments posed by the particular characteristics of the tourism industry. Foremost among these is the wide diversity in scale of operations and the prevalence of small, independent industry components. Even the term 'resort' has different meanings and can refer to large integrated establishments, individual members of a corporate group, or small, independent 'Mum and Dad' enterprises.

Goodall describes the tourism industry as 'a fragmented, competitive, high-risk industry, dominated in tourist destinations by many, small, family-operated firms'. (Goodall, 1995, p. 35). As a consequence, the nature and structure of the industry can act as barriers to the adoption of best management practices, such as environmental auditing.

In this respect, tourism can be compared with agriculture. Each individual farm manager is free to choose combinations of enterprises and management practices according to circumstances. Any best management practice approach proposed for these independent operators must be attractive and flexible enough to be capable of adaptation to a particular farm situation, if it is to gain acceptance and credibility.

So it is with tourism. The multiplicity of small, independent operators must perceive the advantage in the best practices advocated for environmental management; or at least they must be convinced of the disadvantage in not pursuing this approach. Moreover, management practices which allow for the diverse, dynamic nature of the tourism market, and which offer scope for further innovation by already well-performed and environmentally aware operators, stand a greater chance of implementation. The goal is not to have all tourism establishments adopting the *same* approach to environmental management, so much as encouraging all operators to do better environmentally.

TOWARDS BEST PRACTICE ENVIRONMENTAL MANAGEMENT

The expertise, expense and long-term commitment of resources involved in lifting environmental performance inevitably mean that the adoption of best practice environmental management is 'currently, a minority activity, confined, in the main, to a few large firms' (Goodall, 1995, p. 34). This has been borne out in field research in the Coffs Harbour region where the few, major five-star integrated resorts have well-developed programmes for environment management, while the majority of tourism operators remain yet to be convinced that the benefits outweigh the costs. The challenge is to raise concern for the environment among the smaller and more numerous establishments, and achieve something of a 'trickle down' effect in the spread of environmental best practice to all levels of tourism activity.

Convincing disparate elements of the tourism industry to move beyond the minimum of 'passive, regulatory compliance' (Anderson, 1994, p. 9) may call for a range of incentives, and possibly sanctions. Industry groupings, for example motel chains and motoring organisations, could play an important part in disseminating information on environmental policy, and in convincing their members to endorse environmental codes of practice, adopt the means of auditing compliance, and monitor their performance in implementing such codes. Pressure might also be brought to bear indirectly on suppliers of tourism products and services by recognition in promotional material of sound environmental credentials (Stabler and Goodall, 1993).

Peer pressure too can be influential as support and enthusiasm for 'greener' tourism gather momentum. Part of this approach could include awards and incentive schemes for superior environmental practice, and identification of industry leaders for 'benchmarking' to compare and emulate performance.

BENCHMARKING

A successful business enterprise repeatedly compares its performance against competitors. Benchmarking is a more formal expression of this process and has ready application to tourism. Benchmarking is a continuous learning process designed to compare products, services and practices with reference to external competitors and then implement procedures to upgrade performance to match or surpass these

(Thomas and Neill, 1993). Benchmarking is most widespread in the manufacturing industry, but does have application in the services sector and hence in tourism. A ready example is to be found with the accommodation guides published by motoring organisations and the stimulus they represent towards improved facilities and performance, and rating.

The process of benchmarking requires proper selection of the features and practices to target and emulate, and the 'partners' against which to compare performance. Once again, monitoring systems and feedback measures are needed to ensure the improved outcomes anticipated. In the tourism industry, benchmarking could be an effective mechanism to prompt smaller establishments to relate to, adapt and adopt elements of best practice environmental management programs of market leaders.

As support and enthusiasm for 'greener' tourism gather momentum, pressure from within the resort sector for operators at all levels to lift their 'environmental game' could well be reinforced by market forces. It is not inconceivable, in a more environmentally aware world, that visitor preference might be directed towards those resorts which can demonstrate a superior environmental track record. It is here that auditing again can assist in substantiating consistent and successful procedures for ensuring compliance with accepted levels of environmental performance.

Future visitors to the Coffs Harbour region, for example, could well prefer, and be willing to pay extra for, an environmentally compatible product – an establishment located, designed and constructed in keeping with the ambient environment and operated along environmentally 'friendly' lines. The emergence of a generation of more environmentally concerned tourists could reveal neglected market opportunities arising from greater understanding of environmental values in the resort industry. 'With a significant number of consumers translating their environmental concerns into purchasing decisions ... "green marketing" is a viable marketing option' (Townley, 1995, p. 165). Perhaps the current systems used to rate accommodation in terms of comfort and facilities will ultimately be replaced by 'green diamonds' to indicate the degree to which a resort measures up to best practice environmental management. Sanctions,

involving downgrading in ranking, or cancellation of membership of an organisation, could be used to reinforce the message.

Finally, one of the more promising ways in which a higher order of compatibility can be achieved between tourism and the environment which nutures it is through education and communication. As with agriculture, professional personnel can play an effective leadership and extension role. It is not enough merely to inform those involved of the consequences of resource misuse. They need to acquire and demonstrate a sense of social responsibility and concern for environmental quality. Tourist developers and operators not prepared to adopt a more enlightened approach to tourism–environment interaction are likely to be forced to conform by combined pressure from industry organisation, market forces, regulatory agencies and even punitive tax measures.

CONCLUSION

Tourism is assuming an increasingly prominent profile in the Australian economy, and with this emergence comes the expectation that tourism establishments will be developed and managed at the highest standards of environmental excellence. Such expectations need to be tempered by knowledge that significant impediments stand in the way of rapid and widespread implementation of best practice environmental management in the tourism industry.

Anderson (1994) advocates 'environmental co-regulation' as the preferred option for achieving the goal of sustainable tourism development. This implies collaboration between the tourism sector and government in a more relaxed regulatory regime that liberates rather than inhibits initiatives in pursuing higher environmental standards. It could be that, under such a regime, a more feasible, practical and effective alternative to best practice environmental management is an approach which seeks to 'eliminate worst practice'. Removing from tourism management practices which are not environmentally acceptable would make an immediate contribution to improved industry performance, and would be likely to receive more ready acceptance and endorsement as the 'best practicable environmental option' in the short term (Goodall, 1995, p. 36).

In a more environmentally conscious world, the tourism industry faces increasingly stringent conditions on development, reflecting a concern of sustainability and the long-term viability of the resources on which tourism depends. The challenge for the industry is to justify its claims on resources and the environment, which a commitment to their sustainable management.

As global demands on space and resources grow with increased population, technological change and greater mobility and awareness, pressure will emerge for the tourism industry, in Australia and elsewhere, to implement appropriate steps towards best practice environmental management. The task ahead is to put in place effective procedures for introducing and monitoring 'greener', more environmentally compatible forms of tourism development, and so avoid the imposition of sanctions to satisfy mandatory compliance measures.

REFERENCES

Anderson, E. (1994), Towards self-regulation for sustainable tourism, *Proceedings of Ecodollars Tourism Conference*, Environmental Management Industry Association of Australia, Brisbane.

Australian Manufacturing Council (1992), *The Environmental Challenge: Best Practice Environmental Management*, Canberra AMC.

Australian Tourism Industry Association (1990), *Environmental Guidelines for Tourism Developments*, Canberra: ATIA.

Australian Trade Commission (1992), *Best Practice for World Competitiveness*, Canberra: Austrade.

British Airways (1992), *Annual Report*, London.

Buckley, R. (1991), *Perspectives in Environmental Management*, Berlin: Springer.

Checkley, A. (1992), Accommodating the environment: the greening of Canada's largest hotel company, *Proceedings of ISEP Conference on Strategies for Reducing the Environmental Impact of Tourism*, Vienna, 178–189.

Cornwall, G., and Burns, B. (1992), The Greening of Canada, in Edwards, F. (Editor), *Environmental Auditing. The Challenge of the 1990s*, Banff: Banff Centre for Management, University of Calgary Press, 1–6.

Daikyo and Thiess (1992), *Codes of Environmental Practice and General Safety Instructions*, Cairns: Daikyo.

Department of Industrial Relations (1992), *International Best Practice*, Canberra.

Ding, P., and Pigram, J. (1997), Tourism–environment interaction: the greening of Australian beach resorts, in T. V. Singh (Editor), *Tourism in Critical Environments: The Coastal Zone* (forthcoming).

Goodall, B. (1995) Environmental auditing: a tool for assessing the environmental performance of tourism firms, *Geographical Journal*, 161(1), 29–37.

Hawkes, S., and Williams, P. (1993), *The Greening of Tourism*, Simon Fraser University, Vancouver: Centre for Tourism Policy and Research.

International Hotels Environment Initiative (1992), *Environmental Management for Hotels: the Industry Guide to Best Practice*, Oxford: Butterworth-Heinemann.

Kelleher, G. (1993), Sustainable development of the Great Barrier Reef, in Hawkes, S., and Williams, P. (Editors), *The Greening of Tourism*, Simon Fraser University, Vancouver: Centre for Tourism Policy and Research.

Oppenheim, D. (1990), *The Green Resort*, Workshop papers (unpublished).

Stabler, M., and Goodall, B. (1993), Environmental auditing in planning for sustainable island tourism, *International Conference on Sustainable Tourism in Islands and Small States*, Valetta, Malta, November.

Thomas, J., and Neill, K. (1993), Benchmarking industrial R & D, *Search*, 24(6), 158–159.

Townley, P. (1995), Is green marketing worthwhile? in *Waste Management and Environment Source Book*, Sydney: Minnis Business Press.

Troyer, W. (1992), *The Green Partnership Guide*, Toronto: Canadian Pacific Hotels and Resorts.

The Environmental Consequences of Declining Destinations

Chris Cooper

12

ABSTRACT

A number of resorts in the northern hemisphere are experiencing declining tourism numbers as a consequence of both changing market demand and also the inability to supply a product desired by the late twentieth century holiday taker. This chapter examines the environnmental consequences of declining visitor numbers in terms of townscape, accommodation and transport. The chapter goes on to examine the possible strategic options for these resorts in terms of addressing environmental decline and examines a number of selected strategies, in an attempt to elicit common trends and approaches.

INTRODUCTION

It is the aim of this chapter to focus upon the environmental consequences of declining resorts and to assess the strategic response. The tourist area life cycle is assumed as the framework for this paper (Butler, 1980), and in particular the chapter focuses on the decline stage of the life cycle. This stage of the life cycle is receiving increasing attention (see for example Agarwal, 1994), not only in terms of the descriptors of decline, but also from the point of view of the strategic response (Cooper, 1992). The attention paid to the decline stage balances firstly, the historical literature where simple description and historical narrative of the growth stages of resorts is the norm (Pimlott, 1947; Gilbert, 1954), although more recently, serious academic treatment of resorts has emerged (Soane, 1993; Walton, 1983). Secondly, the consideration of the decline stage acts as an important and sobering counterpoint to much of the tourism literature recounting growth and optimistic forecasts; indeed, it could be argued that the tourism industry is facing the problems of declining destinations for the first time. Finally, this perspective also allows consideration of appropriate strategies and responses to decline.

This chapter utilises the British experience of decline in coastal resorts and off-shore islands. These resorts represent a unique urban form created to satisfy Victorian holiday tastes and habits. Much of their built fabric dates from the late nineteenth century – piers, terraces of hotels, promenades and bandstands – and yet remains today as the basis for late twentieth century tourism. Whilst much of this architecture is celebrated and rightly protected (see Lindley, 1973; British Tourist Authority, 1975); it does represent a real (and fixed) constraint for the resorts as they struggle to come to terms with the demands of the tourism market to the year 2000. In consequence, the economic, social and environmental integrity of many resorts is seriously threatened (Smith, 1980; Cooper, 1996). In part this is due to the changing social context.

Urry (1990) has suggested that the original popularity of the resorts lay in the creation of 'extraordinary' leisure landscapes and experiences; landscapes which were in spatial contrast to those of the workplace. In the twentieth century these distinctions have blurred and the places where people live and work are often equally exciting and provide leisure experiences. Indeed it can be argued that falling visitation and the economic malaise of the resorts has created inferior landscapes and urban areas. The level of concern is now such that a range of strategic initiatives is taking place in the last quarter of the twentieth century in an attempt to rejuvenate resorts. These initiatives and the levels of investment involved are beginning to rival that of the last quarter of the nineteenth century in some resorts (see for example Rhuddlan District Council, 1990).

DECLINING DEMAND FOR BRITISH COASTAL RESORTS

Apart from a brief period of prosperity in the immediate years following the end of the Second World War, the British coastal resorts have seen their tourism market decline year on year since the 1950s. This not only reflects an absolute fall in their tourism market, but also a loss of market share and a fundamental restructuring of the British domestic market (Wales Tourist Board, 1994). The main influence here has been the decline of the long-stay holiday market, the one or two week family holiday at the resorts which provided the basis for the 16 to 20 week season and underpinned the profitability of enterprises at the resorts.

Quite simply, the British long-stay holiday market has deserted the resorts for tourism products overseas. Rising real incomes in the post-war period allowed the realisation of

demand for overseas travel; a demand which was ably met by the outbound intermediaries who creatively packaged together flights and accommodation and sold them at competitive prices. By 1961 estimates suggest that 4 million holidays were taken overseas, and the subsequent decades have seen the inexorable rise of the intermediaries who have combined both marketing and financial strength to the detriment of the domestic resorts. In effect this represents a switch to more competitive destinations by a higher spending and more discerning market (English Tourist Board, 1991). However, new competing destinations are also in evidence in the domestic market. Holiday centres which are weather-proofed with fun pools and activities are more often located in rural areas than in the resorts. In addition, rural and heritage products have grown rapidly since the 1980s and taken both staying and day visitors from the resorts.

This structural change in the market is a result of both the supply-side influences noted above and also changing tastes and attitudes towards holiday taking which in turn are rooted in shifting demographic and social trends. First, the resorts' core market has always been the blue collar family, a group which is the most likely to take an overseas inclusive tour (Association of District Councils, 1993). This has left resorts dependent upon a low spending and often elderly long-stay market. Second, this has been accompanied by a switch towards shorter domestic holidays, often taken as a weekend break (Wales Tourist Board, 1992). Whilst it could be argued that this development should partly compensate for the decline in the resorts' long-stay market, this has not completely proved to be the case. In part this is because large increases in the numbers of two or three night stays would be required to match the decline in long-stay holidays, but also the typical coastal resort cannot deliver either the quality of accommodation nor products demanded by this market. As a consequence rural, heritage and city destinations have benefited from the short holiday market (Wales Tourist Board, 1994).

For the off-shore holiday islands (The Channel Islands, the Isle of Wight and the Isle of Man) the problem is exacerbated by access issues. With the exception of the Isle of Wight the sea journeys take at least four hours and thus inhibit attempts to attract the short break market as well as providing a price barrier. The off-shore islands also sharply illustrate the decline in demand and also the changing nature of tourist demand for resorts in the decline stage. Data for the islands is more reliable than that of the mainland (see for example, Economic Advisers Office, 1994; Southern Tourist Board, 1994; Jersey Tourism, 1992; States of Guernsey, 1994).

The islands demonstrate a clear dependence on an elderly and low-spending domestic market where seasonality is acute. In Jersey and Guernsey one third of arrivals are in July and August whilst for the Isle of Wight two thirds of visitors arrive between June and September. In addition the markets are fiercely loyal. Whilst this is heartening, it does imply a lack of new recruitment, and in recession once bookings have come in from the repeat visitors, demand often evaporates. In the Isle of Man for instance two thirds of visitors are on a repeat visit, whilst for the Isle of Wight the figure rises to three quarters. The dependence on the domestic market is also problematic. In the Isle of Wight over 90% of staying visitors are domestic, whilst for the Isle of Man the figure is 85%. These trends drive down the average length of stay (from 9·3 nights in 1977 in Jersey for example, to 8·0 nights in 1987) and reduce the value of tourism to the island economies. In the Isle of Man tourism represented 11% of the island's total income in 1979 compared with 6% in the mid 1990s (Corlett, 1995).

For the mainland the data is less reliable but the trends are clear. In the decade 1978 to 1988 when the outbound market was growing rapidly, the seaside resorts lost 39 million bed nights (Wales Tourist Board, 1992). This represents half of the staying market for some of the smaller resorts and has led to a concentration of both arrivals and expenditure in six major resorts leaving the remaining seventy smaller resorts with often less than 2,000 staying visitors per week (English Tourist Board, 1991; Davies, 1992).

It is both the decline of demand and also an increasing dependence on a low-spending and highly seasonal clientele that has impacted upon the environment of the resorts to initiate a downward spiral of dereliction, poor maintenance and a consequent reduction in environmental quality.

THE ENVIRONMENTAL CONSEQUENCES OF DECLINE

It is ironic perhaps that the Victorian seaside resorts were conceived as high capacity tourism destinations designed to handle large numbers of visitors. Indeed it could be argued that the Victorians were practising 'environmentally friendly' tourism long before it became a fashionable term in the late twentieth century (Turner, 1993). There is for example no doubt that the construction of the resorts, allied to the lack of mobility of the Victorian and Edwardian tourist, protected the undeveloped parts of the British coastline. It is only in the latter half of the twentieth century that the under-use of these facilities has led to dereliction and infrastructure problems (Association of District Councils, 1993). The loss of townscape features and the very buildings and features which characterised the resorts' success is striking. Stallibrass (1980), for example, estimates that up to half of all seaside guesthouses were lost to the tourism market between 1951 and 1971, whilst the number of 'grand hotels' fell by one half during the 1970s and the number of seaside piers was cut by two thirds in the century 1890 to 1990. The environmental consequences of long-term market decline in the resorts has produced a spiral of decline which has put in jeopardy the quality of life of those who live, work and holiday in the resorts (English Tourist Board, 1991). Solutions are handicapped by the inability of the public sector to maintain parts of the resorts' fabric and the difficulty of attracting private sector investment in the face of a falling market. It is possible to view the environmental consequences of decline under three headings.

Townscape

As noted above, distinctive townscape features defined the character of the resorts. In particular, the promenade and seafront areas and the Victorian, Edwardian and even art deco buildings are a critical ingredient in their 'sense of place'. In many resorts the 'recreational business district' is now reduced to a jumble of night clubs, fast food outlets, poor quality amusement arcades and retailing, all of which cater for a low spend and highly seasonal market (English Tourist Board, 1991). These outlets are highly seasonal, poorly maintained in the off-season and create resentment amongst the local residents, particularly where housing is close by.

In addition, replacement of traditional features with mundane street furniture, loss of historic buildings to be replaced with infill blocks of apartments and the simple lack of awareness of the importance of design detail in the resorts has led to a loss of quality in the townscape, and particularly in the recreational and accommodation business districts (Turner, 1993; English Tourist Board, 1993). One reason for this has been the lack of a planned relationship between tourism and other forms of development.

Accommodation

The accommodation sector in the resorts can be characterised as one and two star, small units of ten bedrooms or less, and owner-managed. Whilst this provides a flexible and friendly stock of accommodation, it also represents a sector which lacks the management and professional skills to deliver a high quality product. Also, as barriers to entry are low, many owners came into the sector for emotional reasons (such as a desire to live in a particular resort), rather than for sound economic reasons (Brown, 1987; Shaw and Williams, 1990; Stallibrass, 1980). In the post war period, changing market trends and the desire for quality accommodation have taken their toll on this sector. Simply, accommodation standards at the resorts have failed to keep pace with consumer expectations. There are a variety of reasons for this. There is a clear lack of investment in the sector due to a combination of low occupancy, seasonality and the character of ownership. These factors conspire to drive down profitability and therefore reduce the resources available for reinvestment. In addition, many of the buildings are inappropriate and often past their useful life. Large Victorian guesthouses commonly do not have lifts, en-suite bedrooms or car parking and the rooms themselves are large and expensive to heat. Data from the Isle of Man clearly illustrate these problems. In the mid 1990s, 49% of the bedrooms on the island were not en-suite; 11% of hotels on the island had no central heating; 29% had no television in the bedrooms; and 62% had no lift (Corlett, 1995). In addition the small independent hotel or guesthouse is handicapped in their marketing as they lack access to computer reservation systems and do not have large promotional budgets.

In summary the accommodation sector in the resorts often has a poorly maintained and rundown appearance stemming from the difficult trading conditions they face (Cooper and Buhalis, 1992). In turn this deters new markets seeking quality accommodation and frustrates the resorts' attempts to break into the short break and business/convention sectors. As a result much of the accommodation is being lost to the tourism market and is changing use to offices, nursing homes and emergency accommodation for the homeless – all developments which change the 'tone' of the resorts.

Transport

The post-war arrival of visitors by car rather than by rail has had fundamental implications for the resorts. In a practical sense the provision of road schemes and car and coach parking facilities has changed the nature of the towns. In particular the seafront area is often cut off from the town and the accommodation districts by traffic. This creates environmental problems and frustrates pedestrian access to the promenades (Pearce, 1978; Turner, 1993). In addition, resorts have now become touring centres, as dependent upon their hinterlands to attract business as on the town itself. In the meantime, under-use of public transport leads to poorly designed and un-welcoming arrival gateways such as railway and bus stations.

The best summary of the implications of these trends has been provided by the English Tourist Board (1991):

'Market shifts have produced a negative cycle of falling product quality, reduced prices to hold on to available markets, lower profitability, lack of investment even for refurbishment – and further decline in the quality of the experience provided in resorts. By 1990, much of the more demanding clientele has switched to competitor destinations' (p. 7).

THE STRATEGIC RESPONSE

The public sector faces a dilemma in the resorts. Whilst many recognise the value of supporting tourism, they are dependent upon a residential constituency which is often hostile to tourism; indeed, the highly visible signs of physical and social decline do not help the public sector case (English Tourist Board, 1991). Yet as planning and environmental authorities it is the public sector that holds ultimate responsibility for environmental quality.

Clearly, strategic vision is needed in the resorts. However, the public sector is handicapped here due to twelve monthly budgeting cycles which deter a long-term view, and also often due to a lack of tourism expertise in the smaller resorts. The industry too, finds it difficult to initiate regeneration in the resorts due to lack of an effective voice, bickering between competing trade associations and the general fragmentation of the tourism sector. In addition there is no tradition of strategic thinking in the resorts, either in the public or the private sector. Indeed, the sector has been characterised by short-term, tactical planning approaches. Equally, in the past when the destinations were successful their very success obscured the need for long-term thinking, whilst in the latter stages of the life cycle it is more difficult to justify the cost of an expensive planning exercise. As if these barriers were not enough, the difficulties of implementing strategic planning in the communities which make up the resorts should not be underestimated. The multifaceted economies of resorts, allied to the residential community provide a formidable context where the political interests and conflicts between myriad stake-holders may hinder the process.

It has been against this difficult backdrop that a number of British resort regeneration strategies have been launched in the post-war years. This is a belated recognition of the severity of decline and also reflects the changing role of public authorities as corporate, income-generating agencies. The initiatives represent a belief in the need to re-launch and reposition the resorts and also are testament to recognition of the benefits of taking a strategic approach (Heath and Wall, 1992; Smith, 1991; Travis, 1992). These benefits translate into providing a sense of ownership in the tourism sector, providing a set of performance standards against which success can be evaluated and, above all, providing a guiding set of objectives and a framework for coordinated action in the resort. This coherence of approach

should provide a sharpening of objectives and demands that stake-holders are clear in their role (Kotler *et al*, 1993). In effect, strategic planning for a destination is a sequence of choices and decisions taken about deployment of resources which drive a destination in a particular direction (Brownlie, 1994). It represents a deliberate, integrative plan which recognises the need for goal setting and the need to control change through a higher-order planning exercise (Kotler *et al*, 1993).

The Strategies

Early strategic initiatives are found in the British off-shore holiday islands. This is not only due to the severity of the problems experienced by the islands, but also they lie outside of the British statutory tourist board system. This system was established in 1969 and it was not until their remit for domestic marketing and development led them to take an interest in the seaside resorts that regeneration became an issue on the mainland (English Tourist Board, 1972a).

This interest led to a number of detailed resort studies examining supply, demand and organisational issues and providing both a SWOT analysis and recommendations for future actions in terms of physical development and market repositioning (see for example English Tourist Board, 1972b; 1979; 1981a; 1981b; 1982; 1983; 1986). In Northern Ireland a similar exercise was undertaken but here the emphasis was more upon market research requirements (Northern Ireland Tourist Board, 1971; 1978). In an attempt to maintain this momentum and also to stimulate interest in a strategic approach, the English Tourist Board held a competition 'Resorts 2000' in 1985. This was designed to focus thinking at the strategic level and winning resort strategies qualified for government aid. The initiative has continued into the 1990s with a published resort strategy for Wales (Wales Tourist Board, 1994) and an influential report on the future for smaller resorts (English Tourist Board, 1991).

It would be expected that the strategies would demonstrate a commonality of approach. After all, the problems and issues are similar across all resorts. Here, Jain (1985) and Diamond (1988) provide useful frameworks within which to locate the strategic response to changing markets and the changes in the wider context.

Jain's (1985) approach is to build a matrix of competitive position and industry maturity. Clearly, British coastal resorts are at the mature/ aging stage and generally have a tenable competitive position. **Withdrawal** and **divestment** are cited by Jain (1985) as possible options, however these are difficult decisions for a resort to take, particularly as tourism tends to be interwoven into the fabric and way of life of the town. Nonetheless, the mid-1990s are seeing just such a public debate taking place in both the Channel Islands and the Isle of Man.

Jain (1985) cites other options. The **harvest approach** aims to convert market share into higher returns to provide a sudden boost to profitability. **Turnaround** is an attempt to overcome a weak performance in a relatively limited time scale, leading to stable conditions and average performance. **Find niche** opts for retention of a small defensible segment of the market rather than withdrawing, whilst **retrench** means cutting back investment and reducing exposure to losses.

Diamond (1988) takes Jain's (1985) framework one stage further by classifying the strategies adopted by resorts in decline. He considers four possible responses:

(1) **Turnaround** represents a concerted public and private sector initiative to reverse falling visitor numbers by investment in development and substantial planning and promotional efforts. The Isle of Man's strategy can be classified as turnaround.

(2) For **sustainable growth** the resort's external conditions are unfavourable, perhaps in terms of access or location, and the strategy focuses on maintaining existing markets and achieving a low level of growth by new recruitment of visitors to supplement a loyal repeat clientele. A number of small/medium sized resorts in Northern England fall into this category.

(3) With **incremental growth** the strategy adopts a phased approach to resort development with limited use by test marketing of new products and phased development projects as the resort seeks new markets. Bournemouth's strategy in the leisure segment of its market fits this category.

(4) **Selective tourism** is similar to Jain's (1985) niche strategy where only certain market segments are targeted to capitalize on the resort's

strengths. Swanage, with a concentration on family holidays and the education market, is a good example.

Many of the resort strategies identify both product and market-driven objectives. The product-focused approach is the most relevant to environmental concerns as it is concerned with organising the various public sector and other agencies with responsibility for the destination to coordinate initiatives and work to common objectives: objectives which will maintain and enhance the quality of the tourism product and the environment. Supporting objectives are often also present and relate to issues such as product quality, accommodation grading, management, staff and training. The aim here is clearly to provide a high level of product quality and service.

An example of a product-driven strategy is found at Rhyl on the north coast of Wales. Here a multi agency package, led by the local authority, has transformed the promenade area. By the 1960s Rhyl was in a downward spiral of decline having lost its major attractions, many of its bed spaces and in a town dependent upon tourism, unemployment and economic malaise resulted. By 1985, the town had a male unemployment rate of 42% (Rhuddlan Borough Council, 1990). The Rhyl strategy involved a total regeneration of the town with tourism as a part but not the only element; indeed considerable housing improvement was also included in the scheme. By 1997, the town will have completed a multi-million pound building and investment scheme to rejuvenate tourism which is on the scale of late Victorian investment and vision found in UK resorts.

Less ambitious, but equally effective product-driven strategies have focused on resort environments and townscape (Turner, 1993; Smith, 1991; Davies, 1991). The English Tourist Board and the Civic Trust have assembled an innovative strategy for Weston Super Mare (English Tourist Board, 1993). This strategy takes the form of a highly detailed design guide to combat the loss of townscape features and poor design. It is based upon regeneration of the heritage and environment of the resort. Similar initiatives are under-way in other resorts each with a particular emphasis – for example traffic management in Jersey, Guernsey, St Ives and Tenby; whilst the concept of core visitor areas is suggested by the English Board (1991) to address the visual blight of many recreational business districts. Core visitor areas not only provide the sense of place for visitors with associated facilities, landscaping and interpretation, but they also have to be sustained year round and must therefore have significant appeal to local residents. Rhyl's promenade developments are a good example of this approach.

More all-embracing strategies are found in the Isle of Man and Wales. In the Isle of Man a political commitment to tourism in the mid-1980s stimulated an ambitious approach which involved both a marketing and development strategy and a reorientation of public sector tourism structures (Cooper and Jackson, 1989; Cooper, 1990; Corlett, 1995). Similarly the Wales Tourist Board has a coastal resorts' strategy with the clear objectives of maintaining market share, lengthening the season, developing new markets and promoting environmental initiatives through integrated development strategies for individual resorts (Wales Tourist Board, 1994).

Whilst all the strategies are diverse it is possible to draw a number of generalisations from British coastal resort regeneration. A number of key development issues can be identified which focus on the need to balance competing interests – for example, residential and tourism demands particularly where nightlife and large tourist attractions are being proposed (Merseyside Development Corporation, 1991). Other common features include:

- land acquisition
- development control
- traffic management
- empowering the local community
- core visitor areas
- design briefs
- multi-agency projects and funding; and
- careful target marketing and disciplined marketing strategies and plans.

Experience in the resorts suggests that successful strategies have all been championed and provided an emphasis on local achievement. Equally, it is important to involve as many stakeholders in the resort as possible. This immediately provides a sense of ownership in the strategy, but also secures commitment to

implementation (see for example Isle of \ Tourist Board, 1992; 1994; Borough of Colei 1994).

CONCLUSION

This chapter has examined the particular consequences of the decline stage of the life cycle for British coastal resorts and off-shore islands. The decline has been relatively rapid as demand has switched to alternative destinations, often overseas. The demand-side changes and particular characteristics of the supply environment have conspired to reduce environmental quality at the resorts. On the one hand, the post-war combination of social, demographic and economic trends has rendered the resorts unfashionable and resulted in a market which has deserted the resorts in its search for quality in the delivery of tourism. On the other hand the resorts' amalgam of small businesses and outdated fabric means that neither the expertise nor the investment are available to deliver the quality of service and type of product demanded in the 1990s.

The severity of the problems is matched by the difficulties in devising and implementing an effective response. Barriers to the strategic vision necessary in the resorts are many, stemming again from the supply environment and also the complex political and organisational issues involved. Not the least of these is a residential population which is often hostile to the tourism sector. In the strategies so far developed, the public sector has taken the lead and secured the support of the many stakeholders at the destination. The fact that the problems are similar across the resorts has meant that the room for manoeuvre is limited and many of the strategies rightly see tight market targeting and consequent tailoring of their product as the way forward. Underlying these standard strategic approaches, however, is the need to address the decline of environmental quality which has been triggered by the fall in visitation. This requires a committed response to physical planning and design which in turn demands considerable public sector and private sector funding partnerships. Only by addressing this concern will the resorts be successful in rejuvenating their tourism markets.

REFERENCES

Agarwal, S. (1994), The Life Cycle Approach and South Coast Resorts, in Cooper, C. and Lockwood, A. (Editors) *Progress in Tourism Recreation and Hospitality Management*, Vol 5, Chichester: Wiley.

Association of District Councils (1993), *Making the Most of the Coast*, London: Association of District Councils.

Borough of Coleraine (1994), *Portrush Regeneration Initiative*, Coleraine: Borough of Coleraine.

British Tourist Authority (1972), *British Home Tourism Survey*, London: BTA.

British Tourist Authority (1975), *Resorts and Spas in Britain*, London: BTA.

Brown, B. (1987), Recent Tourism Research in South East Dorset in Shaw, G. and Williams, A. (Editors) *Tourism and Development: Overviews and Case Studies of the UK and the South West Region*, Working Paper 4, University of Exeter: Department of Geography.

Brownlie, D. T. (1994), Strategy Planning and Management, in S F Witt and L Moutinho (Editors) *Tourism Marketing and Management Handbook* second edition, New York: Prentice Hall.

Butler, R. W. (1980), The Concept of the Tourist Area Cycle of Evolution; Implications for Management of Resources, *Canadian Geographer* **24** 5–12.

Cooper, C. P. (1990), Resorts in Decline: The Management Response, *Tourism Management* **11** (1) 63–67.

Cooper, C. P. (1992), The Life Cycle Concept and Strategic Planning for Coastal Resorts, *Built Environment* **18** (1) 57–66.

Cooper, C. P. (1996), Parameters and Indicators of the Decline of the British Seaside Resort, forthcoming in Shaw, G. and Williams, A. (Editors) *Ride the Big Dipper*, London: Mansell.

Cooper, C. P. and Jackson, S. (1989), Destination Life Cycle : The Isle of Man Case Study, *Annals of Tourism Research* **16** (3) 377–3.

Cooper, C. P. and Buhalis, D. (1992), Strategic Management and the Marketing of Small and Medium Sized Enterprises in the Greek Aegean Islands, in Teare, R (Editor) *Managing Projects in Hospitality Organisations*, London: Cassell.

Corlett, S. (1995), *Resort Strategy and Action*, Paper delivered to the Royal Town Planning Institute Conference on the Future of Resorts, Llandudno.

Davies, P. (1991), Wish You Were Here? *Landscape Design*, 21–24 December.

Diamond, N. P. (1988), *A Strategy for Cold Water Resorts into the Year 2000*, Unpublished MSc Thesis, Guildford: University of Surrey.

Economic Advisers Office (1994), *Isle of Man Passenger Survey*, Douglas: Economic Advisers Office.

English Tourist Board (1972a), *The Future Marketing and Development of English Seaside Tourism*, London: English Tourist Board.

English Tourist Board (1972b), *Blackpool Visitors and Tourism Survey*, London: English Tourist Board.

English Tourist Board (1979), *Woodspring Tourism Study*, London: English Tourist Board.

English Tourist Board (1981a), *Scarborough District Tourism Study*, London: English Tourist Board.

English Tourist Board (1981b), *Isle of Wight Tourism Study*, London: English Tourist Board.

English Tourist Board (1982), *Torbay Tourism Study*, London: English Tourist Board.

English Tourist Board (1983), *Brighton Tourism Study*, London: English Tourist Board.

English Tourist Board (1985), *Resort 2000 Competition*, London: English Tourist Board.

English Tourist Board (1986), *Bournemouth and South East Dorset Tourism Study*, London: English Tourist Board.

English Tourist Board (1991), *The Future of England's Smaller Seaside Resorts*, London: English Tourist Board.

English Tourist Board/Civic Trust (1993), *Turning the Tide*, London: English Tourist Board.

Gilbert, E. W. (1954), *Brighton Old Ocean's Bauble*, London: Methuen.

Heath, E. and Wall, G. (1992), *Marketing Tourism Destinations*, New York: Wiley.

Isle of Wight Tourism (1992), *Tourism on the Isle of Wight. A Strategy for the 1990s and Beyond*, Newport: Isle of Wight Tourism.

Isle of Wight Tourism (1994), *Isle of Wight Tourism Strategy*, Newport: Isle of Wight Tourism.

Jain, S. C. (1985), *Marketing Planning and Strategy*, Cincinnati: South Western.

Jersey Tourism (1992), *Jersey Tourism Visitors Survey 1991/92*, St Helier: States of Jersey Tourism Committee.

Kotler, P., Haider, D. H. and Rein, I. (1993), *Marketing Places*, New York: Free Press.

Lindley, K. (1973), *Seaside Architecture*, London: Evelyn.

Merseyside Development Corporation (1991), *New Brighton Area Strategy*, Liverpool: MDC.

Northern Ireland Tourist Board (1971), *Seaside Resort Holidays in Northern Ireland, 1971*, Belfast: Northern Ireland Tourist Board.

Northern Ireland Tourist Board (1978), *Resorts Survey 1978*, Belfast: Northern Ireland Tourist Board.

Pearce, D. G. (1978), Form and Function in French Resorts, *Annals of Tourism Research* **5** (1) 142–155.

Pimlott, J. A. R. (1947), *The Englishman's Holiday: A Social History*, London: Faber and Faber.

Rhuddlan Borough Council (1990), *West Rhyl Regeneration and Development Strategy*, Rhyl: RBC.

Shaw, G. and Williams, A. (1990), Tourism, Economic Development and the Role of Entrepreneurial Activity, in Cooper, C. (Editor) *Progress in Tourism Recreation and Hospitality Management*, Vol 2, London: Belhaven.

Smith M. (1991), The Future for British Seaside Resorts, *Insights* 21–26, London: English Tourist Board.

Smith, S. J. C. (1980), Coastal Planning. Where Next? *The Planner* **66** (1) 143–145.

Soane, J. V. N. (1993), *Fashionable Resort Regions: Their Evolution and Transformation*, Oxford: CAB.

Southern Tourist Board (1994), *Isle of Wight Tourism Facts*, Eastleigh: STB.

Stallibrass, C. (1980), Seaside Resorts and the Hotel Accommodation Industry, *Progress in Planning* **13** (3) 103–174.

States of Guernsey (1994), *Guernsey Statistical Digest*, St Peter Port: States of Guernsey.

Travis, P. (1992), The Seaside Fights Back, *Insights* 11–18, London: English Tourist Board.

Turner, G. (1993), Tourism and the Environment: The Role of the Seaside, *Insights* 125–131, London: English Tourist Board.

Urry, J. (1990), *The Tourist Gaze*, London: Sage.

Wales Tourist Board (1992), *Prospects for Coastal Resorts – A Paper for Discussion*, Cardiff: Wales Tourist Board.

Wales Tourist Board (1994), *A Strategy for Wales*, Cardiff: Wales Tourist Board.

Walton, J. K. (1983), *The English Seaside Resort. A Social History 1750–1914*, Leicester: Leicester University Press.

Community
Issues

The Four *H*s of Tribal Tourism: Acoma – a Pueblo Case Study

13

Valene L. Smith

ABSTRACT

The American Indian pueblo of Acoma is examined in terms of the four criteria of tribal or ethnic tourism development: Habitat, Heritage, History and Handicrafts. The resident population effectively developed and currently manages their visitor industry, and is a model for indigenous leadership and participation.

Tribal Tourism is a new and expanding addendum to such post-modern travel modes as Ecotourism, and Adventure and Wilderness Travel. For the tourist, these new destination concepts posit a vague awareness of diminishing resources that individuals should *see while they still can*. The travel industry, ever alert to innovation, is despatching travel writers and itinerary drafters to popular tribal destinations, and especially to Indian reservations in the American Southwest (Figure 13·1), to the New Guinea Highlands, to China's Yunnan Province, and to the Andean provinces. World Tourism Organization (WTO) is also contributing, perhaps inadvertently, to the concept of Tribal Tourism with its developmental programs for *La Ruta Maya* (through Central American communities), for *The Silk Road* across Central Asia, and most recently, *The Slave Route* in West Africa. All three regions are the homelands of indigenous peoples, whose cultures are featured in tribal or ethnic tourism marketing.

The issues of Tribal Tourism are particularly apparent in the USA because of the current influx of European and Asian visitors, attracted both by a comparatively weak dollar and a residual pent-up desire to find not 'family roots' but the 'dendrites' of historic family migrations to the New World. Decades of American motion pictures, especially the Westerns dating to the 1930s, created stereotypes of dramatic landscapes, and intensified the desire to *see* the picturesque lands of the Indian, so richly depicted by noted nineteenth century artists, George Catlin and Kurt Bodmer. And traditional Indian culture 'lives' today in the novels of Willa Cather and Tony Hillerman.

Land claims settlements in the USA have empowered tribal groups with capital for tourism development (including casino gambling on

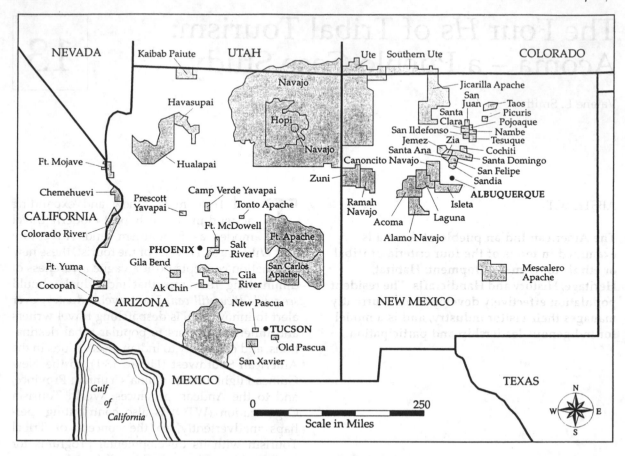

Figure 13·1. American Indian reservations (1995).

Indian reservations) but disparity and doubt persist among the indigenous peoples. Some tribal nations (as they are appropriately defined) have successfully created substantial employment from marketing their cultural heritage. Included in this list are the Pueblo Indians at Taos, New Mexico whose 5-storied pueblo is on the World Heritage List (Figure 13·2); and the 200,000 Navajo whose 17·5 million acre reservation includes some of the most spectacular scenery in the Southwest including Monument Valley (Smith 1996); and the Eastern Cherokee in North Carolina whose history has been theatrically staged every summer evening for more than forty years (Tiller 1992:247). Significantly, tiny Nambe Pueblo (one of the eight Northern New Mexico pueblos, Figure 13·1) advertises itself as the *only Native American-owned tour operator*, and from its Santa Fe office provides tour and guide services to the other regional pueblos, to archaeologic sites, and to other tourist destinations.

The two most traditional American tribal nations are wary of tourism, fearing loss of cultural heritage. The Hopi of Arizona (who occupy a small reservation only a few miles east of Grand Canyon, one of America's most favored international destinations) closed their historic pueblo of Walpi to tourism. An unfortunate negative cartoon, interpreted as ridicule of religious ceremonials, stirred public anger. The Zuni of New Mexico relented on long-standing policy prohibiting visitors at their *Shalako* ceremonies in 1994, but tourists unfortunately openly violated community restrictions against photography, and were escorted off the reservation by tribal police. Subsequently the Zuni Tribal Council closed the pueblo to tour groups and motorcoaches.

To close a pueblo to outsiders means a serious revenue loss for their craftspeople, especially jewelry and *kachina* figures for which both pueblos are justly renowned. Arizona estimates

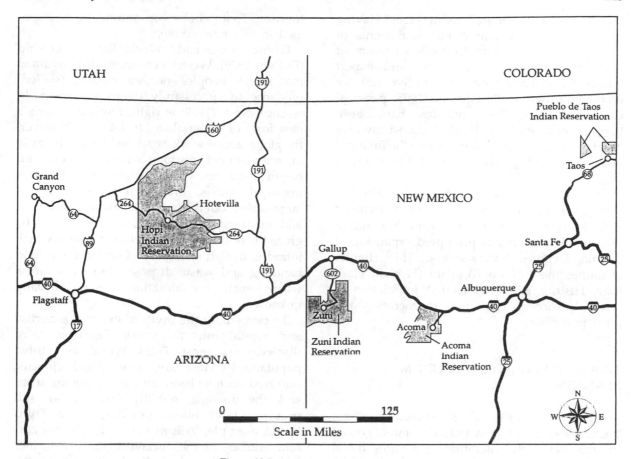

Figure 13·2. Area map of the Southwest.

their 1995 visitor count at 26 million, of whom 3 million were international visitors (Northern Arizona University 1996). New Mexico hosted some 13 million visitors in 1995, and estimated their international numbers at 200,000 (New Mexico State Office of Tourism 1996). When visitors are restricted, tourists shop along highways in Anglo-owned stores whose management benefits from the mark-up on prices. Most tourists (especially foreigners) would prefer to 'buy from an Indian', even if they paid the same or a higher price; Indian mystique favors 'authenticity'. If only a small percentage of these millions of tourists purchased at Indian-owned cooperatives on the reservations, the income would benefit tribal employees and their nation. Many Indians have learned that privacy to protect culture is sometimes dearly bought.

The Hopi nation owns a motel, restaurant and cultural center with craft salesroom, on the highway an hour's drive east from Grand Canyon. One of America's most visited national parks (especially by foreigners), in 1995 the Canyon hosted some 4·9 million visitors, of whom some forty-five to fifty percent were Europeans and Asians. The Park administration estimates the average length of stay in the park at 3·8 hours but notes that passengers on motor-coach tours actually spent only 17 minutes (average), viewing the Canyon from its rim. Most of their visitor time was given to eating, and shopping in concession stores. Visitors repeatedly say that although to see the canyon is a paramount attraction, the desire to see a 'real Indian' (tribal tourism) is a close second (Smith 1996). Yet the tourist facilities at nearby Hopi are empty or little-used most of the year, despite their proximity to this burgeoning sales opportunity.

The Zuni pueblo, a short drive south of Gallup, New Mexico (a famous town on historic Route 66, now Hiway 40), is unsure of investing in facilities even as limited as at Hopi. Having recently won two land claims settlements of US$25 million each, Zuni Councilmen comment that 'after paying the attorneys and expert witnesses, we have only US$20 million left; we fear being swindled' (Ghahate 1995, personal communication). Both pueblos have been tempted and similarly decided against involvement with casino gambling, despite the financial benefits accruing elsewhere (*Indian Gaming Magazine* May 1995:10–11).

Acoma Pueblo, a close neighbor to Zuni and an aboriginal trading partner, has been involved with tourism for over fifty years. The recent increase in visitors has prompted expansion of pueblo facilities and services. This chapter examines the 4 H's of Tourism (Habitat, Heritage, History and Handicrafts) in relation to Acoma's success in cultural regeneration and tourism income.

TRIBAL/THIRD WORLD TOURISM PLANNING

Tribal tourism, originally subsumed as ethnic tourism (Smith 1977) is virtually unrecognized in the scholarly literature although travel industry journals and media writers headline it as a promotional banner. By contrast, the indigenous peoples of Third World countries (who are both ethnic and tribal) have received extensive consideration from scholars too numerous and too well-known to justify listing here. Tribal tourism and Third World tourism share many characteristics: their population is usually factionalized, with one group searching for the benefits of a wage economy, while another rejects modernization to maintain traditional values. Both tribesmen and Third World indigenes have traditionally suffered from high unemployment including a significant population with minimal job skills (unemployment on southwestern Indian reservations can be as high as 40% with a comparable school drop-out rate). Because of these, and other social factors (strong family interdependency, shared religious values, closed societies with minimal intercultural mix from in-migration, subsistence level economies, etc.), much of the existing tourism literature pertaining to Third World societies is equally applicable to tribal

tourism. That scholarship should be re-examined in this new context.

Dating to the early World Bank leadership (DeKadt 1979), Western ethnocentrism assumed that native peoples needed outside (skilled) guidance to successfully develop tourism. In essence, Nash (1989) is right; tourism became a new form of imperialism. In fairness, however, the global air network expanded largely because of international visitors whose comfort and health required Western-style and Western-managed hotels, which ultimately became large-scale models for small-scale locally owned and managed hostelries. Due credit must be given the multinational hotels and resorts which introduced high standards of sanitation in food handling and waste disposal into world areas where such considerations were virtually unknown.

To perpetuate the myth of external expertise and capital into the 1990s, however, is a disservice to most Third World and tribal populations. Most are now global citizens, nurtured on television, and many among them seek the upward mobility that tourism still promises (and often provides). In a Third World example, Wilson (1997) documents current tourism in the enclave of Goa, a former Portuguese colony in India. In December 1994, Goa hosted 220,000 tourists most of whom were *domestic* tourists from India, and who were satisfied with their hospitality in locally owned-and-managed hotels and beach front restaurants. The leakage was minimal and the multiplier effect was estimated at 3·2–3·6, about equivalent to the figure for India (Richter 1989:122), and higher than the world average. Goan tourism is home-grown, developed without expert consultants, and its control rests largely with Goan townspeople whose newspaper speaks clearly on their behalf. Wilson (1997) supports the local opinion that government solicitations for major up-scale resorts will harm, rather better, the economy.

Demographics and cost-effective economy will continue to mandate ever larger cruise ships, airplanes and resorts, the latter projects so ably described by Inskeep (1991). Their creation, however, continues to impose on residents a changed lifestyle and a different economy. Very few projects are funded for *mitigation* or *conflict resolution*, even when shown that it can be successful (Preister 1987). In fact, Inskeep (1991), Shaw and Williams (1994) and Theobald (1994) and their respective authors all fail to even mention either term. This almost universal omission of public concern prompted the following comment:

> 'unless the citizens affected by tourism are included as permanent contributors to the planning process, their protests will grow even more shrill and effective [NB *in destination decline*]' (Plog 1994:46–47).

Tribal tourism and its correlates: ecotourism, adventure and wilderness travel, all focus on small-scale enterprises that are labor intensive for an owner, a family, or a small tribe. Not quite a return to the 'mom and pop' era, these activities are transferring tourism management to local control and maximizing local benefits.

Tribal tourism must begin with and be sustained by internal leadership and group accord. Consensus should be a goal but if not possible, then divisive factionalism must be contained through mitigation. This chapter, an essay in applied anthropology, suggests guidelines (or questions to ask) that could enable tribal/ethnic leadership – at whatever level – to assess their available tourism resources. From a carefully considered and thoughtful self-evaluation, any Third World entity or any Native American nation (or any smaller part thereof) should be able to determine:

(1) if tourism is an appropriate activity for them; or
(2) establish valid reasons for NON-participation; and
(3) if tourism is a viable option, then
(4) in what type(s) of tourism activity
    a) do they have the greatest strengths? and
    b) which type(s) will minimize negative impact?

Several cautionary comments must be made. Many Native American leaders today are highly literate and hold advanced degrees in law, the sciences and economics. If tourism resource persons are invited, colonial 'talking down' is a signal affront. Their mission should be to listen, not advise. The Canadians who have worked for years in Inuit villages of the North have learned the lesson well: most outside 'experts' fly in for a day or two, hold their meeting, lay out a plan, and depart without developing 'any credibility among the natives' (Woodley 1993). From the perspective of applied anthropology, the weakest single link in external evaluation of tourism – including whether to participate in this activity at all – lies in the failure to ferret out and to engage the real decision-makers of the community. Unfortunately that insight is not quickly obtained even by an anthropologist-in-residence; overt status-markers are not always symbols of social authority. Human behavior at planning sessions often resembles a group of seals on a beach: the eager 'barking bachelors' create commotion and noise while the 'beachmaster' quietly sits and watches. Although outsiders might credit the aggressive young seals (or youths) with leadership, every adult seal within earshot and vision knows who wields the power!

THE 4 Hs OF TRIBAL TOURISM

The Four Hs of Tribal Tourism are: Habitat, Heritage, History and Handicrafts. Fully described elsewhere (Smith 1996), the 4 Hs are analytic tools by means of which indigenous populations can assess their strength for tourism, and similarly ascertain their weaknesses. It is the belief of this author that tourism entrepreneurship or involvement is not appropriate for every population. Rather, judicious self-study of the physical and human resources present in any given society can become their guidelines to the reality of tourism development, and the type(s) of tourism promotion that will be (a) successful, financially and culturally; and (b) a positive experience for both the host community and its visitors. Tourism is first and foremost a hospitality industry, dependent upon mutual warm relationships and interactions.

Each of the 4 Hs is associated with a few basic values, and idea around which to base discussion (Table 13.1). Taken together, the composite description of the community resources can define a *culturally-bounded* host-visitor experience which is, quite literally, a micro-study of local man-land relationships. Each community will be geographically, socially and historically distinct. By laying out a chart of (+) and (-) for many of the individual characteristics, the community can develop a self-appraisal to aid in the process of tourism decision-making. Rather than

Table 13·1. The four *H*s of tourism.

Habitat	Heritage	History	Handicrafts
Access	Cultural Resources	Culture Contact	Heritage Crafts
Proximity	Museums	Decision Makers	Innovation
Appeal	Interpretive Centers	Conflict Resolution	Miniaturization
Diversity	Ceremonials	Showcase Today	Marketing
Resources	Experiential	Marginal Men/Women	
Marketing	Marketing	Marketing	

pursue further purely theoretical and definitional prose, the Native American Pueblo of Acoma serves as an illustrative case study.

ACOMA – AND THE 4 Hs

Acoma was selected for the case study because it is a small, homogeneous geographic unit, aptly known as the 'Sky City' which vies with Hopi in claiming to be the longest continuously occupied village in the USA. Tourism dates to the 1930s, was developed by the Acomas and remains today completely within their control. In 1994 the gross receipts for the 140,000 visitors exceeded US$1 million, and the net income provides for supplemental social services for the tribe. Tourism is locally viewed as a positive activity, and is credited with cultural preservation and restoration. A succinct ethnographic overview of Acoma appears in the Handbook of North American Indians Volume 9 (Garcia-Mason 1979). In addition this writer has visited Acoma repeatedly in the past decade, to monitor tourism development and change.

HABITAT AND TOURISM

Habitat as a geographic term usually defines the physical attributes of an area but, for tourism, habitat is expanded here to include the tourist-host region. The Acoma Reservation comprises 245,672 acres (Figure 13·3) and supports some 5000 population, by farming (over half the acreage is irrigable and with a growing season of 118 days, produces alfalfa, wheat, corn, row crops and some fruit orchards). Aside from small Douglas fir reserves, cattle ranching is the other principal activity. Some mineral reserves exist including clay, oil, coal, natural gas and uranium. The altitude ranges between 6000 and 8000 feet, and more than half the annual 10 in of precipitation occurs in July, August and September. Summers are hot (up to 103° F in August), and winter lows may drop to 20° F.

Acoma Reservation lies about 60 miles west of Albuquerque, but only 11 miles via paved road south of Interstate 40, a main trans-continental freeway (Figure 13·2). Tourists using Albuquerque as an air gateway can easily visit the pueblo on a half-day tour. Because of the quality of the road network in the USA, as a rule-of-thumb, USA residents and visitors can/will drive to destinations within a 100 mile radius for a one-day outing; similarly, they will drive a radius of up to 250 miles for a weekend, 2–3 day trip. Acoma is also only about a 6-hour drive east of Grand Canyon, through the Painted Desert and Petrified Forest which are also important tourist destinations. Acoma therefore enjoys easy access to major tourism generating-centers. The proximity to metropolitan Albuquerque, historic Santa Fe (which receives some 1·3 million tourists per year) and the nearby Pueblo of Taos places this community in a prime position to further develop tourism. The diversity of landscape, with the Sandia Range just east of Albuquerque offers excellent skiing for winter visitors as well.

The site of the 'sky city' is the most dramatic of any Indian pueblo, on a flat-top mesa 357 feet above the valley floor . The view from the pueblo is accentuated by an adjacent and smaller table-land, termed 'Enchanted Mesa' about which local folklore recounts a human drama. The paved road (1993) to the pueblo has increased access for the mandatory tour buses (public admittance to the Sky City is by Acoma-owned 25-passenger tour bus only, and visitors are encouraged to walk down the steep historic path). Coronado, the first Westerner to see

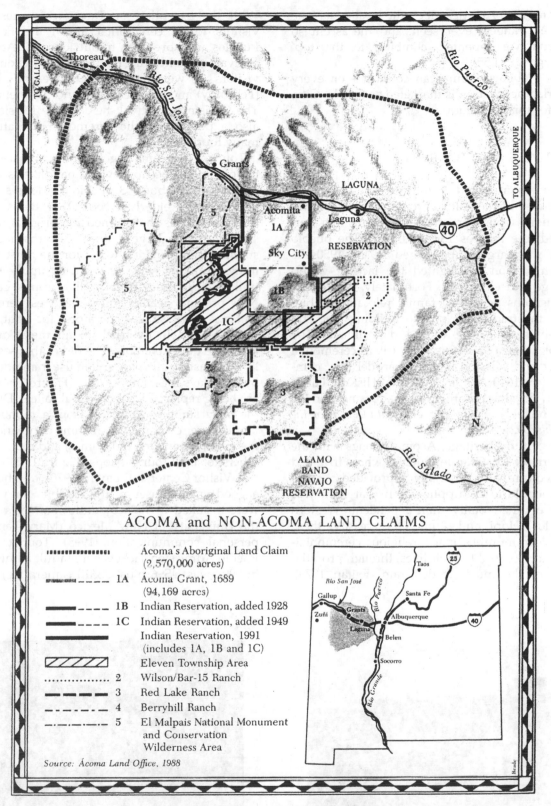

ÁCOMA and NON-ÁCOMA LAND CLAIMS

··············		Ácoma's Aboriginal Land Claim (2,570,000 acres)
─ ─ ─ ─	1A	Ácoma Grant, 1689 (94,169 acres)
── ─ ─ ─	1B	Indian Reservation, added 1928
══ ─ ─ ─	1C	Indian Reservation, added 1949
────────		Indian Reservation, 1991 (includes 1A, 1B and 1C)
//////		Eleven Township Area
················ 2		Wilson/Bar-15 Ranch
─ ─ ─ ─ 3		Red Lake Ranch
─·─·─·─ 4		Berryhill Ranch
─··─··─ 5		El Malpais National Monument and Conservation Wilderness Area

Source: *Ácoma Land Office, 1988*

Figure 13·3. Acoma land holdings (1995).

Acoma (1540 AD) described the location as 'one of the strangest ever seen...and the ascent so difficult we repented climbing to the top' (Metzger 1994:55).

For Habitat, Acoma can count a + on every criteria; the location is marketed as the Sky City, and for this it is unique.

HERITAGE AND TOURISM

Acoma is affiliated with the Keresan Indian identity, and the cultural roots are the Mimbres tradition, whose artistic designs are rich and varied (see Figures 13·6 and 13·7). The pueblo itself was largely abandoned in the 1950s as modernization highlighted the lack of water, sewage and electricity. Fortunately, ranch land acquisitions permitted family relocation. However, the traditional pueblo buildings are still well-preserved due to the dry climate. The pueblo plaza remains the tribal ceremonial center and Mission San Esteban del Rey, completed in 1640 AD, is a National Historic Landmark. The altar painting was made famous in the 1971 novel by Willa Cather, *Death Comes for the Archbishop*.

By cultural heritage, Acoma belongs with the Eastern (or Rio Grande) Pueblos whose irrigated horticulture traditionally provided more dependable food supplies each year than was true of the totally rain-dependent Western Pueblos, Hopi and Zuni. Of necessity, these latter communities made religious ceremonialism more central to their lives, through propitiation for the much-needed rain (Eggan 1979).

With the exception of Taos (which restricts visitors to all ceremonial areas) the Eastern Pueblos are more open to outsiders. At Acoma, festivals are held in the Pueblo Plaza, and outside visitors are welcomed to the Governor's Feast (February) and the Harvest Dance (September). The Christmas Festival, held in the Mission, is also a popular public ceremony that attracts many tourists.

Tourism to Acoma is generating a renaissance in both pueblo occupancy and handicrafts. Until recently, only about 13 pueblo residences were occupied (by elderly Acomas) of the several hundred homes that formed the original townsite. Formerly large natural cisterns fed by summer rain provided water for the horses and mules; drinking water was carried up the steep trail in head pots from wells/springs below. Now propane heaters and cookstoves, kerosene lanterns (even small generators) for light, and water hauled in by truck to fill metal drums make life quite tolerable. The old outhouses that line the eastern cliffs are still in use, reminders of bygone days for many visitors (Figure 13·4), but are being replaced with chemical toilets. During the busy summer tourist season, a number of families are returning to part-time occupancy on the mesa, renovating old homes, and converting others to small tourist shops (Figure 13·5).

A Visitor Center, built in the 1970s, also houses a good small museum, the exhibits for which were installed in 1978 by anthropologists from the University of New Mexico (Mary Tenorio, personal communication, 1995). Tourists buy Pueblo Admission Tickets here (adult admission in 1997 was US$6 plus US$10 camera fee), and

Figure 13·4. Acoma – east slope with outhouses.

Figure 13·5. Acoma – house renovation creating a curio shop.

Figure 13·6. Acoma pottery.

see the Museum. Tours then depart every 20 minutes, and last about an hour. With an Indian driver, 25 persons per bus take the 10-minute ride to the mesa top where they are met by a tour guide, and walk through the pueblo. Various houses (some are used only for day use, and salespersons commute to their ranches) set up stands by their door (Figure 13·5), and the tour guide pauses long enough for shoppers to make quick selections. No photos are permitted of the cemetery or the interior of San Esteban Mission.

In 1994 the Visitor Center leaders sought assistance from an Albuquerque tourism consulting firm, to provide a professional guide training program. For several decades prior,

Figure 13·7. Acoma pottery jewelry in Mimbres designs. Necklace discs 1·3 inches in diameter.

guides were often poorly informed, and visibly embarrassed about their Indian identity. The guides nowadays are articulate, and this author was impressed with the quality of the training, and the newly found self-confidence and pride in heritage on the part of the young people currently employed as pueblo hosts. Their commentary was interesting, accurate, and their ability to answer questions admirable.

With its museum, guided tour, and book store, the Visitor Center provides the Acoma visitor with a positive experience – in an hour or two, there is heritage exposure, an opportunity to ask questions, and to purchase reference reading and buy handicrafts. For US$8, this is a tourist bargain and a worthwhile opportunity to understand Indian culture and tradition. The Pueblo should rate itself + on all accounts – with the recognition that the Visitor Center could be enlarged, better meal selection and service in the small cafe and more craft sales space. They have maximized their heritage, commoditicized it without seriously altering the product ... and for individuals who wish to ask about the complexities of clan organization or tribal politics, the guides are capable. Further, visitors are made welcome to ceremonials, so few host-guest barriers exist.

One important factor to be added: there are no overnight accommodations, no supermarkets, no stores other than the Visitor Center. When the Center is closed, the tourists are literally locked out – they see front stage what the community is willing to show but few visitors wander through the family occupied farms and ranches of the reservation since they look like Western homes anywhere in the Southwest. Privacy is maintained, and the community benefits from the direct sales of their crafts to the public.

In summary, Acoma Pueblo is a veritable heritage center and should score itself with a + for heritage preservation and presentation.

HISTORY AND TOURISM

History as used here refers to culture contact between the resident aboriginal peoples and outsiders. In the Southwest outsiders include the Athabaskan-speaking in-migrants, the Navajo and Apache, who moved south from the sub-Arctic centuries ago. Culture conflict between the resident horticulturists (Pueblo Indians) and these nomadic hunters probably forced many Pueblo peoples to seek defensible mesas that offered safe haven, such as Acoma, the Sky City. Whatever the cause, Acoma was apparently occupied for 500–600 years prior to the Spanish who came looking for gold and the seven Cities of Cibola. Coronado visited Acoma in 1540 AD, described the houses as 3–4 stories high, and a village that was abundantly supplied with maize, beans and turkeys. One of his men described Acoma as 'the greatest stronghold ever seen in the world' (Minge 1991:4).

The Franciscans arrived in Acoma in October 1598 AD, a community then estimated as 6000 population. The padres were peacefully received but in December, the Acomas staged a rebellion; seven Spaniards leaped from the mesa in an attempt to save themselves. Several weeks later, avenging Spaniards scaled the cliffs at night, taking 500 Acomas prisoner. A month later, the Spanish staged a trial, and decided the Indians had been the instigators. They ruled that all males over age 25 should have one foot cut off; males aged 12 to 25 were sentenced to twenty years of personal servitude as were the women over twelve years of age. The population declined rapidly to 1400–2000. The first permanent priest, Fray Juan, arrived in 1629 AD and earned the Indians' respect for he set about rebuilding 'Old Acoma' and also supervised construction of the Mission.

The Pueblo Rebellion of 1680, which blazed through Taos and Santa Fe, brought to Acoma an unusual blessing. The Spanish Governor Otermin interviewed a number of Indians, learned of their desire to reestablish old ways and especially to revitalize their religion. To attain peace, in 1689 AD, Otermin signed a remarkable document – a Spanish land grant to Acoma, which became the basis of their first legal holdings (Figure 13·3). His strategy worked, and nearly a century later when the first Spanish expeditions turned their fire on the Navajo, Indians from Acoma were part of the Spanish armed forces. When Mexico won independence from Spain in 1821, they instituted new government concepts but raids against the Navajo persisted and with the arrival of American troops, the Mexicans agreed to the Treaty of Hidalgo in 1846.

The Acomas then faced a new battle, proving the validity of their land grant to the US government, because the Acoma's claim overlapped with those of the adjacent pueblo of Laguna. Settlement dragged on through American surveys and courts, and meanwhile the first Indian Agent arrived in 1899, and soon thereafter a school opened. Acoma's comparative isolation 'kept her people out of the mainstream of the twentieth century' (Minge 1991:83) except that the railroad needed a right-of-way through Acoma lands and paid the tribe US$1,078·85, then a substantial sum. Indian women began to sell arts and crafts along the railroad, and their children attended pueblo schools. In March 1967, after more than 100 years of legal maneuvers, the Indian Land Claims Commission settled the question of overlapping boundaries, and paid Acoma US$6,107,157 for compensation of lost lands. The Acomas had learned an important lesson: self-determination can be attained through persistence in dealing with government(s), and they were equally determined to preserve their heritage.

Tourism began at the Sky City in 1930 when Paramount Pictures of Hollywood asked to use the mesa-top village as a location for two motion pictures – 'Redskin' and 'Slap!'. To gain access with camera crews, the producers widened trails, then built a make-shift road. Thereafter occasional tourists came to visit the mesa, and the Mission church caretakers assumed responsibility to look after them, asking in return only a donation to help with its reconstruction. Gradually, these tour hosts began to charge US$·50 per person. In the 1950s the road to the top was finally completed, and a guard office was opened; towards the end of that decade, the Tribal Council decided to take charge of tourism. The Visitor Center was built (with assistance from matching grants) in 1978, and tourism has steadily increased, with greater numbers now evident from overseas as well.

In 1984, the Council opened a Bingo and Pool Hall facility on Interstate 40, primarily as a local recreation center. In 1991, the Council decided to extend into machines and slots and, recently, into card games as well. Whereas other nearby pueblos fear possible negative effects upon their youths, according to resident tourism spokesperson, Mary Tenorio (personal communication, 1995), Acoma has not incurred significant problems. 'They have to be 18 to enter'.

The culture contact between Acoma and outsiders (including the Navajo) has been centuries long with a tangled history. The comparative prosperity of Acoma farmers and ranchers reflects their fortitude and will to survive. The fact that the village is well-preserved, the Mission largely restored, and that youth have pride in showing to the public their heritage suggests that the miseries of past generations have been transcended.

Acoma rates a + for the positive manner in which historical inequities are recorded in textbooks but not in personal bitterness.

HANDICRAFTS AND TOURISM

Among its natural resources, Acoma is blessed with quantities of fine clay which, for a thousand years, has been turned into utilitarian vessels for water carriage and storage. The women are considered among the finest potters of the Southwest, and preserve the ancient designs of their Mimbres ancestors (Figure 13·7). Handmade vessels of a gallon or more in size, with extensive decoration, can cost thousands of dollars. Therefore to meet the demands of visitors, especially air travelers, Acoma potters now also manufacture small figurines (the author added a 3ft penguin to her collection for US$7), small plates, and jewelry fashioned of clay discs decorated with Mimbres designs (Figure 13·7).

To their credit, the Acomas have remained true to tradition, and have not desecrated their art by buying silver beads in bulk, to string into trinket-like necklaces, as is true else in the Southwest. By selling from stands by their homes, purchasers can 'meet the maker'. Acoma potters benefit from direct sales (although wholesalers do purchase wares for resale in urban stores in Albuquerque, Santa Fe and elsewhere).

Acoma therefore also rates a + for handicrafts, by maintaining traditional skills, decoration and quality, yet miniaturizing products for tourists, and for their direct marketing.

THE LESSONS OF THE 4 Hs

Acoma has effectively bridged tradition with tourism, and bulwarked both with the strength of self-belief. They are managing this facet of their economy well. The net earnings go back to the tribe as needed – for Head Start (pre-school) programs, for social assistance to the elderly, for emergency funds to help individuals, and as needed. The pride shown by all who work for and with tourism in Acoma is self-evident, and the future ability to cope with increasing numbers seems assured. Plans are already in place to enlarge the Visitor Center, expand the craft industry, and encourage more visitors.

Acoma is a worthy model to explain the analytic merits of Habitat, Heritage, History and Handicrafts as factors in the development of tourism. Here, tourism is locally controlled, financially profitable and culturally supportive, as well as sustainable and environmentally appropriate. Admittedly their striking landscape, combined with location near major tourist routes have favored the modern development, but the Indians themselves have contributed to their success through the development of a heritage interpretive program, and judicious selection of new handicrafts. Acoma illustrates the validity of indigenous leadership and participation as integral to tourism.

REFERENCES

Cather, W. (1971), *Death Comes for the Archbishop*. New York: Random House. de Kadt, E. (1979), *Tourism: Passport to development*. New York: Oxford University Press.

de Kadt, E. (1979), *Tourism: Passport to development*. New York: Oxford University Press.

Eggan, F. (1979), Pueblos: An Introduction, in Alfonso Ortiz, (Editor) *North American Indian Handbook Volume 9, SOUTHWEST*, pp. 224–235. Washington DC: Smithsonian Institution.

Garcia-Mason, V. (1979), Acoma Pueblo, in Alfonso Ortiz, (Editor) *North American Indian Handbook Volume 9, SOUTHWEST* pp. 450–466. Washington DC: Smithsonian Institution.

Ghahate, Rueben (1995), Personal Communication, Pueblo of Zuni, New Mexico.

Indian Gaming Magazine (1995), Indian Gaming Dollars – Where are they going? May 1995: pp 10–11.

Inskeep, E. (1991), *Tourism Planning*. New York: Van Nostrand Reinhold.

Metzger, S. (1994), *New Mexico Handbook. 3rd Edition*. Chico, California: Moon Publishing Company.

Minge, W. (1991), *Acoma: Pueblo in the sky*. Albuquerque: University of New Mexico Press.

Nash, D. (1989), Tourism as a Form of Imperialism, in Valene Smith (Editor) *Hosts and Guests: The anthropology of tourism.* 2nd edition. pp 37–52. Philadelphia: University of Pennsylvania Press.

New Mexico State Office of Tourism, Personal Communication, 1966.

Northern Arizona University, (1996), Arizona Hospitality Research and Resource Center, Flagstaff, AZ: Personal Communication.

Plog, S. (1994), Leisure Travel: An extraordinary industry facing superordinary problems, in Theobald, W. (Editor) *Global Tourism: The next decade.* pp 40–54. Oxford: Butterworth-Heinemann.

Preister, K. (1987), Issue-Centered Social Impact. in R. Wulff and S. Fiske, (Editors), *Anthropological Praxis: Translating knowledge into practice.* pp 39–55. Boulder, Colorado: Westview Press.

Richter, L. (1989), *The Politics of Tourism in Asia.* Honolulu: The University of Hawaii Press.

Smith, V. (1977), Introduction, in Valene Smith (Editor), *Hosts and Guests: The anthropology of tourism.* lst Ed. pp. 1–14. Philadelphia: University of Pennsylvania Press.

Smith, V. L. (1996), Indigenous Tourism – The 4 H's. in Butler, R. and Hinch, L. (Editors), *Tourism and Indigenous Peoples.* London: International Thomson Business Press.

Tenorio, Mary. (1995), Personal Communication. Acoma Pueblo, New Mexico.

Theobald, W. (1994), *Global Tourism: The Next Decade.* Oxford: Butterworth-Heineman.

Tiller, V. (1992), *Discover Indian Reservations USA: A visitor's welcome guide.* Boulder, Colorado: Council Publications .

Wilson, D., Paradoxes of Tourism in Goa, *Annals of Tourism Research,* **24**:1, 52–75.

Woodley, A. (1993), Tourism and Sustainable Development: The community perspective. in Nelson, J. G., Wall, G., and Butler, R. (Editors). *Tourism and Sustainable Development: Monitoring, Planning, Managing.* pp 135–148. Waterloo, Canada: Department of Geography, University of Waterloo.

Tourism Development: Still in Search of a More Equitable Mode of Local Involvement

14

Kadir H. Din

ABSTRACT

The meaning of tourism development, from the host community's point of view, has rarely been subject to critical analysis. This chapter examines the concept of 'development' within the context of the Malaysian host community with a focus on the distributive aspects of growth. Observations from four situations suggest that benefits from tourism development have tended to by-pass ordinary members of the local community in favour of entrepreneurs who come from outside. In order to encourage a greater level of involvement among the locals it is recommended that a suitable action plan be implemented to ensure a more equitable measure of resident participation.

INTRODUCTION

The subject of equitable involvement in tourism development has been discussed in the literature for more than two decades (de Kadt, 1979, p. 2; Hughes, 1995, p. 59). Yet there is little progress so far towards addressing the question of whether there can indeed be a general model for managing the development process in the host communities. To be sure, there is considerable coverage given to the practice of tourism planning at the macro level, such as those offered by Kaiser and Helber (1978) and Inskeep (1994). Although many of these recent texts on tourism planning do allow some space for a discussion on the relationship between tourism and community development, usually expressing the desire that tourism should benefit the host community, they say very little on how to actually mobilise local involvement. Even the term 'local' is rarely defined. It appears as though the subject is a moral issue which objective analysts would try to avoid.

The purpose of this chapter is to reactivate interest in the above subject through a discussion of the situation in Malaysia. It begins by looking at the meaning of 'development' and its relevance and application to a number of host situations in the country. This is followed by a review of available development options and some reference to strategic issues which constrain the search for an equitable approach to tourism development.

THE MEANING OF TOURISM DEVELOPMENT

From the standpoint of the host community, 'development' refers to the process or stage of realising its full potential. This potential is defined according to the goals that the community members share and aspire to achieve. It has several identifiable dimensions, namely environmental, economic, social, cultural, political and spiritual. The value assigned to each dimension differs from one community to another, even though each community exists as part of the national society.

From the Malaysian government's point of view, the primary objective is to bring about sustainable development in the tourism sector so that it can contribute towards economic development of the nation. In explicit terms the federal government's tourism policies are directed towards sectoral growth and image building at the macro level. At the state level each of the 14 territories in the Federation have their tourism portfolios. Perhaps with the exception of the Kelantan State, which is under the control of a religious-based party, every state strives to 'develop' its tourism resources in the same constructionist mold, notwithstanding the more frequent exhortations on the need to bring benefits to the local community.

A search for the most favorite terms used in government documents for each decade would yield 'foreign exchange earnings' (1960s), 'employment and promotion' (1970s), 'economic multiplier' (1980s) and 'sustainable development' (1990s). While the meanings of these terms were rarely subject to closer examination, the interest of the local community is rarely mentioned. This neglect has continued since the early 1970s when the Malaysian government first started to pay attention to tourism. Two of the six functions assigned to the Tourism Development Corporation in its enabling act (1972) were to conduct research and to facilitate a balanced development of the tourist industry. The meanings of the terms 'research' and 'development' appears to have been understood solely in the marketing and promotional sense. Until very recently considerations on equitable involvement have always been left out of the political and administrative agenda.

In one sense the neglect of the distributive aspects of development contradicts the policy directions as outlined in the Second Malaysia Development Plan 1971–1975 (the national development policy) which recognised the problem of interethnic inequality and sought to remedy this through affirmative policies which were to apply to all sectors in the economy. It is reasonable to suggest that the group that gave advisory inputs to the formulation of new economic policy as contained in the above plan, and as was re-emphasized in the subsequent four (5 year) plans, did not communicate well with the groups that produced the four consecutive tourism development plans which first appeared in 1969. These documents presented the results of studies and recommendations in a pattern familiar to most tourism consultants.

As Malaysia is a newcomer to the tourism scene, local residents have always displayed a positive attitude to both tourists and the tourist industry. However, of late there have been some local opposition in many parts of the country; the issues of contention usually revolved around the displacement of original settlers in the areas acquired for the development of resorts. There were also cases of opposition due to objection to tourism being perceived as morally undesirable. More recent protests have surfaced in island and upland destinations on account of environmental considerations; much of these protests have been inspired by opposition groups who are well linked to other movements based outside the country.

Thus the ideas on tourism development, whether it is the mainstream or the alternative, mostly originated from outside and have now assumed adversarial positions so that what is recommended may not necessarily reflect the priority need of the local community. It is very rare for consultants to recommend that tourism in particular areas should not be pursued when their terms of reference (TOR) dictates otherwise, as it is equally rare to find protest groups that would push for their preferred type of tourism development. Such pervasive influence of outside players means that local issues are given, at best, palliative attention. Despite the emphasis given to poverty alleviation in the sustainable development concept as originally popularised in the Brundtland report (World Commission on Environment and Development, 1987), most of those who use the new-found term 'sustainable' tend to forget the social and cultural sustainability. For the same reason the issue of equitable host involvement is seldom invoked in the local debates on tourism – it has eclipsed to become a nonissue, except when one reads the Malaysian

5-year development plan. For the policy implementers it is perhaps much easier to remain silent on such subjects even if they are duty-bound to address them. In this way the constructionist meaning of development as ascribed by tourism advisors serves to further obscure equity issues which are highlighted in the higher-order national development plan.

SOCIO-ECONOMIC DIMENSIONS OF TOURISM DEVELOPMENT

Socio-economic dimensions refer to stakeholders and their interests in tourism. The question to raise here revolves around who controls tourism at the destination, who should tourism be sustainable for? Which group loses and which gains? Is there family monopoly or exclusive entrepreneurial networks in the industry? These questions are clearly relevant and have rarely been addressed in the various plans; for instance, the structure plans usually carry a chapter on tourism. Environmental impact assessment of major tourism projects are also required to cover these dimensions. The review process for both plans calls for mandatory public reviews. Herein lies the opportunities to air residents' views on equitable involvement.

A scan through available reports in these two categories of reviews suggests that because these are 'pre-' evaluation procedures, there are no grounds for complaint among most local residents since they are unlikely to attend the sessions, let alone understand the shortcomings of the reports. Even among the better informed members of the public, they are usually placated through the inclusion of perfunctory statements such as 'the project will bring great benefits to the locals'. Such near empty pronouncements will always be included since the risk of complaint is almost absent. After all the local public is always ignorant and such reviews are usually held in big towns, which makes it irrelevant to the peripheral host community.

As pointed out elsewhere, even if the public is coaxed to participate in the review process, the process is not necessarily without shortcomings (Din, 1992). It can be tempered by the placement of review committee members who are undisclosed stakeholders in the 'development' process.

EQUITABLE INVOLVEMENT: A REVIEW

By equitable involvement I mean a fair access to participation in the decision-making process and in taking advantage of the economic opportunities that arise from the arrival of tourists. This implies an open opportunity structure that is not tempered by undue advantages on account of economic, social or political influence. It should permit the local host community to share the benefits of tourism in such a manner as to even:

> Permit the poor to reacquire the power and control over their own lives and the natural and human resources that exist in their environment ... If social and economic development means anything at all, it must mean a clear improvement in the conditions of life and livelihood of ordinary people. There is no intrinsic reason, moral or otherwise, why large numbers of people should be systematically excluded from development in this sense or, even worse, should become the unwitting victim of other people's progress. (Friedmann, 1992, pp. 9, 72)

A few successful examples of reasonably equitable involvement have been reported (Saglio, 1979; Ranck, 1987; Gonsalves, 1987; Rodenberg, 1980; Ooi *et al.*, 1994). Most of these are small-scale operations which rely on collective efforts, either through family ties or through village cooperatives. As Butler (1980) suggests, locals will get involved in small businesses which offer service to a small number of tourists during the inception stage of tourism development. Available evidence indicates that locals will seize the opportunities after learning about them from some outsiders, and rarely as a spontaneous response in the community. In most situations such 'free-for-the-taking' scenarios end up in some pecuniary jealousies and bickering once a certain individual manages to accumulate wealth to rise above others. He will have the advantage of a pioneer and may himself display 'natural' entrepreneurial traits. It will abruptly upset the traditional leadership structure and lead to a gradual demise of reciprocity sanctions once social relations become increasingly influenced by pecuniary considerations. The situation will lead to a deterioration of the community as traditional obligations to the community become weaker. Social control and organisation will change rapidly based on a new order where power relations are built on emergent forms based on merit and wealth. The process of community break-up will be exacerbated with the influx of outsiders as the area develops into a popular tourist destination. The process will lead to the marginalisation of the ordinary onlookers in favor of the family members of the pioneer entrepreneurs who may also lose subsequently in the competition with the better funded, better linked and better informed investors from outside the region.

Ultimately the process will lead to proletarianisation of the locals, who, as a rule, will assume the low paying jobs while suffering the burden of consumerism and inflation that come with the expansion of the tourist industry. This leaves the original inhabitants alienated and powerless in their own places of birth. They will no longer be able to take part in the decision-making process affecting their lot, as most functions and decisions will be rapidly assumed by institutionalised bodies, public or private. The end result will be an opposite situation from the model of participatory involvement as suggested by Friedmann.

The rapid destruction of the traditional host community may take place as predicted above, but the usual situation evolves at a slower pace, owing to political intervention which is mobilised by the original community members who can use their voting rights to induce remedial measures by the local representative in the state legislative assembly.

The following are four examples which illustrate variations in the capacity to absorb tourism in terms of local involvement.

Sarawak longhouse safari

There are a few places in Sarawak where one can sample the experience of living in an indigenous longhouse. The trip involves travel by road from the staging point in towns and further upstream by boat to a chosen longhouse for an overnight stay. In the Skrang river, entrepreneurial initiative came from Kuching-based Chinese tour operators who managed to persuade the longhouse dwellers to build separate dwellings (hostel style) for the tourist. Food, a guide and land transportation are provided by the tour operators; the villagers take turn to stage

traditional welcome dances while the majority of the women also are involved as peddlers of traditional crafts, many of which are purchased from the town. Through the years the Iban tribesmen are beginning to complain about the inequitable share of income from the tours. They would prefer to go all out on their own. At the inter-group level a paid stage performance is equitably shared through the rotation of performers. There were traces of individualistic tendencies when competing for customers in the handicraft trade, each *bilik* or household would try their level best to woo for maximum sale. In some of the less popular longhouses the *ketua* or headman usually monopolises the business transactions with the tourist.

The longhouse host community is generally happy with visits by tourists. There is, however, some resentment with tour operators who use underhand moves to pit one longhouse against another over the hosting business. In the Mulu and Niah areas longhouse dwellers were unhappy with the state authorities for interfering with their traditional activities. Some of the swift nest collectors (the activity is a tourist attraction) at the Niah Caves object to recent regulation of their nest collection. In the Mulu area two of the power generators installed by the park management were burned down as a show of protest against the state government's decision to acquire 'their' land to be occupied by a resort developer from outside. In this example the Iban–tourist encounter poses articulation problems, a problem of linking a subsistence economy in the lower circuit to a modern tour operation in the upper circuit.

Instant development in Langkawi

The island of Langkawi to the northwest of Peninsular Malaysia was declared a duty-free zone (1987) in an effort to turn it into a popular tourist destination. The local population of about 26,000 have since been overtaken by rapid developments which was beyond their expectations. Over a dozen tourist-class hotels have appeared on the shoreline of the island, resulting in bullish sales of properties which left a handful of islanders rich. With the exception of a few islander families who are connected to entrepreneurs on the mainland, most Langkawians became anxious onlookers as developers and speculators from outside took advantage of the government-led development process. Many of the hotels faced acute shortages of labor, but the percentage of islanders who gained employment in tourism was minimal. Most islanders, being fishermen and farmers, were not preadapted to the business culture to be involved. The only impact they had to face was a steady rise in the cost of living despite the duty-free status of the island. The prices of basic household items such as sugar, fish and vegetables had soared, although of course islanders can now acquire brand items and cigarettes at duty-free prices. The rows of shops that have been built in the two large centers on the island have been occupied by nonislanders, mostly Chinese entrepreneurs from the mainland. With the exception of tourist transportation almost every activity is dominated by outsiders.

The Langkawi case suggests that there is limited local involvement in the newly created tourist industry. Among those islanders who benefitted, families of beach property owners had windfall bounties from the sale of land which in certain prime locations experienced increases in price by over one hundred fold in 10 years!

Cherating and Melaka

In Cherating and Melaka tourism has a much longer history. Melaka has appeared in tourist brochures since the late 1950s, while Cherating started as a backpack traveller's favorite destination in the early 1970s. In Melaka most of the tourism businesses are in the hands of long-established family-owned enterprises. With the exception of a few corporate owners, the entire hotel industry is owned by local Chinese families. The Malays, Indians and Portuguese have remained more as attractions rather than beneficiaries. In Cherating, the dominant group is the Malay elite from outside, who since the 1980s has taken over from the original landowners who are now relocated in a new settlement towards the interior part of the district. The initial chalet operations continue, but the beach resort activities are now dominated by a string of modern resort centres which occupy the beach areas stretching from Cherating down to Kuantan.

In these two cases, tourism never grew on the initiative of the indigenous group, and the expected trickle-down effect never developed to the degree envisaged by regional planners and tourism textbooks. Again, the original inhabitants became merely disadvantaged spectators in the process.

The fact and fantasies of agrotourism

Agrotourism (and ecotourism) have appeared as catchwords in the media and in tourism since the early 1990s. One of the rationales for promoting these activities is that it promises to spread tourism benefits to the rural population. In Malaysia most of the rural dwellers are Malays, other tribal groups numbering about 30 or so in East Malaysia, and the aborigines in the interior parts of Peninsular Malaysia. The idea is to link up rural villages, parks, farms and fruit orchards to the tourist market, so that foreign visitors can visit them and make local purchases (fruit, handicraft, fish, local food and flowers). In the process tourists were expected to seek accommodation, services (especially guide service) and purchase local handicrafts. The above ideas were never developed into any meaningful projects, mainly because of a lack of local initiative and poor marketing. However, the main problem lies in the fact that villagers, like the longhouse dwellers, do not have any experience in the conduct of business, and few can even communicate in English. This means that if the project is going to take off it will have to depend on urban-based initiatives, and when that happens it is difficult to imagine how the locals can withstand competition from the far more experienced urban entrepreneurs.

The above four examples illustrate that the economic benefits from tourism rarely spread readily in favor of the original population in the destination areas. There are nonetheless other instances where substantial benefits accrue to the local host, but when such situations present themselves they are often controlled by a few ethnic or kinship-based family concerns. In this way tourism promotes an inequitable spread of income and employment even at the community level. Public resentment has recently arisen in about 12 cases in the country over tourism-related equity issues. The two most protracted cases were, first, in Jerai which was directed against the state government's decision to build a US$7 billion international tourist resort, and in

Pulau Redang which involved the relocation of a fishing village to make way for an island gold resort. The missing items in such development context is the distributive and sustainable aspects of development.

Given that the spread effect from tourism is rarely addressed in the literature, it may be useful to examine the various options available to the development planners in the hope that the expected benefits, often announced repeatedly by politicians, can be carefully scrutinised. The following options, though not exhaustive and may even be overlapping, are some of the possible policy choices for state tourism authorities to consider.

DEVELOPMENT OPTIONS

Laissez-faire

In practice this has been the mode of development in Malaysia before the 1980s. Although the state had maintained the old colonial rest houses and had set up hotels through the Tourist Development Corporation since the early 1970s, there was practically no effective intervention in the market beyond routine licencing of businesses and promoting Malaysia overseas. There was no attempt to encourage locals to be involved, let alone to address equity issues in the industry. It was nevertheless pronounced in the second and subsequent 5-year development plans that the government intended to encourage more indigenous involvement in the industry. Much of this is devoted to training of *bumiputeras* (meaning 'son of the soil', referring to the autochtonous population including Malays, aborigines of Peninsular Malaysia, native groups of Sabah and Sarawak) in diploma and certificate level hotel and catering programs at the Council of Indigenous People (MARA) college, and at the National Productivity Center.

The above programs succeeded in producing over 400 graduates each year, but less than 20% sought occupation in the non-*bumiputera*-controlled tourism sector. Even if they did, they bear little relevance to the need of the local community at the resort destinations, since they either come from urban areas, or at best were taken in to occupy the lower-skilled positions in the hotels. Virtually all the small- or medium-class hotels, owned by non-*bumiputeras*, as a rule, do not employ them except in the menial categories.

Public enterprises

Since the late 1970s a number of government-funded bodies have shown interest in the accommodation sector. Because the Malaysian government is dominated by the *bumiputera* group, the hotels managed by government agencies, or those connected with the ruling party, were obliged to hire *bumiputera* workers. They have managed to encourage more involvement, even at the upper level. Unfortunately many of the government-backed outfits did not perform as well as expected, resulting in the closure of many of them, usually to be taken over by non-*bumiputera* companies.

As a rule the government agencies position themselves in the upmarket establishments, with several of them located in untested areas. This focus on the star-rated establishments meant that there was no government support given to potential *bumiputera* entrepreneurs who sought to operate budget facilities with low overhead costs. Before the 1990s the few *bumiputera* establishments in the country were not given space in government brochures or statistical bulletins. On the islands of Penang and Langkawi (late 1980s) the authorities ransacked at least two of these small-scale establishments, forcing them to close shop.

The situation has changed markedly; there are now a sprinkling of successfully operated '*bumiputera*' hotels owned by the elite. As a rule these operators do not display visible support for the government affirmative policies in the tourist sector. In the case of Melaka, for example, while the government machinery (planning and administration) is dominated by the Malays, there are no Malay or *bumiputera* hotels to speak of. Even the state-owned hotels are mostly run by non-Malays. State administrators continue to face the dilemma of having to chalk healthy annual profits while at the same having to address affirmative action directives. The same can be said of the handicraft sector where government corporations are both overbureaucratised and unprofitable. By and large the issue of equitable involvement – where members of the local community have fair access to opportunities for income and employment – does not arise. The locals continue to remain largely in the rôle of passive onlookers.

Consortium and cooperatives

There is no shortage of *bumiputera* chambers of commerce. It has been suggested that they ought to come together to explore and exploit the opportunities that arise from tourism. Unfortunately, few of the chamber members have shown an interest in tourism, and the very few that did tended to limit their involvement to small family-run hotels. This will not help the local community in peripheral destinations. While it is plausible to suggest that the local community, for example the longhouse safari hosts, could combine their resources and organise their own operations, thereby side-stepping the role of the middlemen tour operators for a bigger profit margin, in reality members of the host community are often envious of one another, and do not have the necessary network, education and experience to compete with urban-based tour operators on whom they have depended in the past. There is conceivable scope for the formation of cooperatives which enlist members who subscribe shares according to their means. Such cooperatives should be encouraged by the government and advisory and supervisory assistance should be extended during the formative stage.

It would appear that if the state is seriously intent on encouraging local involvement (as beneficiaries of tourism), a special unit in the Ministry of Culture, Arts and Tourism should be set up to ensure that local interests are protected and that equitable (and therefore sustainable) modes of development are promoted. The most critical areas to be addressed are business intelligence and marketing. Since the locals do not have network linkages with foreign tour operators, the state, with its 18 promotional offices overseas and its numerous participations in tourism fairs abroad, should have the capacity to establish these linkages for the local community, at least at the inception stage.

It will, however, require more groundwork besides the building of the market linkages. The locals who have no experience in business, not even the familiarity with the discipline demanded by such involvement, need training and exposure to many skills in tour and business management. Without such preparation it will be very easy for other stakeholders from outside to manipulate local sentiments to their advantage, pitting one host community against their neighbouring tribesmen. There is also an inherent risk of one or two individuals or families succumbing to greed, preferring to operate on their own rather than through cooperatives.

Equity shares

Equity share refers to the value of input(s) by subscribers to a venture. These can be in the form of capital share, land, labor or whatever inputs that can be converted into units of shares. Potentially, this mode of local involvement is not only equitable (each according to ability), but also practicable. Because tourist-related businesses, like any other productive enterprise, need the basic input of factors of production, households in the host community are mostly in the position to contribute and derive benefits from tourism. They can either purchase shares from their savings, take up loans for the purpose, offer sites or rooms, and provide labor or services (e.g. dancing, guide or transport). It is flexible and at the outset, implementable.

For this proposition to be realised, it has to be fully backed by the government to ensure that the locals are not unduly shortchanged. The likelihood of trickery is remote in the long term since the business in question will have to depend on local inputs.

General trust companies

For a general trust company to take off the government will have to provide the seed funds and the initial managerial expertise. In the long run the company will have to operate on a profitable basis and be run by its members, and failure of which will be the market verdict on whether tourism should be developed at all in the local community. To be equitable, the goal should be directed towards improving the standard of living for the entire host community. This can be achieved through bulk purchases of construction materials which can then be used for building tourist facilities and public facilities such as kindergarten, library, workshop, cooperative sundry shop, playground, public hall, clinic, and other items which are outside the scope of government functions. Saglio's 1979 report on this subject is instructive.

In this model share subscription may come from outside, but the majority share should be held by the community as a collective, even if government support is required in the beginning. At the state level there have been a number of successful models; most of the success stories arose from preferential treatment given to state trust companies in the purchase of blue chip and new shares released in the open stock-exchange market. The same principle can be (and in fact is) extended to the trust companies organised by the host community.

This mode of development appears viable since urban-based tour operators can also be included, thus making them equally committed to the welfare issues of the host community. It is a better proposition since in the long term it does not tie locals to an exploitative and dependent mode of tourism development.

Local fraternity

One of the key ingredients in the success of Asian immigrant communities overseas (Chinese, Japanese, Koreans and to a lesser degree Indians) is that they operate along ethnic lines usually on the basis of kinship ties. The same applies to some extent among other Asian migrant communities in Europe and Africa. Among peasant communities in the rural areas the above mutual-aid business network does not exist to a significant extent, mainly because the subsistence mode of production does not require networking for purposes of sharing capital and business intelligence.

In the absence of such mutual-aid fraternities, the host communities should identify and solidify the bases of their bond of solidarity. This can either be religion, root syndrome, old boy's alumni or ideological commonalities. It would seem that the most persuasive call is to be found in the root syndrome which is usually reinforced by the local school alumnus sentiment. This model requires each host community to solicit support, especially ideas and leadership, from their kinsmen who have left the village to carve out a successful career after leaving the local school. Based on the writer's experience with colleagues at work and members of his Alma Mater Association which has a chapter in Kuala Lumpur, virtually every successful man/woman who left their village would want to help develop their place of origin, but does not know how. They may be in the position to contribute as a big shareholder and possibly volunteer to relay business intelligence and strategic information. Since

these splinter groups are usually too busy with their urban career and living, the initiative will have to come from the local leaders who will have to approach the former face-to-face.

From the above six options, the last three appear to be viable, either pursued individually or in combination, depending on the local situation. Whichever the choice, the process of promoting equitable local involvement needs to be generated methodically through an action plan initiated by the state, assuming that each state is serious in wanting to spread the benefit of tourism to a wider spectrum in the host community.

ACTION PLAN

Given the exploratory nature of the subject, the following are seven steps recommended for promoting a more equitable pattern of local involvement in the tourist industry:

(1) Definition of goals and objectives to be initiated by the government agency in charge of tourism development: locals must decide, after clarification by a tourism official, whether to accept or reject the proposition. The decision must be a rational one, whatever the explanation.
(2) If the decision is affirmative, a short study which scans the level of demand and resource capability should be carried out to identify areas of strengths and weaknesses.
(3) Choose a workable approach and an institutional framework: set up a cooperative? Call meeting of influential and successful ex-residents? Set up trust funds?
(4) Awareness campaign among local residents on the benefits that can be derived from tourism – what are the exploitable opportunities?
(5) Call for participation through extended dialogues; make sure the proposed programs are transparent and fully understood. Take note and address reservations raised by locals.
(6) Obtain support/cooperation from politicians and tour operators. Elect a village trustee committee through consensus.
(7) Identify and implement short- and long-term strategies.
  (a) *Short term*:
    • inventory of potential household inputs and capability;

- seek advisory input from tour operators and successful urban-based
  ex-residents;
- begin network linkage with industry
  insiders, including suitable overseas
  tour operators;
- begin building basic facilities incre-
  mentally based on a communal
  enterprise.

(b) *Long term*:

- set up a trust company and promote sale of shares;
- train locals on the relevant aspects
  of business management;
- monitor and review progress – study
  recurrent problems and attend to
  bottlenecks;
- hand over entire operation for local
  takeover;
- continue marketing and product
  development.

CONCLUSION

This chapter takes an advocacy position in the
belief that researchers ought to interpret the issues
examined, not only from their objective perspective, but also from the subjective perspective of
the group they study. In the case of the host–guest
encounters, previous findings on the subject have
rarely reached the relevant audience in Third-
World destinations beyond the ivory tower.
Tourism planners and policy makers seldom
pay attention to issues considered relevant
among academics. As for the host, they have
never sought to understand the subject except on
their terms, and their terms, like others, usually
revolve around the question of what good does
change bring to their midst? What's in it for them?

In this chapter I have avoided a critical review
of the relevant literature, some of which are
listed in the bibliography. The chapter attempts
to direct attention to the distributive and sustainable aspects of tourism development; these
two interrelated themes have appeared in the
literature for over two decades (although the
latter term has gained currency only recently).
It is suggested that there is an urgent need
to reexamine the benefit structure so that the
growth in the industry can be presumed to
be 'developmental' (development used here
extends beyond the constructionist notion). The
contention here is that equitable involvement of
the host community is a prerequisite to sustainable tourism development. A mode of tourism
development that displaces or marginalises the
original host community is more of *mis-
development* than development.

In order to ensure that tourism development is
reasonably equitable it may be necessary to
examine closely local capacities in terms of the
factors of production: land, labor, capital, entrepreneurship, institutions, exogenous ideological
influence, community support and entrepreneurial
leadership. Which factors are critical and which
factors are weak and need to be beefed up, and
how? Such a line of enquiry may be more useful
in making tourism deliver what it should – the
time-worn claim of the trickle-down effect.

REFERENCES

Butler, R. W. (1993), Pre- and post-impact assessment
of tourism development, in Pearce, D. G. and Butler,
R. W. (Editors), *Tourism Research: Critiques and
Challenges*, London: Routledge, 135–155.

de Kadt, E. (1979), *Tourism – Passport to Development?*
New York: Oxford University Press.

Din, K. (1992), Dialogue with the hosts: an educational strategy towards sustainable tourism. In
Hitchcock, M., King, V. T. and Parnwell, M. J. G.
(Editors), *Tourism in South-East Asia*, London: Routledge, 327–336.

Friedmann, J. (1992), *Empowerment: The Politics of
Alternative Development*, Cambridge, MA: Blackwell.

Gonsalves, P. S. (1987), *Alternative Tourism*, Bangalore:
Equitable Tourism Options.

Hughes, G. (1995), The cultural construction of sustainable tourism, *Tourism Management*, **16**(1): 49–59.

Inskeep, E. (1994), *Tourism Planning: An integrated and
sustainable development approach*. New York: van
Nostrand Reinhold.

Kaiser, C. Jr., and Helber, L. E. (1978), *Tourism Planning
and Development*. Boston: CBI.

Ooi, S. T., Kohoi, G. and Yapp, J. (1994), Local par-
ticipation in a nature tourism project: the Batu
Punggul experience. In Ti, T. C. (Editor), *Issues and
Challenges in Developing Nature Tourism in Sabah*, Kota
Kinabalu: Institute of Development Studies (Sabah),
69–78.

Ranck, S. R. (1987), An attempt at autonomous devel-
opment: the case of the Tufi guest houses, Papua
New Guinea. In Britton, S. and Clarke, W. C.
(Editors), *Ambiguous Alternative: Tourism in Small
Developing Countries*, Suva: University of the South
Pacific, 154–166.

Rodenberg, E. (1980), The effects of scale in economic development: tourism in Bali, *Annals of Tourism Research*, 7(2): 177–196.

Saglio, C. (1979), Tourism for discovery: a project in Lower Casamance, Senegal, In de Kadt, E. (Editor), *Tourism – Passport to Development?* New York: Oxford University Press. pp. 321–335.

World Commission on Environment and Development (1987), *Our Common Future*, London: Oxford University Press.

Index